For d Uwaku

INFREQUENT FREQUENCIES, RARE RESONANCE

Arohanui

(✱)**green**hill

https://greenhillpublishing.com.au/

Poole, G. E. (author)

Infrequent Frequencies, Rare Resonance

ISBN 978-1-923156-56-2 (paperback)

ISBN 978-1-923156-57-9 (hardback)

PHILOSOPHY | PERSONAL-TRANSFORMATION

Cover and Book design: Green Hill Publishing

Typesetting Calluna Regular 11/18

UNTRAVELED PATHS THROUGH NATURAL,
PRACTICAL AND ALTERNATIVE UNDERSTANDINGS
OF YOUR LIFE, PURPOSE AND MEANING.

INFREQUENT
FREQUENCIES
RARE
RESONANCE

G. E. POOLE

Contents

This work is dedicated to each of my children
and grandchildren and to
each of my teachers who came before.

CHAPTER 1

What is Knowable?
Stepping into the Breach

*"If you only read the books that everyone else is reading,
you can only think what everyone else is thinking."*

HARUKU MURUKAMI

First and foremost, believe nothing at all written in this book. Believe nothing indeed written or said or communicated in any form anywhere else as well. If you have no relentless critical faculty, no due scientific scepticism, balanced with an objectively open mind, this or any collection of words can be of little benefit or value to you.

In the 21st Century nearly anyone can write a book or otherwise express their thoughts to mass audiences. Never before in human history has there been so much information, so much knowledge, so much opinion, so much truth and untruth, everything so freely and widely available in so many accessible forms. So, what is the point or the value of yet another volume of subjective musings by yet another clown in the circus?

Well, so this then is a book that the author never intended or wanted to write. Sure, of course they all say that. Yet, in this case it happens to be the sincere truth. The book is not written by the author nor even through the author, but rather in good faith through necessity and sheer happenstance. In other words, simply because of compelling necessity.

You are on the journey already traveling through exposure to quite unconventional, decidedly alternative, and seemingly preposterous, outrageous ideas, notions, facts and observations that will challenge all your fixed attitudes around nearly everything you have been conditioned to assume by your upbringing, your education, your culture, your religion, including many of your basic assumptions, values and your former understandings of life as a human being.

On the other side of the same coin, you will also simultaneously see or recognize these truths from vastly different angles as an "aha, of course," moment.

The only requirement for the journey is to keep an open mind and believe absolutely nothing you read or hear or learn. Ever. That is, until and unless you have eventually thoroughly and rigorously put it through yourself and confirmed for yourself the truth, the validity and the vital relevance of each singular bit of it, no matter how seemingly preposterous or different, or unconventional.

COMPETING IDEAS AND ENDLESS THEORIES ABOUT EVERYTHING

Probability is you have come in with an enquiring mind and a relentless quest for knowing or it's unlikely you would have chosen to either spend or invest your time, currency, and energy on reading anything such as this. A proportion of the 8-9 billion or so fellow human primates presently inhabiting the surface of our common organic life-sustaining planet are content to more or less graze in the pastures, grow up to adulthood, reproduce, engage in work and pastimes, grow old and die much as members of a herd of animals feeding in a field of grass do.

But you are in a bit different, part of a smaller group of thinkers or seekers with an indefatigable thirst for knowledge. Your heart's desire *is to find out.* The gulf, however, between acquiring huge stores of information and gaining any understanding is vast. Naturally enough, first comes the information, then comes the processing, the assimilation and the knowledge. But in the current times, way too much, an avalanche of data from all directions.

Yet, through developing a critical faculty you begin to sift and sieve through the bewildering barrage of information seeping filtered through to your conscious awareness. What is truth and what is falsity? What is wheat, what is chaff? What is evidence-based and, equally, what is nothing more than the folly of human conjecture, prejudice, suggestibility, imagination, superstition and whim? What follows the laws of logic and reasoning and what is based on fallacy? What is objective and what is subjective knowing? What is balanced and what is unbalanced knowing? What to keep and what to jettison? Is it not all about discernment?

THE HUMAN LIFE OWNERS' MANUAL

From the time and day, you were born you and your brain have been learning constantly every day in every way. Yet, unfortunately, your body, your brain, your heart, your ego idea, your name and whatever

3

else there is of you didn't come with an Owners' Operating Manual. From the very beginning when you were thrown into the world you have been left to figure it all out for yourself. A substantial percentage of people cannot be bothered pondering about why they are here, what is the purpose or meaning of their average 60 to 80 or so terrestrial years on the planet, or what happens at the end of their given organic lifespan.

But you are slightly different because you have such a strong desire, a need, a hunger and, an insatiable thirst to find out something more about what is this gift, this burden, this challenge, this joy, this cosmic, comic tragedy, this master riddle, of what life as a human being is about and what is the reason for or the point of it all. Your need is to find out. So how? Where to begin?

CAN SCIENCE AND SCIENTIFIC METHOD HELP YIELD CRUCIAL INSIGHT?

Most definitely yes and most constantly is science proving and improving its value. Particularly over the past 150 years, the course of rapid and accelerating systematic advances in physics, biology, chemistry, genetics, and mathematics through the application of the scientific empirical method has yielded exceptional insights into how the known universe operates from the sub-atomic to the cosmic scale. The empirical scientific approach brings a spectacular strength in its rigorous requirements for hard evidence and refutation with the aim *to better get closer toward the truth.*

The development specifically of quantum mechanics, relativity physics, and more recently string-theory have advanced ideas, theories, and understandings of the nature and the fabric of space, time, materials, chemistry, energy and the relationships between them as far as the human primate mind can presently understand how they operate.

Breakthrough revelations around evolution, natural selection and the advances in biological sciences are leading to constant increase in knowledge about the human biological machine, the natural world around, as well as the intricacies of with the body and brain. Through to understanding the genetic code within the double helix of DNA, and all that is flowing from that discovery, science advances stepwise, and nature is gradually unravelling and revealing deeper secrets.

Many recent writers and observers have noted that as physics advances, it moves into new and unfamiliar quantum territory where the once firm boundaries between the seemingly real and the unreal begin to melt. This human mind is designed to constantly look for patterns, whether they objectively exist or not. That same mind is also designed to place labels on things in order to try to grasp meaning in them.

So, science and the human intellect contributes exceptionally, but should you solely invest all your faith in it for understanding of the most important questions of your life and purpose?

The intellect is proved conclusively a highly effective tool as a blade for cutting, dissecting and analysing. Little doubt about it. At the same time, science has revealed its weaknesses when taken to the logical extreme where unbalanced adherence to the empirical method has led to reductionism. Reductionism simply means that everything is reduced to its three-dimensional basic material components. A prime example: "The mind is nothing but the brain."

Such "nothing-butism" leads to a cul de sac as material fundamentalists and empirical atheists have shown in their capacity to be just as bigoted, limited, and biased as any extremist religious zealot.

EXTREME MATERIALISM, REDUCTIONIST DOGMAS, AND NOTHING-BUTISMS

"Refusal to believe until proof is given is a rational position; Equally, denial of all outside of our own limited experience is absurd."

ANNIE BESSANT

What is your belief about the existence of cosmic rays or of dark matter or dark energy? Why do you believe or disbelieve? Who told you a gravity-dense vortex black hole exists in space or time? How do you know it's true? Do you also believe in the existence of 'fairies', leprechauns or 'water sprites?' On what basis?

Through the 19th, 20th and 21st Centuries the empirical **scientific method** arose in force and gathered increasing momentum Methods of critical analysis had passed down through many thinkers, scientists and philosophers since the mathematics and logic of the Pythagorean and Aristotelian Greeks and on through other civilizations. The deductive reasoning of syllogisms and logic was applied to identify fallacies or baseless claims to begin the long, painstaking process of separating fact from fiction.

Scientific method delivered a system of rational thought and logic through to practical application leading to industrial revolutions, and technological innovations transforming human societies. Scientific Method as an empirical (evidence based on observation) approach has powerfully driven science since the 17th century and deep into history. It applies careful, measurable observation, together with rigorous scepticism about what is being observed.

The essential element of scientific scepticism acknowledges how assumptions, fixed attitudes, and cognitive differences can distort the accuracy and truth of how observations are interpreted. The Science Method involves forming ideas, theories and hypotheses and then applying experiments to test the truth, or falsity of their validity through observation and empirical evidence. There is also the distinction between deductive and inductive reasoning. The purpose here is not to provide further information on the topic beyond the minimum necessary for setting the context and foundation.

The principle of falsifiability was associated with 20th Century science philosopher Karl Popper. Ideas that might be wrong in fact are the lifeblood of science: you test them, find evidence to support or undermine them, and learn something in the process. But hypotheses that can't even ever be wrong, Popper maintained, can't tell you anything. This limiting principle would present problems for the recent 'string theories' of the universe (or multiverse) emerging in physics, where the models often cannot be tested by experiment.

For Popper, knowledge only progresses when falsifiable claims about the world get proven wrong. In his classic example, you can never confirm the statement "all swans are white", (or all crows the colour black) because there might always be some non-white swans (or albino crows) you haven't yet encountered. It only takes one black swan (or one white crow) to falsify the claim definitively.

WHEN THE RESULTS THUS OBTAINED FROM THE RIGIDITY OF SCIENTIFIC METHOD LED DOWN A CUL DE SAC TO A DEAD END

The success of the scientific method and its underpinning and overarching due scepticism led to a swing of the pendulum by the middle to late 20th Century away from religion, faith, metaphysics, mysticism and philosophy toward extremist materialism, empiricism, and what might be understood as three-dimensional' reductionist, dogmatic atheism, not even allowing for agnostic doubters on the margins.

In this reductionist trend, everything could be boiled down to materialism. For example, in one university course entitled 'the philosophy of mind' the evidence for the case was presented that the human mind was 'nothing more' than the brain. The total was nothing more than the sum of its parts. The physics and creation of the universe, evolution and all phenomena were 'nothing- but' complex physical, electro-chemical processes generated by 'nothing more' than sheer spontaneous happenstance.

There was no necessity nor place for any god, a creator, or any higher dimension, or any supreme being, force, source, or entity in that causeless, spontaneous, reductionist, gross material universe. Materialist, empirical atheism was its logical, consistent conclusion and its fundamentalist adherents espoused it with disdain for those unbelievers.

Extremist fundamentalism of any sort- religious, political, or scientific is unbalanced. Why or how? Because it builds a wall of fixed attitudes, then locks the vault door trapping and sealing its adherent victims inside.

THE PROGRESSION OF SCIENCE AND THE SEARCH FOR TRUTH

Science is still young and progressing. Humility requires acceptance that there are mysteries and riddles that cannot be unlocked in the present point in history because of the limitations of finite human primate minds. But ponder an equally intriguing possibility that this is because humans are not yet meant to know.

Knowledge of the technology of splitting the atom via fission historically led to development of nuclear weapons of mass destruction by the end of the Second World War. This high tech 'invention' has shadowed the human species since 1945 with the prospect of self-annihilation or at the least the end of civilization.

Was it wise to unleash the nuclear technology spectre to an immaturely evolved hominid species bearing the remnant of a chimpanzee-like trait of a penchant for aggression and violence? Would it be a sensible idea to entrust a four-year-old child with a deadly weapon such as a pistol? Might those very same due cautions apply to biological genetic manipulation technologies, bioweapons, or the development, application and rise of artificial intelligence?

The Fermi Paradox posed in the 1990's considered the inconceivable vastness of the known universe, and asked why there had been no evident or conclusively provable contact with any other species of life so far. Robin Hanson's response to the Fermi Paradox was what he called *the Great Filter*. The Great Filter theory posits that life and particular intelligent species may evolve up to a point where their technological prowess supersedes their wisdom and evolutionary maturity.

For Hanson, tacit development and adoption of new and potentially self-destructive advanced technologies could have caused the extinction of older extraterrestrial civilizations through the Great Filter. Hanson went on to suggest that the human primate species may well be rapidly approaching the threshold of the Great Filter test. Would the human primate experiment end by reciprocal self-destruction (war) or by the whimper of human-made pollution and destruction of the environment and biosphere? The latter Chief Seattle best of all presaged in 1885:

> "Contaminate your bed, and you will one night suffocate in your own waste."

What are the objective criteria determining if a species is a 'successful' experimental life form or an 'unsuccessful' one? Is it the Great Filter? Big enough question? What original thoughts and ideas come through to you?

Just as nuclear weapons mounted on missiles and fired in war could easily lead to the destruction of humankind, and much of life on the surface of the planet, equally those same technologies could potentially be marshalled to defend Earth from the mishap of a rogue asteroid impact. Such an impact as believed to have occurred approximately 65 million years ago around the Yucatan Peninsula. That epic event was believed to have brought about the extinction of the dinosaur age, and to have cleared the way for the evolution of mammals.

Because we live in the *pairs of opposites*, all these things have blades which can cut both ways where nuclear and missile technology, for example, could be applied to self-destruction of life, or protection of life on the planet. So, all the rapid technological advances bring enormous challenges, enormous risks, and the double-edged blade of immense progress or complete self-destruction as the species approaches the Great Filter. Yet human beings keep on learning and building on that knowledge, and it was Hope that was crucially also contained in that Pandoras Box.

So, by being curious, persistent, diligent, patient, and open-minded and by building on what is reliably known, it can be possible for successive generations living in the future to progressively and gradually discover more answers through time. That is if they are at least left a habitable, stable world worth living in.

CLEARING OUT THE CONDITIONING, THE ASSUMPTIONS, AND THE FIXED ATTITUDES FOR OPENING THE MIND TO POSSIBILITY THINKING

All is Vibration

All things in the known realm of existence are constantly in motion and vibrating. Even objects that appear to be stationary are in fact at the molecular level vibrating, oscillating, resonating, at various frequencies. Resonance is a type of motion, characterized by oscillation between two states. And ultimately all matter is vibration of various underlying fields and frequencies. As such, at every scale, all of nature vibrates.

Something interesting happens when different vibrating things come together: They will often start, after a little while, to vibrate together at the same frequency. They "sync up," sometimes in ways that can seem 'mysterious'. An observation described as the phenom-enon of spontaneous self-organization.

Mathematician Steven Strogatz provides some examples from physics, biology, chemistry and neuroscience to illustrate *sync* – his term for resonance – in his 2003 book *"Sync: How Order Emerges from Chaos in the Universe, Nature, and Daily Life,"* including:

- When fireflies of certain species come together in large gatherings, they start flashing in sync, in ways that can still seem mystifying
- Lasers are produced when photons of the same power and frequency sync together
- The moon's rotation is exactly synced with its orbit around the Earth such that we always see the same face of the surface.
- Resonance and synchronicity have also been observed when birds flock together, or fish school together, or insects hive or nest together

Examining resonance can potentially lead to insights about the nature of consciousness and about the known and knowable cosmos more generally.

Neuroscientists have identified sync in research on the human brain as well. Collective patterns of neuron activity can occur in human brains at measurable frequencies, with mammalian consciousness thought to be commonly associated with various kinds of synchronization.

It's simply Nature, just as Nature is simple, natural.

———————

"The Book of Nature is the Only Book."

H.I. KHAN

———————

A RESONANCE FREQUENCY NOTION OF CONSCIOUSNESS

Resonance theory builds upon the work of Fries and many others, with a broader approach that can help to explain not only human and mammalian consciousness, but also consciousness more broadly.

Based on the observed behaviour of the entities that surround us, from electrons to atoms to molecules, to bacteria to mice, bats, rats, and on, we suggest that all things may be viewed as at least a little conscious to some extent. It sounds strange at first blush, but *panpsychism* – the view that all matter has some associated consciousness – is an *increasingly accepted position* with respect to the nature of consciousness.

A panpsychist might argue that consciousness did not emerge at some point during evolution. Rather, it's always associated with matter and vice versa – they're two sides of the same coin. But the large majority of the mind associated with the various types of matter in our universe is extremely rudimentary. An electron or an atom, for example, enjoys just a tiny amount of consciousness. But as matter becomes more interconnected and richer, so does the mind, and vice versa, according to this way of thinking.

Biological organisms may rapidly exchange information through various biophysical, electrochemical pathways. Non-biological structures might exchange information internally using heat-thermal pathways or gravitational fields – slower and less rich in information in comparison. Living things leverage their speedier information flows into larger-scale consciousness than what might occur in similar-size things like boulders or piles of sand, for example. There's possibly greater internal connection and thus far more "happening" in biological structures than in a boulder or a pile of sand. Or that has been the assumption.

Within that line of thought, boulders and piles of sand are *mere aggregates*, just collections of highly rudimentary unconscious entities at the atomic or molecular level only. This in contrast to what happens in biological life forms where the combinations of these micro-conscious entities together create a higher level macro-conscious entity. For the human mind, this combination process is the hallmark of biological life.

The central thesis of this approach is this: the particular linkages that allow for large-scale consciousness – like those humans and other mammals enjoy – result from a shared resonance among many smaller constituents. The speed of the resonant waves that are present is the limiting factor that determines the size of each conscious entity in each moment.

As a particular shared resonance expands to more and more constituents, the new conscious entity that results from this resonance and combination grows larger and more complex. It follows that the shared resonance wave frequency in a human brain that achieves threshold gamma synchrony, for example, includes a far larger number of neurons and neuronal connections than is the case for beta or theta rhythms alone.

What about larger inter-organism resonance like the cloud of fireflies with their little lights flashing in sync? Researchers think their bioluminescent resonance arises due to internal biological oscillators that automatically result in each firefly syncing up with its neighbours.

Is this group of fireflies reaching a higher level of group conscious-ness? Probably not, since the phenomenon can be explained without recourse to intellect or consciousness. But in biological structures with the right kind of information pathways and processing power, these tendencies toward self-organization have the potential at least to produce larger-scale conscious entities.

This emerging resonance theory of consciousness attempts to provide a unified framework that includes neuroscience, as well as more fundamental questions of neurobiology and biophysics, and also the philosophy of mind. It gets to the heart of the differences that count when it comes to consciousness and the evolution of physical systems.

So yes, it's all about vibrations and frequencies, but also about the form and scope of vibrations and, most importantly, about shared common vibrations and **rare frequencies.**

CHAPTER 2

What is the underlying value of Faith, Religions or "Spiritual" Endeavours in Pursuit of Truth for Answering the Big Questions?

In every religion there is love, yet love has no religion.

RUMI

Religions have been trying and vying for thousands of years to explain the reason, the purpose and meaning of human existence and experience. Although an unduly tired metaphor, a religion could accurately enough be considered simply a form of vehicle. There are numerous vehicles of various shapes, sizes, compositions, emphasis and utility on offer to deliver you to your desired destination. There is also surely always an ample supply of used vehicle sales reps hawking their brand as the only one that will get you there.

If your destination or aim is in seeking the eternal reward of a 'heaven' or avoiding the aversive infinite punishment of a 'hell' then the Abrahamic religions may be well-suited as your chosen vehicles. If you are seeking to know more about yourself, existence itself, life and death, and how to achieve some higher purpose or state then there are these and many others equally readily accessible such as Buddhism and Taoism.

You may have noticed how religions tend to go on about a god? This god, that god or the One-and-Only-God, or this form or that form, or this dogma or that ritual?

The endless and constant and ceaseless search is for The Source. Mere words, in any language, inevitably, fall far short for naming who or what The Source is. *Hallowed Be Thy Name* is in the beginning invocation of the Lord's Prayer.

And so it was that the word that is for so long at the core of the Quest remaining has long been – G O D. Why? Because words fail.

The uncaused Cause, the One, the Source of All. The All in All of All. In their outer forms, most of the major religions will generally agree on at least a first universal truth:

"Everything comes from God and Everything goes back to God."

All the disputes, the debates, the controversy, the schisms, the politics, centuries of wars, the rancour and bitterness, all that inevitably follow when human beings try to delve into the detail of the how, the when, and the where of that nearly universally acceptable first principle. All the ceaseless debates futile.

At the Core of Existence, Everything is God and God is All

Faith is a deeply personal matter for an individual. The worst thing you could ever do to another person is to try to take away their faith or try to undermine it in any way. This principle applies to each religion and equally to the adherents of more recently emerging prominent ones commonly known as Materialism or Atheism.

THE UNITY OF TRUTH UNDERLYING RELIGIONS AND FAITHS ONE LIGHT OF TRUTH, MANY WINDOWS

H.I. Khan in the early 20th of Century reached exceptional insights, built knowledge bridges and generated astounding breakthroughs in unifying diverse religions, teachings, philosophies, and ideas. What he did was to shine light on the unity of the underlying Truth in the scriptures of various religions and teachings given out at different times and places over the course of thousands of years of human history.

H.I. Khan was no ordinary man but rather an example of an exceedingly rare, different, and highly conscious and developed human being operating on a far higher frequency of existence. Never accept the claim in this statement without researching and putting it through yourself until you find the truth or the falsity of it for yourself.

In any case, H.I. Khan provided in his remarkable insightful writings such as in the *Gayan, Vadan, Nirtan* a key to understanding the unity of faiths and the single truth underpinning each and all of them, but expressed in so many different ways at different times.

Succinctly and elegantly, he summarized the essence and core teaching of each great religion emerging throughout recorded history:

- The Hindu Faith - among the oldest and the religion of Wisdom
- The Buddhist Faith - the religion of Compassion
- The Zoroastrian Faith - the religion of Purity
- The Judaic Faith - the religion of the Law

- The Christian Faith - the religion of the Self-Sacrifice
- The Islamic Faith - the religion of Unity

There is also in the writings and services of H.I. Khan, the acknowledgement, tribute and homage to the 7th realm of all other faiths for those "known and unknown to the world which have held aloft the Light of Truth during the darkness of human ignorance."

SO HOW IS THE COSMOS CONSTRUCTED AND WHAT COULD BE THE PLACE OR PURPOSE OF HUMAN BEINGS?

"Each human personality is like a piece of music, having an individual tone and a rhythm of its own."

H.I. KHAN

A Natural Map for Understanding How It All Operates and Connects OTHER MEN'S FLOWERS

This small book and the pure sources it references can potentially point you to new insights into yourself and truth about the often perplexing and baffling world you find yourself in.

Yet, there is most definitely no substitute for the pure sources of knowledge and teaching that are, as faithfully and accurately as possible, transmitted here. In each and every instance, the strongest recommendation, will be to seek, study and ponder the knowledge directly from the purest sources.

As much as the sincerity of intention to accurately and faithfully transmit the knowledge as accurately as possible, there will inevitably come through some distortion, some subjective interpretation and some error.

Each generation has an aim and duty to try to translate worthwhile knowledge in a form that will be understandable and digestible to the contemporary people living at the time.

Foremost, the source of this stream of knowledge which the writer has been a student of for nearly 40 years was a human being living an externally ordinary life. Genuine Teachers, original thinkers, and particularly highly evolved, or developed conscious beings are extraordinarily rare at any one time on the planet and they remain mostly hidden from the mainstream life of media and publicity for essential reasons. They are operating on a vastly different frequency, and don't seek the limelight, power, wealth or fame and, indeed, shun all of it.

The sources and references to this stream of knowledge will be revealed toward the end of your reading journey, but the writer wishes to pay homage and deep gratitude to the exceptional, extraordinary Teacher who sought, earned, grasped and lovingly shared it.

In his talks he used to refer to "other men's flowers" in which writers who often falsely present ideas and esoteric knowledge as their own. He also drew from Teachers before him whom he fully acknowledged, but was also an exceptional original thinker inspired and guided from the rarest and purest sources. These flowers came from others far higher than this writer but were always meant for you.

CHAPTER 3

The Natural Order, How Is the Cosmos Created, Existing, and Operating?

*"A candle never diminishes its own light
by lighting another candle."*

RUMI

On most mornings, 365 days each year, you will wake up, attend to hygiene, showering, teeth brushing, donning clothes, eating breakfast, or engaging in any of your mechanical early day habits. You may notice the Sun shining in the sky and usually not take much notice. You might take it for granted. You will have learned in school how the Sun is believed to be an average size star which supplies the inhabitants of Planet Earth light and life. You learned the sun is a burning furnace, a sphere of hydrogen and helium running on atomic fusion.

Our ancient ancestors worshipped the Sun and the Earth as Gods. *How quaint and primitive you may think?* Today, we supposedly superior 'moderns' can understand how this was not surprising when our distant ancestors had to struggle to forage and hunt for food, and later to farm in order to survive and reproduce. So, their reverence for the Sun and Earth was logical, natural and even predictable.

Ancestors worshipped the forces of nature which shaped and determined their lives. The difference between a sufficient or failing crop season leading to starvation would make the difference to survival. They learned to pray to the Sun and Earth deities and sometimes make sacrifices to them in the devout hope of a good crop, abundant food and resources and safety from the weather and the elements and the predators.

The creation stories and myths of the ancient ones give context and perspective as articulated so succinctly by the insights of Joseph Campbell. What people believe today in the world is still consciously and subconsciously influenced by the creation myths as they have handed down generations.

"Is not the Sky a father and the Earth a mother, and are not all living things with feet or wings or roots their children?"

BLACK ELK (HEHAKA SAPA) OF THE OGLALA LAKOTA SIOUX NATION

CREATION STORIES AND THE SUBTLE MYTHS

The Purpose of Allegory and Storytelling Is To Crack Open the Windows of Mind in New and Different Ways in Preparation for Something

---

"People forget facts, but they remember stories. Myth is much more important and true than history.

JOSEPH CAMPBELL

JUDEO CHRISTIAN

There remains a trove of many myths, creation stories, parables, and teaching tales from so many different times and ancient cultures told and retold through the ages to explain the origin of life. The *Garden of Eden* in the Torah and in Biblical Genesis is the story indelibly inscribed in the minds and essences of many of Judeo-Christian, Abrahamic cultural heritage, widely well known, and requires no retelling. Most will recall the great fall caused by the eating of the forbidden fruit of the Tree of Knowledge.

There are, however, alternative, Talmudic esoteric interpretations of the ancient story explaining the fall from grace for the first couple in eating from the forbidden Tree of Knowledge. An alternative, esoteric interpretation is that it was a conscious choice, not just a violation of Divine prohibition, but a renunciation, a conscious self-sacrifice to descend into lower worlds through birth, death, and suffering for fulfilment of the highest noble purpose of re-ascension.

The triad is seen in Adam, the affirming force, in Eve the denying force, and the snake, which is the third, reconciling force.

HINDU

For Hindus, existence was willed by Brahma, the Creator who made the universe out of himself. After Brahma created the world, it is the power of Vishnu which preserves and operates the world and sustains human beings. As part of the cycle of birth, life and death it is Shiva who will ultimately judge and destroy the universe.

MAORI

The Maori of Aoetearoa New Zealand and related peoples of Polynesian (Hawaiian, Rarotongan, ancestry have the creation story of Ranginui (the Sky Father) and Papatuanuku (the Earth Mother). The Maori creation story begins with a description of the darkness and nothingness out which the Sky Father and the Earth Mother emerge from their embrace. Interestingly and intriguingly, the Maori word for the Sun is **Te Ra** which is the same as from the Ancient Egyptians.

EGYPTIAN

The Creation Story for the Ancient Egyptians also began with a primeval ocean of darkness and nothingness out of which life would spring. When the entity Atum decided it was time for Creation to begin, an island emerged to support this divinity who manifested itself in the form of **Ra**, the Sun God of Egypt.

When Ra appeared at dawn in the Eastern horizon, taken was the form of a falcon, known as Horus of the Horizon, (Horus - one who is high up.) But Ra also had other forms. He also could be represented as a scarab called Kheper, the one who comes into being—an analogy based not only on the pun between the name of the scarab and the verb "to happen', but also because the scarab, arises from desert sands at the first rays of the sun, was believed to be self-created. By midday the sun-god was again Ra and represented by the sun-disk. At sunset he became Atum, an old man who had completed his life cycle and was ready to disappear to be regenerated for a new day. All the other of the many Egyptian Gods had their genesis from **Ra**, the Supreme God.

ABORIGINAL AUSTRALIA

The Australian Aboriginal (from Ab-origin - the original) peoples are believed to be among the oldest continuous (60,000 -80,000 years) genetic and cultural lines of human beings alive today. Although there are many tribes and languages among those identifying as Aboriginal, there are common threads of arising going back from the *Dreamtime*. The source and essential nature of the *Dreamtime* is subtle and often misunderstood. One creation story of one Aboriginal community tells of the Two Wise Men and the Seven Sisters.

In the beginning of Yulbrada, the Earth, and the Creator, Jindoo-the Sun, sent two Spirit Men ancestors to shape it. They were from the far reaches of the Milky Way galaxy. They made hills, valleys, lakes and oceans. When they had nearly completed their work, Jindoo, the Sun Creator, sent seven sisters, stars of the Milky Way, to beautify the Earth with flowers, trees, birds, animals and creatures.

The Seven Sisters were busy making honey-ants when they got thirsty and needed water. The youngest sister was sent in search of the water. She came to a source of a spring and met the two Spirit Men. The youngest sister 'fell' in love with the Spirit Men. But the other six sisters were still so thirsty and went looking for her as they wondered where she had gone. After a while, they found her together with the Spirit Men.

The Creator, Jindoo the Sun had warned them that if such a thing would happen to any of the Sisters, she would not be able to return to her place in the Milky Way, so only six of the Sisters returned to their celestial home. The two men and the young sister remained here on Yulbrada, the Earth. Their divine powers were taken away and they became mortal. These were the Ancestors who became parents of the inhabitants of the Earth and who made the laws that are lived by through generations. This is the reason why the people of the desert have such knowledge and respect the stars of the universe.

STAR PEOPLE AND NATIVE NORTH AMERICA CREATION STORIES

From the early 21st Century authors from indigenous North American backgrounds are writing books for sharing their creation stories which feature legends about visitors from extraterrestrial origin referred to as the *Star People*. Contemporary authors such as G.W. Muller, Nancy Redstar and Ardy Sixkiller Clarke have revealed that there has always been a familial connection with travellers originating from other worlds beyond the Earth. Some of the writers have suggested that the 21st Century is the point when the previously hidden stories, parables and legends must be made widely known during times when humanity may be reaching a pivotal crisis point.

The writers offer evidence that the ancient people of North and Mesoamerica long believed they have been visited by unexplainable beings from the heavens. G.W. Muller states that the experience of tribal individuals with the link to the Pleiades star cluster is featured quite prominently in legends and teaching parables across many tribes including Cherokee, Onondaga, Lakota and Hopi.

In some instances, there exists a longstanding belief among some tribes that the "Star People" had interbred with humans, just as early homo sapiens had interbred with other species of hominids such as the Neanderthals, and Denisovans, and as yet undiscovered others, with the result to mix hybrid DNA blood lines. Some oral traditions of Native North Americans speak of strange crafts coming from the skies as "ascension vehicles."

G.W. Muller recounts one Lakota legend telling of seven maidens who are pursued by a bear. Just as they are about to be killed, they fall to their knees and pray for intervention. Just as the bear charges, they are lifted high into the air, and the bear is left to claw at the risen ground. The basis of this story is Devil's Tower in Wyoming. The seven maidens became the Pleiades, and the bear's claws are said to have carved the geological features of the rock.

ANCIENT GREECE

One of the most intriguing, complex and insightful creation stories has come down from the Minoan Civilization through the Greeks.

In the beginning, there was the empty darkness. The only thing in the Void was the Nyx, a bird with black wings. She laid a golden egg, and for ages she sat upon the egg. Finally life began to stir in the egg, and out of it rose Eros, the God of Love. One half of the shell rose into the air and became the sky and other became the Earth. Eros named the sky Uranus and the Earth he named Gaia. Then Eros made them rise in love.

Uranus and Gaia had many children together and eventually they had grandchildren. Some of their children become afraid of the power of their children. Kronus, in an effort to protect himself, swallowed his children when they were still infants. However, his wife Rhea hid their youngest child. She gave him a rock wrapped in swaddling clothes, which he swallowed, thinking it was his son.

Once the child, Zeus, had reached adulthood his mother instructed him on how to trick his father to give up his brothers and sisters. Once this was accomplished the children fought a mighty war against their father. After much fighting the younger generation won. With Zeus as their leader, they began to furnish Gaia with life and Uranus with stars.

Soon the Earth lacked only two things: man, and animals. Zeus summoned his sons Prometheus (fore-thought) and Epimetheus (after-thought). He told them to go to Earth and create men and animals and give them each a gift.

Prometheus set to work forming men in the image of the gods and Epimetheus worked on the animals. As Epimetheus worked, he gave each animal he created one of the gifts. After Epimetheus had completed his work Prometheus finally finished making men. But when he went to see what gift to give man Epimetheus shame-facedly informed him that he had foolishly used all the gifts.

Distressed, Prometheus decided he had to give man fire, even though gods were the only ones meant to have access to it. As the Sun god rode out into the world the next morning Prometheus took some of the fire and brought it back to man. He taught his creation how to take care of it and then left them.

When Zeus discovered Prometheus' deed, he became furious. He ordered his son to be chained to a mountain and for a vulture to peck out his liver every day till eternity. Then he began to devise a punishment for mankind. Another of his sons created a woman of great beauty, Pandora. Each of the gods gave her a gift. Zeus' present was curiosity and a box which he ordered her never to open. Then he presented her to Epimetheus as a wife.

Pandora's life with Epimetheus was happy except for her intense longing to open the box. She was convinced that because the gods and goddesses had showered so many glorious gifts upon her that this one would also be wonderful. One day when Epimetheus was gone, she opened the box.

Out of the box flew all of the horrors which plague the world today - pain, sickness, envy, suffering, war, greed. Upon hearing Pandora's screams Epimetheus rushed home and fastened the lid shut, but all of the evils had already escaped.

Later that night they heard a voice coming from the box saying, "Let me out. I am hope."

Pandora and Epimetheus released her and she flew out into the world to give hope to humankind.

Ancient myths and creation stories from the native peoples of North and South America, from Africa, and from ancient China and around the world hold and express similar explanations with common themes.

Reflect for the moment on what patterns and underpinning themes that you can you discern from this collection of ancient creation stories and then relate that from others that you personally know? What creation myths or allegories or parables have shaped your own ideas and perspective?

CHAPTER 4

Another Circle Closes In The Arising And Advance Of Quantum Physics

"Any intelligent fool can make things bigger, more complex, and more violent. It takes a touch of genius— and a lot of courage—to move in the opposite direction."

E.F. SCHUMACHER

Advances in quantum physics dealt classic materialist adherents an untended yet serious setback in the latter part of the 20th Century. Quantum theory as conceived and constructed by the work of a breakthrough generation of Human Number 3 intellects (the term later explained) including Niels Bohr, Paul Dirac, Erwin Schrödinger and Werner Heisenberg in the 1920s and 1930s changing forever the predictable assumptions of Newtonian mechanical physics.

As it happens, at the extreme smallest scale of the subatomic particle level, even seemingly ordinary matter can show some strange and even extraordinary properties.

For example, CERN Physicist John Bell eventually arrived at the view that quantum physics cannot be solely local – that is to say that it permits phenomena to be correlated and connected at arbitrarily large distances from each other. For Bell, there were unknown variables operating as a possible explanation. Einstein had presaged it with his description: 'spooky-action-at-a-distance." The phenomenon was demonstrated experimentally and led to what is known as 'quantum entanglement', essential in the development of artificial intelligence and quantum computers. On one level, quantum entanglement can be directly understood as being about interactions and relationships.

What could it mean in practical application? Quantum physics has been described as "magic without the lies." Why so? Possibly because matter is energy and energy is matter, or manifested as waves and particles simultaneously? Or what is hidden inside the subatomic cupboard of protons, electrons, neutrons, quarks, muons and the Higgs fields hinting at such seemingly 'magical' properties? Is any sufficiently advanced 'technology' actually likely to be indistinguishable from 'magic' as Clarke once proposed?

A time-travelling visitor arriving from life in the 21st Century to the 14th Century bringing contemporary gadgets and technology inventions might be considered an 'alien god' or some mystical apparition by the inhabitants of era of human history? But do our technological gadgets which allow us to transport our planetary bodies flying in mechanical machines through the air, to communicate instantly over vast distances, or to send robots to Mars actually make us in any way objectively superior to the ancestors living in the 14th Century? As a species have humans actually evolved any further in 500 years, or are we simply just rather arrogant 'Clever Apes.'

Physicist and rigorous thinker Richard Feynman notably was

purported to observe in 1964 that anyone who pretends to understand quantum mechanics would have to be "lying or mad." Feynman equally warned that "first you must not fool yourself, as you are the easiest person to fool."

Feynman observed that the scale of light can be described by numbers, which are called the *frequency*. Although human eyes can't see ultraviolet light, its presence can be detected by photographic plates. It's still light, just the number of the *frequency* is different. Hold on to this concept of frequency as it will unfold further in coming pages.

Studying Feynman's tests of truth, and his method of four steps to learning is certainly worthwhile and commended for anyone seeking a system in the search for it. The second of his four techniques for learning requires nothing at all like formatory apparatus or rote learning, but deep understanding on such a level as the most advanced complexity could be explained to a young child. This was the test he often gave to his graduate students.

"If the universe is the answer - then what is the question?"

This was the riddle posed by physicist Leon Lederman and his collaborator science writer Dick Teresi in their 1993 popular book "The God Particle" which brought the Higgs Boson into widespread public awareness.

Lederman was an original thinker and an early proponent of particle accelerators leading eventually to the CERN project in Geneva. *The God Particle (Lederman reportedly remained an avowed atheist through life)* and his subsequent books are highly informative and provide one of the superior and most readable overviews of the foundations, history and progression of physics and science. Some of the best insights of his long and distinguished career came later in *"Quantum Physics for Poets"* (2010) which he co-authored with Christopher T. Hill.

Although Lederman may have named his book the "God Particle" in his compelling story of the search for evidence of the elusive Higgs Boson, the ever-present and much overlooked reality is that *every particle of every nature and every composition, everywhere in or out of existence is a God particle.*

A CONTROVERSIAL CONVERGENCE OF THE HINDU UPANISHADS, BUDDHIST AND TAOIST THOUGHT WITH QUANTUM PHYSICS

Heisenberg reportedly read, studied and came to respect some of the ancient Eastern philosophies and ideas, perceiving parallels with quantum mechanics. Whether that was literally true or contrived, it is more certain that he was influenced by his contact with Rabindranath Tagore and his introduction to the ancient Hindu Upanishads. Heisenberg was quoted by Austrian Physicist Fritjof Capra as saying that after that introduction some of the far-flung ideas of particle physics made sense in the light of the ancient Vedic writings (*Capra 1989 – Uncommon Wisdom- Conversations with Remarkable People*).

Fritjof Capra wrote a highly insightful, pivotal and controversial book released in 1975. *The Tao of Physics: An Exploration of the Parallels Between Modern Physics and Eastern Mysticism* (1975), Capra's first book, upended and challenged conventional thinking by demonstrating striking parallels between Vedic and Eastern mystical traditions and the discoveries of 20th century physics. Originally printed by a small publisher with no budget for promotion, the book became a bestseller by word of mouth until it was picked up by a major American publishing house. It was subsequently published in 43 editions in 23 languages.

It was a brave move by a physicist in 1975 as the reaction from many of the critics and academic contemporaries at the time and subsequently could be described by the term "pecking-out-his-eyes-by-other-jealous-chickens-in-the-coop." Essentially, most of the criticisms were based on the negation that Capra had taken several steps too far to draw parallels where none existed or could be conclusively proven.

Capra can be fairly and accurately credited with taking an important, overdue step in breaking through boundaries, connecting 'dots,' and opening doors and minds to free thought and new lines of inquiry and understanding.

Another influential popular writer who was a contemporary of Capra was Gary Zukav, author of the *"The Whirling Wu Li Masters (1979),"* Zukav experienced a life journey of personal transformation from a time of struggle as a discontented war veteran to introductory physics and alternative thought through his friend Jack Scarfatti, from Lawrence Berkeley Laboratory. *Whirling Masters* generally was well received, even in the scientific community, as it was Zukav's skill to render and translate the arcane complexities, concepts and equation language of physics into a comprehensible English inter-pretation that appealed not only to a wide public audience, but also to a number of academics.

Zukav reportedly went into natural retreat for contemplation and reflection for period of time from 1987 where he lived in a cabin on a mountain and emerged to subsequently write his 1989 book, *Seat of the Soul.* The second book became a best seller as he gained fame and popularity from discussions of his ideas via a series of media interviews. One particularly insightful interview Zukav gave was with psychologist Jeffrey Mishlove in his "Thinking Allowed" program.

In the historic "Thinking Allowed" public broadcasting series Mishlove, had interviewed several leading original unusual thinkers and exceptional teachers including Irina Tweedy and Joseph Campbell. The interviews and insights from the *Thinking Allowed* series are referenced as commendable and worthwhile. One of Zukav's key insights is summed in the quote:

"We are spiritual beings, we have always been spiritual beings and we will always be spiritual beings. The difference is that now we are becoming aware of ourselves as spiritual beings and that is making all the difference."

PROXIMITY - GETTING CLOSE TO THE MARK

What do you imagine these thinkers, researchers, scientists, poets, avatars and adepts share in common in their search for knowledge and truth? Some have most definitely come close to the 'mark.'

What could getting "close to the mark" mean?

The English term "sin" meant in ancient Greek, Hebrew and Aramaic sources of the Jewish Talmud and the Christian Bible have the meaning to "miss the mark' (harmatia or hata) as used in archery or spear throwing. Missing the mark, from the centre of the target, was also understood in metaphor to be away from, falling short of the divine, holy perfection of the Supreme Divine. Can the same principle can be applied to knowledge, understanding and wisdom? There are few popularly known exceptional contemporary thinkers and writers who have come spectacularly close to the mark. One of these 'living treasures' James Lovelock, became best known as he conceived and went on to expound and articulate the Gaia Hypothesis.

"The biosphere and I are both in the last 1% of our lives."

JAMES LOVELOCK AT AGE 100 IN 2020- HE DIED AT 103

James Lovelock, independent scientist, practical, innovative thinker, and a pioneering environmentalist and contemplator of the future, came very close to the mark. Lovelock invented the *electron capture detector*, (applying gas chromatography as a tool to measure chemical structure and composition of matter) which later revealed the presence of ozone-depleting gases in the stratosphere and human-caused pollutants in the air, soil and water.

Further in his career while employed by the US Space Agency NASA, James Lovelock began to conceive and formulate the famous Gaia theory, the iconoclastic idea that all life on Earth is a self-regulating, unified complex community of organisms interacting with each other and their surroundings.

Lovelock went much farther to understand and describe the 'ecosphere' of the Earth as a self-regulating, complex aggregate of interacting systems maintaining balance and regulation which allows organic life to arise, survive and thrive.

Some 'air apparent' examples cited by Lovelock in his early writings were in relation to the regulation of salinity in the oceans, or of the proportions of oxygen, nitrogen or carbon dioxide in the atmosphere. Lovelock and his collaborator, microbiologist Lynn Margullis, questioned why the salinity of the oceans has long remained at 3.5% and how such regulation is even possible. They queried by what mechanism oxygen remains at a constant 21% of the atmosphere around the planet, and were pioneers in warning of the dangers of carbon dioxide pollution produced from human activities and fossil fuels.

The notion that that the ecosphere of the Earth could be capable of purposeful, finely coordinated integration in which living things interact, co-evolve and are regulated in delicate balance by complex systems was considered 'outrageous' by some at the time of its introduction. The Gaia Hypothesis (derived from the Greek Earth Mother in the creation story) continued to be broadly disdained by the mainstream scientific and academic communities. Dr. Lovelock best summed it up in his quote:

"I would love to be able to speak to Galileo to understand how he felt. I think Galileo's problem was with the church rather than people at large. It was so contrary to their dogma that they hated it. I have felt for some time that universities are getting dangerously like the early church.

There are dozens of different sects, if you are a chemist, you don't know anything about biology. It's a division into bits. It's amazing how much objection there is to Gaia. Nobody fully comprehends Gaia, and that includes me, but it's an easier thing to understand than God and religion. With Gaia you can go out in the world and start measuring things."

JAMES LOVELOCK IN 2021

CHAPTER 5

Believe It Or Don't

A fair warning. The following introduction to a succession of ideas on the coming pages may well potentially generate a sense of shock and outrage within you. Why? Because they may alter or directly contradict most of what you have been educated, conditioned and led to believe and hold true during your lifetime so far, and at the same time, may confirm what yet another part of you has always known.

Again, don't believe a word of it. First put it through yourself for as long as it takes, reflect and ponder and come to your own considered conclusions on each point. If it doesn't fit with your map of life, reality and meaning, then fair enough, go well.

There are a proportion of persons having the inclination and habit to deny with their intellect. That is, they will tend to take the contrary position to any idea, theory, fact, or even universal truth coming into their field of attention. They will typically argue incessantly, sometimes arguing against their own original position on some topic. The simple message for such folks: "Believe it or Don't." It doesn't matter if there is no matter.

Equally, it is just as important to pay due homage to the members of the "Sceptics Society", as this membership plays a vital role in the quest for knowledge and truth. There have been so many delusions, diversions, myths, fairy tales, scams, medical quackery, delusions, exaggerations, and outright lies perpetrated on the gullible masses that sceptics are essential for contributing the vital voice of reason, and critical analysis.

The principal problem with entrenched sceptics is that too many tend to be fundamentalists with a narrow-fixed view always denying with the Intellect. Scientific fundamentalism can be just as limiting, unbalanced, and 'one-brained' as any religious variety.

This knowledge is not a philosophy, nor is it a religion or a system. It defies categories. It can be understood at one level as a transformational technology. Although it's true enough that 'faith can move mountains,' it is not necessary to believe or disbelieve anything in order to apply and use it for benefit of self and others.

So always keep remembering to 'Believe It Or Don't'. Entirely over to you.

TWO STRIDES AND A LEAP FROM THE KNOWN TO THE UNKNOWN: FROM THE FAMILIAR TO THE STRANGE, FROM THE COMMONLY-ACCEPTED AND ASSUMED TO THE ARCH-PREPOSTEROUS

Up unto this chapter, the journey has simply tilled the ground in the garden, or set the stage, so to speak, for direct unconventional knowledge that is now going to be revealed nearly full strength. Full strength, undiluted Truth needs no 'sugar-coating' to make it more palatable.

The sole purpose for briefly traversing science, religion, philosophy, quantum physics and modern, more recent mainstream ideas

41

and discoveries is to illuminate a path revealing how a contemporary circle in science is gradually closing with an ancient wisdom.

THE EARTH IS LITERALLY THE HOLY MOTHER

If you are alive, you have a planetary physical body. Most human primate planetary bodies come equipped with 5 sensory portals known in English language as sight, hearing, smell, taste and touch/feeling.

Your human primate planetary body is a miraculous, extraordinary, remarkable work of evolution and biology. The body is a complex biological machine. Your brain a miraculous marvel, a work of extraordinary evolutionary celestial art.

Your biggest hurdle is predictable and inevitable. You identify yourself with the human primate body you occupy. The very same one you have occupied since your birth. You imagine with conviction and certainty that you and your body are one and the same. Some believe that the body is all they are. Others imagine they have a 'soul' but then act and live as if they are still nothing but their body.

Your planetary body does not even belong to you. *Your body belongs to the Earth, has come from the Earth and will return to the Earth.* You have a short-term lease on it. Even space-travelling human primates landing on the Moon, or Mars or other planets are surviving because they have taken some of the material and atmosphere of the Earth with them and are sustained by that alone.

In the 21st Century human primates transport the physical bodies around in inventions called 'terrestrial vehicles' such as cars, buses, or trucks or trains. Few human primates have mis-identified their cars, for example, as being themselves, (although there exceptions even to that rule!).

You are not your body. Your human planetary body is a temporary vehicle which was born, grew, lives and dies. Your planetary body experiences pleasure, pain, and suffering, happiness and misery, and every sensation of the spectrum. Most everything you take to be what you own and are – your body, the biological machine, miraculous and wondrous as it is, is completely and totally part of the Earth and not you.

Your body exists in the *third* dimension. You also have a mind which exists in the *fourth* dimension. Yes, you have a mind but are also not even your mind. The only real you exists in the *fifth* dimension, with both common and unique qualities.

Spanish philosopher George Santyana may have earlier come close to the mark in his observation that the "mind" is a phenomenon of sentient consciousness generated by the physical, three-dimensional brain as sound created from a stream running down a mountain.

The ancients, the common ancestors whom many today consider 'primitive' literally worshipped the Earth as their Mother. The thinking and writings of James Lovelock presage a return to our beginnings.

The Earth is not only an extraordinary, exceptional, miraculous, extremely complex interconnecting, self-regulating set of eco-systems. She is dramatically far beyond any and all of that.

The Holy Mother the Earth is a highly evolved, superior-conscious being on a far higher zenith in the cosmos in relation to her offspring. Our Holy Mother the Earth is a manifestation of God more on a level human beings can relate to and have at least some tangible concept of. Yes, it is also Truth that we all are created in the image of God – the Earth has a Moving/Instinctive Centre (located around the surface), an Emotional Centre (located in the vicinity of the South Pole) and an Intellectual Centre (located in the vicinity of the North Pole).

Although human beings are modelled on the Holy Mother the Earth, come from the Earth and are part of the Earth, she is so much more great, so far more conscious and advanced, so vastly more wise and powerful, than it is possible for ordinary terrestrial beings to even grasp or comprehend.

And all this time, you were led to believe She was nothing more than an inanimate aggregate material sphere of rock, magma, minerals, elements, water, soil and materials somehow bound together by gravity and hurtling through space and time, located in what is called the Solar System or the outer fringes of a Galaxy.

You may have been conditioned to believe that the Earth is only an inanimate ball of rock, water, magma, and elements existing for the benefit of human primates to exploit, use, make profit from, to pollute with waste and to have little reverence or consideration for. You may well also have been conditioned to believe that the ancient ancestors who worshipped the Earth Mother were primitives who knew no better.

But occasionally fragments of truth and direct experience have seeped through. The reported sightings over time of the Holy Mother Mary in the Christian religion, the visions of Kali that Hindu Sage Ramakrishna received during his remarkable transformation, the objective art of the great works, all of these have come directly from the Earth.

There are many more examples from other religions and cultures. Although some vainly imagine their own particular faith, culture, or religion holds the monopoly, such a notion is sheer delusion.

Some human beings, the rare few, have reached a level of evolved consciousness to be able to communicate with our Holy Mother the Earth. Yes, of course, this is an extraordinary notion. Why or how is this phenomenon even possible? It is because such human beings have earned it and equally because grace also descended upon them at the same time. Or put differently, it is simply because they have tuned in because they voluntarily evolved to operate at a different, much higher frequency.

A rare and rarified frequency.

OUR HOLY FATHER THE SUN, CREATOR AND SUSTAINER OF OUR WORLDS

On this day, ask yourself, then ask anyone around you the universal question, "have you ever seen God?"

Many will say with sincerity and honesty they have never seen God. Others will respond that they have not seen, but still believe in the existence of the invisible. Others more will claim they have not only seen God but have regular conversations with the Supreme Source as a routine matter of course.

Everyone who is alive or has lived has most definitely seen God, but most have not realized it.

If you are sincere in your heart wish and desire to see God, then simply wake up early in the morning and watch in stillness the Sunrise. Do this without fail for 365 days. One thing you will notice is the quiet, the Silence of everything at the moment before the sphere of the Sun arises over the horizon. The quieter and the stiller inside you can become, the more you will witness and experience.

Most people in ordinary life have witnessed and marvelled at the extraordinary beauty of the Sunrises and the Sunsets. Artists over thousands of generations have tried to express something of the majesty and the mystery.

Everything living on Earth is given life by the rays of the Holy Father the Sun.

Yes, when you look up into the sky and out into the wonder of the Cosmos on a dark night, there are trillions of stars and galaxies at distances and numbers inconceivable to the human primate capacity to comprehend. *Experience the sheer Awe.* So, the Sun is one amongst countless trillions of stars.

Yet it's the unique relationship of finest balance between the Holy Father the Sun and the Holy Mother the Earth created the conditions that allowed and caused natural biological life to arise and evolve. Astronomers and scientists in the 21st Century are always searching for observable planets in the 'Goldilocks Zone' or the balanced distance between a star and a planet that would allow biological life as it's presently known to arise, be sustained and to evolve. Discovering the existence of even rudimentary biological life such as bacteria on other celestial bodies, such as the planets or moons of the Solar System would simply extend the known scope and range of the Goldilocks Zone. The main thrust worth carefully considering is that the arising and generation of biological life requires unique conditions and very fine *Balance.*

And it is the exquisite, finely balanced dance between our Holy Father Sun and our Holy Mother Earth that created and sustains biological life and that which inspires sheer awe and profound reverence.

THE SOLAR SYSTEM IS THE FAMILY OF HUMANITY AND GOD ON OUR LEVEL

Are there higher levels of God than the Holy Father the Sun and the Holy Mother the Earth? Yes, naturally there are, but manifestations of God on those highest levels are far beyond the capacity of the presently limited but evolving human mind to even have a chance or choice to comprehend. To reach a consciousness of the magnificence, mystery and majestic nature of our Solar System is the gradation of the step required to first be granted any understanding of what is higher still in the beyond.

THE HOLY ENDLESSNESS

The source and destination of all, the Perfection of Perfection, The Atman, The Timeless, The Infinite, The Eternal, The Omnipotent, the Uncaused Cause, The Omniscient, Alpha and Omega, The One, The All Pervading far beyond mere words. The closest that human beings have come to apprehending some of the infinite gracious qualities of The Endlessness are in Sanskrit words like *Om* and *Atman* or the Arabic *Allah*.

If you want to be able to learn at least something of God at the highest vibrations then study and ponder and repeat those two primal words and consider how this manifests as Brahma. Or study in the Koran the 99 names of *All'ah the One* God. Or study and ponder the Yaweh in Jewish Talmud and the Christian Bible. Or consider the Buddhist idea that belief in any arbitrary conception of a supreme entity is only a distraction for humans seeking enlightenment.

It is sufficient only to know that The Endlessness is the Atman, the ultimate reality and source and destination of all and that The Endlessness manifests and descends into lower gradations of vibration through the Ray of Creation in order to know Self and ascend back up the scale of existence and non-existence. This is solely and only because of Perfect Love, Harmony, Beauty and Compassion. The Sufi poetry of Rumi succinctly, artistically paints it best of all:

> *I Died As A Mineral*
> *Rumi*
> *I died as a mineral and became a plant,*
> *I died as plant and became animal,*
> *I died as animal and I was human.*
> *Why should I fear? When was I less by dying?*
> *Yet once more I shall die, to soar*
> *With angels blest; but even from angelhood*
> *I must pass on: all except God perishes.*
> *Only when I have given up my angel-soul,*
> *Shall I become what no mind has ever conceived.*
> *Oh, let me not exist! for Non-existence*
> *Proclaims in organ tones, To God we shall return.*

All that a human being can do is to ponder in awe, revere, give praise, gratitude and homage and send All Love to The Endlessness.

LAW OF TWO AND THE PAIRS OF OPPOSITES

We exist under a set of universal laws. The Endlessness descended from the ONE into the TWO. We live in the Pairs of Opposites under this Law. For day to exist, there must be night. For somethingness to exist there must be nothingness. For light to exist, there must be darkness. For good to exist, there must be its opposite. For right to exist, there must be left. For up to exist, there must be down. For hot to exist, there must be cold. This principle goes on and on through so countless many examples you can immediately recall to mind.

THE LAW OF THREE AND THE TRINITY

The Endlessness further descended into Three. There is the Holy Affirming, the Holy Denying, and the Holy Reconciling.

There is the Active, the Passive and the Neutralizing.

There is Brahma the Creator, there is Vishnu the Sustainer, there is Shiva the Judge and Destroyer from the Hindu religion.

There is the Father, the Son, and the Holy Ghost of the Christian religion.

For transporting electricity, there is the Positive, the Negative and the Earth terminals for the copper wires to connect.

When you understand and apply the Law of Three, you will begin to see something of how this world you find yourself alive in actually operates in harmony and your own place in it. The Law of Three is manifesting and operating at the gargantuan Cosmic scale and at the smallest subatomic level in everything we can observe and experience.

There are a good number of other universal laws operating, some more complex, and these will be later considered, but to understand these primary principles alone is a very big task that will open my doors to your possibilities.

AHURA MAZDA

God Manifests at the Level of the Galaxy

When the ancestors gazed out into the clear night skies, the countless stars their eyes beheld, the sheer wonder of the Firmament they drank in evoked the sense of awe and reverence.

To try to map and make some sense of it all, some civilisations gave familiar earthly names to the patterns and clusters of stars and constellations like Orion, the Pleiades, the Goat, the Archer, and so many others.

Noticing the dense, wondrous band of so many stars in one area of the night sky, it seemed to the ancestors like milk. Milk was the revered food, a sustenance, a source of nutrition and survival, so much that some peoples designated the mammal animals producing it to be sacred cows. So, the Milky Way became prevalent down through the generations as the name of the Galaxy where our Holy Father the Sun and our Holy Mother the Earth are located along the periphery.

Copernicus, the revolutionary historic science pioneer is credited with challenging the widely held historic assumption of the authorities of his time that the Earth was the centre of the Universe. Gradually, the proof that the Earth revolves around the Sun, and that the Solar System is part of a vast Galaxy became indisputable. The Copernican Revolution. The development of the optical telescope and later radio telescopes only further confirmed it all, and also led to yet further discoveries of innumerable other vast galaxies and innumerable celestial objects throughout Space.

But thousands of years before that, before the civilizations of Mesopotamia or Egypt, an extraordinary human being emerged in Ancient Persia, one who ascended to the highest levels of consciousness who gave out the objective teaching of Ahura Mazda. The original Zoroaster (Zarathustra) was a Human Number 7, the rarest and highest evolved being for a human to aspire to (AD). Perfection at the level of the Sun and the Solar System. This model of gradations of human beings will be given some attention later, but the purpose for now is to give some notion of the natural scale of existence. Coming down through so many religions from that original teaching came the concept of the struggle between good and evil, and the foundations of ideals of all that came through thereafter.

The Presence of Asha, the Holy Ahura Mazda is within the Centre of our Galaxy. Evolved teachers have indicated that Ahura Mazda may be seated within the physical body of the giant red star known as Antares (AD).

The Centre of the Galaxy is an extraordinary zone where located is not only the supreme positive force of The Endlessness in the form of Ahura Mazda, but also the extreme negative force of the natural polarity as well, seated in the star Betelgeuse (AD). At the Centre are also located massive gravitational vortexes (or 'black holes' in the vicinity of Sagittarius A) which serve as the neutralizing force of the Galaxy, unfolding the full Trinity of the Law of Three.

These phenomena anyone can try to put into words, but the reality far exceeds anything the human mind could even remotely comprehend. We simply have to pay deepest homage and gratitude to Ahura Mazda and leave it at that. At the same time, very high forces from within and beyond the Galaxy have intervened from time to time in humankind's evolution and progress.

To try to get some initial grasp of this, consider constantly remembering the universal insight of the direct Emerald Tablet teaching of the Sage Hermes Trismegistus (Thrice Great): *"As Above, So Below."*

From another angle, it may help to gain some understanding of how the Divine Light, and the Spirit of Guidance descends from The Endlessness, through to Ahura Mazda and our Galaxy, and then on through to our Holy Father the Sun through to our Holy Mother the Earth, of which you are one minute particle of a part.

CHAPTER 6

The Sun and The Earth and the Great Experiments of Consciousness

"Just as ice is a dense state of water, and vapor a finer state, all matter is a state of Spirit. The miracle of life is the exquisitely fine balance between the Sun and the Earth."

G.E. POOLE

As Above, so Below. You have a dense physical body. You also have a real part that is not of this three-dimensional plane and exists in finer, other dimensions.

Our Holy Father the Sun also has a very great physical body as does our Holy Mother the Earth. For lack of a better or more precise language, we tend to call these higher, finer levels "Spiritual." Just as you have a mind and a 'soul,' so does our Holy Father the Sun and our Holy Mother the Earth as well, just at a far higher and greater exalted level.

Our Sun reflects and emanates the purest vibrational light from Above through Ahura Mazda, just as Ahura Mazda, reflects the Divine Light from higher still. The Sun Absolute.

THE SUN IS ACTIVE AND THE EARTH IS PASSIVE

If you can gain some understanding of what this means, you will come to know much about how natural life emerged and evolved, and something around the purpose of it all.

To be Active means that the Sun shines. The Sun gives out its light and its love to all without favor or any bias. The Sun continually radiates light and love without pause or rest and without any reward. Sinner and Saint are bathed in the rays of the Sun Absolute.

The Earth Passively receives the light and the love radiated by the Sun. To be passive is to be immensely, extraordinarily strong. If you want to gain some understanding the remarkable and astounding power of the Earth, then try to grasp something of the concept of passivity in the natural order.

Human beings who want to become more truly powerful and effectual in life can learn everything from the Active Holy Father the Sun, and Passive Holy Mother the Earth. For women and men, learning what this means and how and when to be Active and how and when to be Passive can give the keys to a new level of operating and living.

Due caution. Human beings can easily become 'caught up' on genders and language around gender. This is simply because of the pernicious attachment and identification with the human primate planetary body. In the Real World there are no genders or races or distinctions. These are constructions of Maya, the world of illusion.

The three-dimensional world in which the planetary body exists is real enough on one lower level, but Maya or sheer illusion in the higher reality of the fine spiritual macro-dimensions.

In the spiritual macro-dimensions of reality, any notion of gender is non-existent as an artificial construct of lower animals along the evolutionary spectrum.

We call the Holy Father the Sun Active and the Holy Mother the Earth Passive because this reflects in words, as closely as any words can, the special qualities of each. This natural order also provides the model for how balanced beings exist, operate and relate in an objective sense.

YOU ARE AN EXPERIMENT OF CONSCIOUSNESS

Yes, that's most definitely accurate, truthful and correct in every sense.

Do you remember giving your informed consent to being a subject in a great cosmic experiment?

Well, it may well have possibly slipped your memory but you volunteered and gave your full consent before and when you emerged into this world. You were also born into the exact circumstances best suited for you. It was not done through the vibration that attracted you.

Here is the reality: Our Holy Father the Sun and our Holy Mother the Earth consciously created the conditions for biological life to emerge and to evolve eons ago.

So from rock and mineral and elements, next came the chemistry of carbon, hydrogen and oxygen. Then from scratch, from carbon, from chemical potions, and from energy came organic molecules. Then from organic molecules sprang the miracle of life. Then from the most rudimentary forms of life, came evolution, change and complexity.

This is Truth and a truth far more miraculous than any religious dogma of an old grey bearded grandfather creating life in 7 days, but each explanation is equally truthful on some level.

And what uncaused cause caused it all? It was Consciousness, and it was Purest Love and Perfection.

So, if you really always wanted to know? Herein is your answer if you can assimilate it.

The species of human beings is an *Experiment of Consciousness*.

So, are human beings so special that they are the only Experiment of Consciousness between the Sun and Earth in our Solar System?

Yes, Human Beings are remarkable products of evolution, but Nature can only take a vehicle of consciousness so far on the evolutionary path. The next evolutionary stages human beings must comprehend and consciously and voluntarily take themselves through. This is about *Voluntary Evolution.*

And are human beings the only *Experiment of Consciousness?*

It may come as a disappointment to some but no, human beings are not the first Experiment of Consciousness, and unless successful as an experiment, will not be the last either.

What it means to be 'successful' as an *Experiment of Consciousness* and something about the forms of prior experiments that were unsuccessful will be explored to some extent in future pages.

But for the present, try to simply grasp the profound truth that the Homo Sapiens species and you personally as one member of the species most definitely have higher purpose, or at least potential.

So, God descended into ever lower frequencies and into denser states for the greatest purpose conceivable or imaginable.

Why? In order to willingly and knowingly ascend back up the cosmic scale. Why? To know Self. Why? Love. Love is the only answer.

The profound suffering of the Eternal Creator is because of this conscious separation. The end of the suffering will be through eventual reconciliation and reuniting with the Source.

Everything existing and non-existing will go back to the Source. The purpose of an Experiment of Consciousness is to go back knowingly, willingly and directly, having first fulfilled Divine Purpose.

Remember: Believe it or Don't. And Choose it or don't. Entirely over to you.

How Do Human Beings Operate As An Experiment of Consciousness?

So, always again, *As Above, So Below.* Some models are more helpful than others for understanding ourselves and the world we live in ways that maps are helpful for travelling. But always keep in mind that helpful as they are, *the map is not the territory.*

Human beings were gradually, through stepwise evolution, imbued with the Third Brain of the Intellect as an *Experiment of Consciousness* by the Sun and the Earth. Concurrently in the evolution from primates with tails climbing in trees through to descending to the savannah, through to standing upright, walking on the ground and developing dexterity of the thumb and the fore-finger, the intellect 'hardware' was installed in development of the brain and the complex central nervous system extending deep into the spine. The 'software' for operating this third brain also developed and refined through time and generations.

But first stop the bus, for just the moment, to acknowledge your-self as a remarkable *Three-Brained Being*. At the present time you are an example of the only Three-Brained Being on Planet Earth. Yes, that makes you significantly unique, and yes you are a marvel of natural evolution. But no, it most definitely didn't happen by sheer, spontaneous happenstance or accident.

An amoeba, a lizard, a crocodile, a fish, possess only the faculty of the *Instinctive-Moving Centre*. They operate on mechanical instinct as they were evolved to do. This Instinctive-Moving is Centre Number 1.

A dog, a horse, a cat, a rat, a rhesus monkey, an elephant, a whale, a dolphin possesses not only the faculty of the Number 1 centre, but also the faculty of the *Emotional Centre*. This is Centre Number 2. So, a horse or elephant is an example of a Two-Brained being because they also have the capacity to feel. If you think about it, you can understand how a horse or a dog have both centres and are emotional beings.

Human beings are unique animals in a number of ways but mostly so because they have the third brain of the *Intellectual Centre*. The intellectual centre evolved principally through the frontal regions of the brain enabling reasoning, but also through the unique capacities of the *pituitary gland* and the *pineal gland*. The pituitary deep in the brain is also the clearing house for connections with non-material phenomena. That is not to suggest that other creatures of the Earth, such as chimpanzees, dolphins, the octopus or crows don't have intelligence. They do, but what they presently lack is the full Third Brain of the Intellect required for a vehicle of consciousness. That sets human primates apart.

Prior *Experiments of Consciousness* were, via evolutionary trans-formation, such as radiation bursts leading to mutation, given the third brain by the Sun and the Earth. But after they failed as exper-iments, the third brain was allowed to atrophy and deteriorated. It happens to be the case that a species of parrot native to Africa was one such failed experiment, and exists in physical form to this present modern day, retaining some remarkable features hinting at its ancient form as a Three-Brained being.

The remnants of such long-failed experiments can also persist in spiritual forms, and can be a cause of mischief and a contributor to distraction and mental unwellness in human beings. These are also the unseen beings that the Arab world has long referred to as the Jinns. But the reader would have to research more about that from other direct sources as that is more a curiosity and not the main thrust of the present purpose.

CHAPTER 7

Arrivals And Departures
Coming In Going Out

*"All situations in life are tests, to bring
out the real and the false."*

HAZRAT INAYAT KHAN

Consider and ponder this: there are approaching more than 8 billion three-brained human beings living on the surface of the Planet Earth at the time of this writing in what is commonly known as the 21st Century. Of this number on an average day (natural measurement of time the Earth revolves over a 24-hour period) there are approximately 380,000 to 400,000 born. The newly born are joining a living planetary population at the rate of 140 million per year, projected (at present levels) to reach 10 billion by year 2056. That's around 4 births for every second of every 24-hour day.

That daily number of births is balanced against an average 150,000 deaths each 24 hours. The average number of departures (deaths) for the total of a year, (another natural measure of one completed orbit of the Earth around the Sun) is estimated to be roughly 60 million.

Death rates fluctuate by natural events such as outbreaks of disease or earthquakes, or human-generated causes such mutual reciprocal destruction (also known as wars).

With a yearly birth rate of 140 million and a death tally of 60 million the population of human beings is growing and has been doing so exponentially since year 1900 when the Earth sustained only 2 billion people.

All that makes for many mouths to feed, a lot of waste to dispose of or recycle, and massive use of the Planet's air, water and resources. Prior to the 'industrial revolution' of the 19th and 20th Centuries, a simple sustainable lifestyle of mostly subsistence farmers would not have all that substantial effect on the Planet's biosphere.

You may also consider it from another angle: If the Earth's history of billions of years is compared to a calendar year, modern human life (the Anthropocene Era) has existed for 37 minutes and human beings have used one third of the Earth's natural resources in the last 0.2 seconds. At the present rates of population and consumption, at least 1.7 Earths would be needed for meeting demands. There is always plenty for human need; there will never be enough for human greed.

So why all this activity in the arrivals and departure lounges and why so many human beings alive at this time in the course of natural history?

Well, homo sapiens are truly remarkable beings, artistic works of evolution and nature it has to be acknowledged. But is it all too much of a good thing?

Human beings over countless generations have adapted and successfully created the conditions for their survival and for repro-ducing and thriving as well as for their physical comfort. At the same time there is vast disparity of wealth and resources with millions living in abject want, hunger, need and poverty.

There is emerging a common consciousness that the rates of consumption of the natural bounty of Mother Earth and the pollution and destruction of the environment are both unsustainable and objectively wrongful. The Great Filter test facing the species of human primates is whether this fact will be recognized and intelligently addressed in time to change course, to circumvent the seemingly inevitable from occurring.

But equally, it is not only that the remarkable species of three brained beings known as humans has created the conditions for their own proliferation. Birth and Death are sacred opposite ends of the one same stick.

Yet, on a more objective alternative explanation is the simple fact that a large number of human beings are actually required in modern current times by higher forces and higher beings for a specific objective purpose.

DO NOT BE ALARMED, BUT YOU ARE BEING FARMED

The natural order of the Solar System operates from the Holy Father the Sun through all of the planets with Mercury, Venus and Earth within the first tier. Humans are more capable of understanding through relating with something tangible that can be seen such as a family. Thus, the Sun has "wives" which are the planets of the Solar System including especially our Holy Mother the Earth.

In reality, Jupiter is actually a passive sun acting in polarity to our Holy Father the Sun (AD). Each of the planets is a highly conscious being far above the scale of human beings. On one primitive level you might consider them "aunties." Not the physical planetary body of the planets, but their conscious higher dimensional lives. Each of the planets has a particular unique vibration, a purpose and operates at a specific set of frequencies.

Science will eventually come to the 'discovery' that Jupiter is actually the Passive Sun to the Active Sun at the Centre of the Solar System.

Many of the Planets have moons orbiting them. Mother Earth has one moon and other planets multiples. There are believed to exist at least 181 known moons in our Solar System.

Strange as it may seem, each of the moons is a child just as human beings are the child of the Sun and the Earth. These moons, over vast eons of time, are gradually and slowly evolving according to natural principles.

These moons in the Solar System have to be fed in order to grow and to evolve. The food they require is a very fine vibration. Moons are, in a sense, children peers to human beings on the scale of the Ray of Creation in the Solar System.

If there were enough evolved, (Human Number 4 and above) conscious living beings on Planet Earth at any one time, the moons could be fed directly by the finer vibrations and emanations produced. This would largely put an end to the widespread ongoing suffering on Earth.

Because there are so few evolved, conscious human beings present, the bodies of the Solar System have to be fed through the fine vibration coming from SUFFERING.

The ongoing enormous amount of unconscious suffering given out by animals and human beings goes directly to feed the moons of the Solar System through a very fine vibration. Yes, this sounds outrageous but it happens to be truth. It also happens to be the truth that if you are a human being, you are being farmed, and no, not by 'aliens' in space ships.

By example, the cattle or sheep grazing in a field are farmed and harvested by human beings for their food. They are taken in trucks to abattoirs where they are slaughtered, dismembered and frozen and distributed and sold as meat for humans. When a forest is being cut down for timber, the trees suffer and send out a vibration.

When human beings suffer from hunger, from disease, from war, from pain, from anything, where does all this vast suffering go? The answer is to feed the Moon of Earth and the many moons of the Planets of the Solar System. No? Some moons may seem just lifeless rocks, but all have a consciousness and their atmospheres are slowly, gradually evolving.

So, the next time you witness or experience or observe terrible sufferings which all human beings come to know in life on Planet Earth, try to get some understanding of how all this is being used and how everyone alive on "The Holy Planet Purgatory."

The "great" political "leaders" who so briefly stomp and storm upon the stage of life by starting wars, playing geopolitics, and garnering wealth, fame and power are nothing at all but mere unconscious instruments as well as fools. The Planet has an' itch' in Vietnam, in Iraq, in Afghanistan, in Ukraine, so a war starts. The terrible man-made widespread suffering of innocent children, women and men creates a vibration which pays the taxes, pays the tolls by creating a very fine vibration needed to feed higher planetary bodies in the Solar System. **It is a pain factory.** Accept the evidence?

It doesn't have to be that way. But changing it will never come through politics, science or human Endeavor. Change will only come when enough human beings transform to operate at a rare frequency in the state of pure consciousness

"The Holy Planet Purgatory" was the name for the Earth given by the Highly Developed Man Number 5 George Gurdjieff in his book "All and Everything." The Holy Planet Purgatory has azure skies, is of exquisite beauty and scenic grandeur and offers every sensual bounty and pleasure. *Equally, the Earth is a Pain Factory.*

This pain factory you were born into is a very tough place and an extraordinarily beautiful place all at the same time. You were born into Heaven and Hell at the same time. You also have the option of creating your own Heaven or Hell. *Why did you ask to be born into a place such as this*? – and yes you absolutely asked and gave your full consent even though your deep memory is suppressed for logical necessary reasons.

EARTH - THE ONLY PLANET OF CHOICE

As long as you are living in a human primate biological body on the Earth you have *choice*, because you are alive on the *Planet of Choice*.

Yes, it's certainly true enough that most of your habits, your emotions, your thoughts, your biological functions are purely mechanical, but not entirely and not necessarily forever. Yes, you are a mechanical, biological machine as you are. You are not even a bus, you are a tram, a train on a fixed track. You are mostly a complex biologic-mechanical robot.

But the *miracle of it is* that while you are alive in a human body living upon the Earth for whatever period of time allotted to that planetary body you have available to you, you have CHOICE.

The Choice you have is whether to evolve voluntarily upward or downward.

The Choice remains with you every minute and every day of your life as long as you are conscious and have life.

You are given so many breaths until the point of your last one. Each inhalation is a little life and each exhalation is a small death. It is vital to understand and to absorb the Truth that you do not breathe at all. Instead, you are breathed.

When your biological machine, known as the Planetary Body withers away and dies, which it inevitably does, your time of choice is finished. Your last inhalation and final exhalation mark the passing.

You will be involuntarily, irresistibly drawn away at the point of death to the vibration and the frequency that you are in resonance with.

If you have made some conscious choices during your brief lifetime on the *Planet of Choice*, if you have worked on yourself, improved yourself, furthered the perfection of self, you will be drawn upward to a higher frequency than when you came in.

If you have lived and done the opposite, made unwise choices, passed your life in virtual slumber, pandered to sensory pleasures and attachments, or harmed other beings without remorse, you may well find yourself traversing downward on the evolutionary scale to coarse and coarser vibrations.

In other words, in the precious time you have available in a lifetime on the *Planet of Choice*, you have the option of working to move upward or downward on the scale of evolution. At this stage, it is *Voluntary Evolution*. Nature has taken you as far as possible, the rest is over to you.

Yes, so what comes from the Earth goes back to the Earth. Ashes to ashes and dust to dust just as from the Scriptures.

The higher parts of what was you, the ethereal elements existing still in the *macrodimensions* will be inexorably drawn to the frequency they are in resonance with. You may have to do your time between organic lifetimes attracted to another planet to which you are vibrationally attuned. If you are vibrating a coarser frequency, you could be drawn to the outer planets or even one of the more than 150 moons, asteroids or other celestial bodies in the Solar System. You have to do your time wherever you have attracted. At that point your choice will be gone until a rebirth within a planetary body on Earth.

If you have made a finer and higher vibration you may be attracted to one of the planets closer to the Sun. If you have attained the very rare frequency, you may finally reach escape velocity, and transcend the rounds of lives and deaths and never have to come back to Earth involuntarily again.

Some unfortunate individuals are left in a dense form of confusion or 'purgatory' around the Earth for a quite limited span of time because of the conditions of their death or attachments to their former lives for approximately 21 years. They are temporarily held by the gravity of intense attachments to the desires of the former bodies they inhabited. In some instances, it could be the shock of sudden, violent or tragic circumstances in which they died. These are the earthbound 'Hungry Ghosts' that some have perceived and others claim to have witnessed. Inevitably, these phenomena will be

eventually drawn back to some source of the vibration they are resonating with, but must undergo more earthly suffering before. Those
among the spiritually dead lose all chance of further individuality
and return to the 'great galactic compost heap' for recycling. Never
is anything wasted.

The Magnetic Centre

Although many religions, faiths, and philosophies refer to the
notion of a Soul given to each human being as of right, that is only
a half-truth. While it's most definitely true that every individual
human being has the Conscience, which is the *Active Force of the Sun*
within, not every person has the Soul (AD Probings 1981).

About half of the population of the living inhabitants of Planet
Earth come in with or have acquired and retained the *Magnetic
Center*. The Magnetic Centre may be understood on one level as the
Seed of the Soul. The Magnetic Centre is located around the *Solar
Plexis* area of the physical planetary body.

Reflect for a moment on a large, old oak tree growing in a park.
The old oak had long ago started off as an acorn. Every autumn
season, the old oak produces many thousands of acorns which
contain the DNA code for a new oak tree to take root and grow.
From the thousands upon thousands of acorns produced in a single
season by the oak, how many of them will fall or be spread at the
right place, and under the right conditions of moisture, soil, and
climate to yield an oak sapling? How many of the acorns are fertile?
How many of the acorns will become food for other life forms? How
many of the saplings will survive grazing, disease, drought, or any

number of hazards to become young trees? How many young trees will grow on to maturity to produce more acorns?

The analogy of the oak tree equally applies to human beings through nature and natural law. The potential of each little human infant arriving on the day of birth is unlimited.

The little being comes into the world pure and fresh and nearly perfect through the miracle of conception, gestation and birth. The slate is clean, and everything in life is before the infant who has come into the world of the Earth.

But how many of the 400,000 little acorns arriving each day will grow to evolve farther? How will the conditions the child is born into effect the trajectory of their life? How will whatever the child has brought with them into the world affect the course of their life? How may so many conditions, parents, teachers, learning, experiences and living affect the course of the stream of their life?

Those who are born with a *magnetic centre* or later acquire or attract or earn one will have some belief in a higher power or higher source, however it may be expressed in myriad ways.

Those with *magnetic canters* may not necessarily be overtly religious or drawn to a particular faith, they may be agnostic. Others may practice whatever ordinary mainstream faith they were born into with sincerity and devotion. The common thread for those with the magnetic centre tend to be their belief, or faith, or conviction that there is something more than this three dimensional, organic, biological life of their planetary body. They also tend to hold the idea that when they die it does not end with the death of their body. They hold the belief or the faith or the conviction that they are something more or beyond their body.

CHAPTER 8

Why is There Apparently So Much Suffering, Adversity Difficulty For Life On the Earth?

"Opportunities to find deeper powers within ourselves come when life seems most challenging."

JOSEPH CAMPBELL

There are some natural and logical reasons in understanding this universal question of why life on Earth can seem or appear sometimes so difficult, so cruel, so unfair, so hard and unforgiving, and so uphill.

The reason very simply is because water flows downward.

The laws of gravity and physics applying in our Galaxy, our Solar System and in our World are tilted downward. That is, our Galaxy exists in a negative polarity line along the *Ray of Creation*. We live under the Law of 7.

Negative does not mean "bad," just as Positive does not mean "good" just as Neutral does not mean "nothingness." Arbitrary notions of "Good" and "Bad" remain trapped in the *Pairs of Opposites*.

These are the natural polarities of the Universe that we live in and the natural laws we live under and through.

Theoretically, across the inconceivable vastness and warps of space and time, there may well be galaxies and multiverses which operating under the positive and neutralizing polarities, but it's pointless to only speculate about it at this stage in our very limited frame of reference. If and when our species is meant to know anything about them eventually, the knowledge will be sought and given. The enormous practical test before humanity is knowing how to live and work in order to fulfil purpose **on this Planet in this Solar System.**

To get your body up a steep slope, you have to climb against the force of gravity. Water flows downward and seeks the lowest level, true. But water can also be pumped back up to great heights. As the Taoists observed, water is humble and seeks the lowest places, but can equally erode away entire mountains of granite.

So it is that in this negative line of polarity in our particular Galaxy, it is quite easy to go downward but it requires effort and will and persistence to go upward.

The various famous "Murphy's Laws" illustrate this well enough in observing that if something can 'go wrong,' it probably will. Humans can invent all manner of impressive technologies such as aeroplanes which allow their planetary bodies to soar above the clouds, or chemical rockets which can even reach escape velocity beyond the gravitational field of the Earth. But a single defective part in the sophisticated mechanism can bring it all crashing back to the ground or exploding in space.

Our self-congratulatory technological 'cleverness' as a species has also risked everything by succumbing to vanity and arrogance.

Human beings do have an important enough role as an Experiment of Consciousness but on the cosmic scale are very far down the Ray of Creation or as a highly astute, practical and a most wise Teacher once put it: "We're very small potatoes."

Because we live in a Galaxy along a negative line of polarity, everything requires struggle. To create you in the form of a foetus, 200 million or more sperm cells had to struggle up the expanse of a fallopian tube in the quest to fertilize the ovum. Most of them perished along the way, but the strong survived and persisted. Now what an extraordinary miracle that one swimming tiny cell finally succeeded in fertilizing the egg, and a zygote began to form and grow. Then nine months of gestation in your mother's womb and your planetary body was born through another miracle and you entered into it.

Although everything seems tilted against you, and the odds seem stacked against you, somehow you were able to overcome them all. And here you are still searching for evidence of miracles?

Your body's immune system, tested, improved and perfected over thousands of generations of your ancestors is every day and night in a constant, unending battle against bacteria, viral infections and parasite invaders. Any one of them could potentially end the living of your planetary body, but still here you are. What kind of machine could be invented that would operate 24 hours each day 7 days of each week and go on functioning for 70, 80 or more years? A human biological machine can do all this and much more.

So yes, life is more difficult and tougher in this particular world. Mother Nature and Life can seem, hard, unforgiving and ruthless. Yes, everything certainly requires more struggle and the path is uphill and steep. Yes, gravity is such that it is most definitely easier to fall than to rise.

Yet, through all of this, it only makes the victory of consciousness all that sweeter and life and evolution all the more miraculous.

THE ACTIVE FORCE OF THE SUN

The Conscience – God Within

Every single individual human being from anywhere at any time who is alive in the Here-and-Now on Earth has within the *Active Force of the Sun.*

This truth is remarkable in and of itself. The Active Force of the Sun is what some religions and faiths and philosophies have generically referred to as the *Conscience.*

The Conscience is the internal guidance system and present in every single human being alive.

The Conscience discerns the difference between what is objectively right for you and what is objectively wrong for you. The term "objectively" is the keystone here in the sense that most morality of good and evil, right and wrong is completely based on subjective criteria. Much of the moral code in "Western" culture has come down from various interpretations of the Judeo-Christian religions of reward and punishment.

It was necessary for conscious, historic leaders such as Abraham and Moses (who were influenced by the Sumerian and Egyptian inner teachings) to bring some order and civilization to the brutal conditions of the time. For the simple ancient societies, they had to lead, the crude basic model of reward and punishment was the method required. The message of the Commandments was eternal heaven for those keeping the laws, and eternal damnation for those violating the laws.

It was a powerful enough incentive and permeated the consciousness of successive generations of the regions, countries and cultures within the sphere of widespread influence of the Abrahamic faiths.

Next and later in the Abrahamic line the power of Love, Forgiveness and Self-Sacrifice came through to transcend the old model of reward and punishment through the Christian religion. Next came the third force in the form of the religion of Islam which was meant and intended to unify the Judaic and Christian teachings.

The Solar Conscience is God Within

Deep within each and every human being is the Conscience which is the "Voice that Constantly Cometh From Within" of Hazrat Inayat Khan. This Voice Within is emanating from a very high source, and is immensely pure and inconceivably powerful. It is the Spirit of Guidance, Alpha and Omega, beginning and end, and is the path to realizing God.

Many cultures and religions have pictured an external god as a wise, grey-bearded old man, or as a muscular god with multiple arms and hands, or carrying a trident, or a beautiful goddess with supernatural powers, or in many images of peaceful or wrathful deities. Is it not natural enough for human beings to try to grasp something of the inconceivable majestic divine nature of The Endlessness by relating to something anthropomorphic, something tangible that can be seen, touched, and sensed such an idol, a symbol or image.

Others use sacred words or mantras to help them seek and remember God as they understand the meaning.

As everything is God, there is no wrong or right in worshipping in any form, and forming an ideal or God image as a logical step to whatever may come next in the quest to return home to the Source.

Returning back to God consciously is the apogee, the perigee, the apex and the purpose of all living beings on every level and scale. It is the Master Purpose, and anything else is nothing but trivial distraction.

As *Everything is God, and God is Everything*, then it is inevitable that all will come from and return to God.

Yet, most will return to God unconsciously and unknowingly. But for those coming through and living a life on Earth, there is a brief time of precious choice. Choice of voluntary evolution, Service to the Existence, and the choice of ascending over descending.

So why then doesn't everyone listen to this truly remarkable, internal guidance system which is the divine birthright?

Many reasons, but mostly because we "bury the conscience" when we go against it. The deeper the Conscience is buried, the less chance you will have hear it.

The *Myth of Atlantis* is the teaching allegory, a parable left from ancient sources and is all about the Conscience (AD). Whether an ancient land of Atlantis, as referred to by Plato, literally existed was never the point or the central thrust. It is the teaching allegory about raising Atlantis which is the Conscience or burying Atlantis that is paramount.

The guards at Dachau, Buchenwald or Auschwitz had to bury their Conscience deepest in order to carry out the horror of their atrocities against fellow human beings in the 20th Century. Another historic example, the Khmer Rouge minions of Pol Pot in the Killing Fields of Cambodia. There are all too many other extreme human tragedies of genocide and brutality illustrating the point throughout history and in contemporary life. All of it shall be repeated over and again unless and until humankind awakens to change and conscious transformation.

All so many of the prominent people, politicians, and so-called 'great leaders' operating in the world today have also buried their Conscience to a deeper or lesser extent also. This truth can be seen by the results of state of the world. They are principally driven by negative motives with vibrations of selfishness, power, fear and greed. The results thus obtained demonstrate with flawless clarity the conclusive proof of this.

How can these things possibly happen? Purely because those human beings failed to see the universal truth right under their noses. The Universal Truth that all is God and all is One and All is connected.

Myriad external human-made laws attempting to regulate the boundaries of human conduct but are usually purely subjective. Just as there is Absolute Truth and Relative Truth, this are Objective Absolute Laws and Relative Subjective Laws in force.

The Active Force of the Sun which is the Conscience, or God Within is wholly and purely Objective. If you do not listen to the Voice from Within or when you go against it, you sink and bury our own Atlantis. But, at the same time, every thought and every action is recorded. Not by some external Deity keeping a ledger outside you but from within your deepest Self. *This higher part of you remembers everything and thus you will absolutely judge yourself ultimately*, no matter how deeply the Conscience has been buried. More will be explained later about this in the unwinding of the Consciousness at the time and the point of the sacred process of Death.

THE GUIDE TO THE CONSCIENCE

The Active Force of the Sun is so immensely, inconceivably powerful that a puny human being could not withstand a direct encounter on any level.

For reasons and purposes, every single living human being is also given not only the Conscience, but also an Inner Guide known as the Voice Within. Your personal Guide to the Conscience dwells or is located within your own Pituitary Gland deep in your central brain (AD).

The Pituitary is the clearing house, a receiving and transmission station. Personal prayers, for example, go through the Pituitary (AD). Not only is this pea-sized double-lobed remarkable organ medically the "master gland" for the endocrine system, but it is the link between the material and ethereal dimensions.

The pine-coned shape Pineal Gland is also very important with separate, related unique functions of its own, as it has become an subject of much study and speculation.

Many various religions, faiths and philosophies hint at some kind of "Guardian Angel" or a "Spirit Guide" or some other descriptor in their teachings and myths.

You absolutely have an individual Guide to the Conscience which is the voice "which constantly cometh from within," described in the prayers of H.I. Khan. Yet, the voice within is passive, wholly passive. You do not hear because there is so much clutter and noise in your head, in your consciousness and in all competing parts of you. How can anything come through that din?

Nothing is volunteered or given out without you asking the question. In order to make any contact with your Guide, you must make the persistent sincere effort from the best motives and not allow yourself to be distracted or diverted by any vain imaginings.

Every Guide to the Conscience would have reached a stage of conscious attainment in a prior life somewhere. If and when you progress in your own development and evolution it will directly benefit your Guide to progress to a higher level.

Systematic methods such as meditation, fasting and yoga, properly applied consistently over time can achieve a result to quieten the mind, attract stillness and create the conditions for the ultimate aim of Silence. When the inner noise is quietened and the channels are opened to a higher frequency, the Guide will come through to communicate with you *only if and when you actively and persistently ask the questions.*

You, alone, must make the sustained effort and take the steps to contact your Guide, because the Voice Within is completely passive. There are certain methods such as application of the Pendulum that can be applied to make contact with the Guide to the Conscience as well as your Subconscious Mind, but there are risks of self-delusion, interference by malevolent entities, and your efforts must be sincere as well as sustained. Each answer must be check and double-checked to assure accuracy. Many are the charlatans who claim some kind of communication from a 'higher source', but are actually deluded by vain imaginings or by distractive lower entities.

CHAPTER 9

Night Of The Living Dead –
Those Without Magnetic Centers

Now you are more aware of how the unconscious suffering and negative vibration being produced from human beings has a purpose and is being naturally harvested for reasons, and the fact that we exist in a Galaxy along the line of the negative polarity, you can begin to understand more about why life on the Planet of Choice can sometimes seem so tough, so unforgiving and so uphill.

But there is a further enormously important factor operating as well contributing to and producing this effect.

Again, don't be unduly alarmed, but not only are you being farmed, you are also being controlled and ruled mostly by "Dead People."

You may have possibly been strangely attracted to watching horror movies or reading books with scary ghost stories throughout your life?

The reasons for that attraction will be explained later, but the reality is that you have been in vivid everyday reality living in a land inhabited and mostly run by "zombies".

Yes, it's unfortunately true. The world is being ruled mainly by dead people.

About 50% of the human being population on planet Earth are without the Magnetic Centre. That will, in 21st Century scales, be about 4 billion or so "zombies" wandering about. Many of them are 'prominent' people, and particularly many are the Power-Possessed who are the politicians and the holders of wealth and power who exert the most influence.

Yes, there are some rare and notable exceptions to even this rule, but by and large it is true and relentlessly real.

Human beings come in one of three states: the *hyclic* or the dead; the *psychic* or the people following ordinary outer forms of religions and looking for miracles; and the *pneumatic*: those working and struggling to awaken, to voluntarily attain consciousness and evolve (AD).

A dead person without the Magnetic Centre will be totally identified with and attached to the body. Typically, but not always, a living dead person without the Magnetic Centre will be a materialist-atheist in personal beliefs about life and death. They will not believe in any 'higher' power or deity, or anything beyond the material body, although some insincere hypocrites may outwardly claim to. So when their body dies, they die with it, and they are most definitely correct enough about that point.

On another objective level, spiritually dead people *could be seen as failed individual Experiments of Consciousness* as a single member of their species. A species can succeed or fail as an experiment of consciousness and so can individual members of that species.

Concepts of 'success' or 'failure' in this instance simply mean fulfilling or not the divine purpose for which they have been created or manifested.

But, equally, don't ever be too hasty to judge the "Quick and the Dead" as some people whom you may imagine to be dead could indeed have a weak magnetic centre, such as the Agnostic who does not claim to know, but believes in "something." People who believe sincerely in some undefined 'higher power', who follow some ethical code, and have some interest beyond their human primate body may well be among the living.

In so many other cases, people displaying all the outward religious institutional trappings who profess 'great spiritual knowledge', great Piety, or are high officials in the Church, the Mosque, the Temple or the Synagogue can be absolutely as dead as the extinct Dodo Bird. The horrible abuses by priests and other authority figures within the various churches and religious institutions over centuries bear conclusive witness to this truth.

As half the population, you will find the living dead drawn to many fields of endeavour such as criminals prone to violence, illicit drug manufacturers, dealers, and users, and many politicians, religious zealots, the excessively wealthy, greedy, and 'successful', cyber hackers, scammers and thieves, and other course, the power-possessed individuals. Many find themselves shocked and saddened to learn that some of their close relatives, associates or friends are among the living dead. Some of the living dead can appear or manifest as perfectly nice people as well.

How does "some-body" not have a Magnetic Centre, or how do they lose it?

Well, about half the people coming into the world are coming in without a Magnetic Centre. This is their last chance and last go around in the Wheel of Life which is the process of incarnation, the birth and rebirth of the spiritual part into a human primate body upon Earth, the Planet of Choice.

What happens to people with Magnetic Centres when they die?

For those with Magnetic Centres who have not more fully evolved, they will be drawn back into the Wheel of Life and attracted through Karmic Law to the vibration consistent with what they have made during their lifetime living on the Planet of Choice. They will be given further chances to learn and evolve by being reborn again, in due course, into a human body, and under the conditions best suited for their development (AD). At the same time, there will be a nearly impenetrable veil drawn between the previous existence and the next.

The Dead without a Magnetic Centre are essentially transferred into the "Great Galactic Compost Heap" so to speak, as a failed experiment of consciousness. Nothing is wasted or lost. Their physical bodies go back to Mother Earth. Whatever was of their individuality in the various parts will be broken down to be recycled again in some other form. Nature is ever efficient and never wastes anything. But they will be drawn back down the scale of existence and return unconsciously and unknowingly, losing individuality.

The Parable of Lazarus in the Christian Gospels is the teaching story familiar to millions around the world, but usually only in its literal, first level meaning.

When Jesus raised Lazarus from the Dead, it was a remarkable miracle of the Messiah for reasons that ordinarily long eluded most orthodox, mainstream Biblical scholars. Lazarus was simply among the Spiritually Dead and the Teaching of Jesus performed the miracle of raising him from that dense state. Nothing happened to his coarse Planetary Body, nor was it at all even relevant.

A person who has no Magnetic Centre and is dead could easily and immediately be given one miraculously, *just for the asking (AD)*.

The reason it was a miracle is because of the problem is that most of the Living Dead will not perceive the need or want a Magnetic Centre. There will be others who may be given a weak Magnetic Centre but will later lose it again through their subsequent actions and descent back into dense vibration.

There are, however, many inspiring real-life stories of redemption in which a Lazarus is raised from the Dead. One simple, practical example may be a person born into a life where they were abused, mistreated, injured, or traumatized by people and circumstances. Later on, they may have become addicted to drugs, for example, and then have reached rock bottom. They then somehow undergo an awakening in crisis after years of tribulation. The 'awakening' may have been through an orthodox or exoteric religion which might be quite narrow, literalist and dogmatic in nature. Nevertheless, the flicker of the spark within, the Magnetic Centre was reignited, and the person is far better off in an objective sense than they ever were before. They have learnt something. It is salvation, it is redemption. Their journey will continue.

DEVELOPMENT OF THE SOUL

The tiny Magnetic Centre must be fed, nurtured and maintained, as it is the Seed of the Soul and the only thing in a human being which is close to being real.

A Soul Has to Be Earned

Orthodox exoteric (outer form) religious doctrine is quite wrong in espousing and perpetuating the false view that every human being is born with Soul. It is simply untrue, inconsistent with reality, and fanciful. It is not how Nature works. A Soul has to be *earned* and grown from the Seed of the Magnetic Centre.

Only half the human beings born on the Planet of Choice Mother Earth will come in with the Magnetic Centre. Fewer still will ever go on to actually develop a Soul.

A Soul is far more evolved, potent, and enduring, and can create the foundation and conditions for the individualized self to evolve much farther.

Any ordinary person could evolve to the stage of developing a Soul just by sincerely following and practicing any of the mainstream orthodox religions. Or by following a moral code largely consistent with objective justice, by practicing devotion to some ideal of God in whatever way it is understood, and by showing some love care and consideration for fellow human beings, a person can lead a worthwhile life and progress on the path, anyone could earn and develop a soul.

A Soul has a significantly longer durability of existence than a Magnetic Centre and a more potent range of gravity and force.

The Body Kesdjan

The development of the Body Kesdjan (the word from Persian origin) can be understood as the creation of a vessel or a 'ship' for the Soul. Although there are notions and explanations for an 'Astral Body' coming down all the way from the writings of Plato, the truth is usually far removed from the popular fanciful conceptions and conjectures. It is enough to know that there are subtle bodies beyond the physical.

At the point where a Body Kesdjan is develops *through combined* sustained *super* effort and *Grace,* a human being undergoes an initiation into the "Real World" and through an extraordinary transformation of consciousness, becoming "Born Again."

The parable Teaching Stories of the Gospel of Saint John are overflowing with multiple levels of Pure Objective Truth which came down through the Essenes for very specific purposes and intended effects and impacts on the course of history. The exoteric, or outer form of the structure of early institutional Christian Church embraced the Scriptures at the first level of literal interpretation, missing entirely the underpinning richness of multiple levels of fine, esoteric knowledge contained in each Parable. Teaching parables always were and will be vital and essential to break through the ego, to break through the mind chatter known as 'inner considering,' to break through all the conditioning, fixed attitudes, and the many barriers to understanding, awareness and awakening. We learn at a different level through objective teaching stories.

When the Christ speaks to Nicodemus in the Gospel of Saint John Verse 3 he declares "**I tell you the truth, no one can see the kingdom of God unless he is born again.**"

Nicodemus asks further: "How can a man be born when he is old."

The Christ answers, "**I tell you the truth, no one can enter the kingdom of God unless he is born of water and the Spirit.**"

Born of water means, **born in biological life**, born in a planetary body on the Earth, the planet of choice (AD). This means that the rebirth is of both water and Spirit. This is the state of the Ascendance of Consciousness.

As another related salient teaching directly from the Gospels: when the Christ was performing the miracle of 'walking on water' it refers to the extinction of the attachment of all desires. Water is referred to throughout the Gospels as life in a mortal, three-dimensional, human primate body. That is, a life of and upon the Earth. Walking on water is motion suspended above life in a body.

In other words, the birth of the Kesdjan body enables another order of 'work' or voluntary evolution to proceed from the being and the consciousness, actualizing the potential to participate in and experience directly other forms of 'space and time' at a very high and unusual vibration and frequency. The Body Kesdjan does not have at all in the same way the limitations as the physical planetary body.

The birth of the Body Kesdjan allows transcending of the limitations of causality and linearity. This is because it is not limited in space and time in the lower dimensions in the same way as the physical body. The Body Kesdjan operates naturally at far higher frequencies and much finer vibrations which specifically allows for the reparation of the past and preparation for the future.

The 'higher worlds' are not elsewhere. Higher worlds of the macrodimensions are in the **Eternal Here and the Everpresent Now** (AD).

Your planetary body exists in the Third Dimension. Your thoughts and mind exist in the Fourth Dimension. The Spiritual part of you which is actual and 'real' exists in the Fifth Dimension.

If you fall on the track in front of an approaching train you will soon enough learn that it's real enough in the third dimension as it will crush and disintegrate the bones and flesh of your three-dimensional planetary body. Your matter will be once again suddenly transformed. But the parts of you that are of a higher reality will not die with your body if you have made something within.

But what is Time? Volumes and entire libraries have been written speculating about it as well as about the famous *arrow-of-time or the Merciless Heropass.* In response to a pupil's questions about the various theories, arguments and ideas about what Time actually is and how it operates, a highly consciously developed and most wise *Teacher replied: "There is a past, there is a present, and there is a future. And then there is Real Time. And that's all you need to know about it (for now)."*

The Kesdjan Body is a high consciousness, a rare state of frequency enabling experience through and participation in Real Time. Bursting beyond limitations of temporality, the Kesdjan transcends the boundaries of causality and linearity.

This is not to be confused with any fanciful so-called "celestial body" referred to by misguided "psychics" cranks, or charlatans. There is a subtle causal body like a shadow body, there is an astral body, but this is entirely of another order. The Body Kesdjan is a rare but natural and attainable very high level of consciousness where a literal *Rebirth* has taken place. In this Virgin Birth, one of the forces of the Sun (Active, Passive, Neutralizing) has come in. The Body Kesdjan can develop by the results of conscious sustained work on self from below combined with Grace from above.

This is not possible in Human Number 1, Human Number 2, or Human Number 3. Only a balanced **Human Number 4 who** has ascended the octave and evolved to this exceptional, and very rare high frequency level of consciousness and individuality is in reality reborn with the Kesdjan.

And such remarkable human beings actually exist at this very time across this planet but they are very rare, likely as few as 800 to 1000 evolved beings out of the huge population of homo sapiens on the planet. You will be most unlikely to find any of these remarkable, transformed people prominent in the media or known to the public. Most operate from Selfless Service to humanity quietly and anonymously. There are occasional exceptions to this rule as well when a genuine Teacher may be more widely known in some circles, but generally they operate well below "the radar." They live in "**Modest Stillness and Humility.**" (AD)

If you are ever fortunate enough to come into direct contact with such a conscious evolved person you may first not initially be able to recognize their remarkable nature as they may seem outwardly quite ordinary. There are subtle ways, however, to recognize such highly developed people. As a little clue, usually they generally don't come equipped with flowing robes, hordes of acolytes, a fleet of luxury cars, opulent material wealth or social media followings.

CHAPTER 10

Know Thyself - Knowing Your Own Makeup and Nature and How You Are Constructed

Human Number 1 - The person who favours operating from their Instinctive-Moving Centre. Adept at physical work, sports, limb coordination, stamina and strength. In psychology and approach, tend to be practical, straightforward, direct. Occupations attracting them may include: builders, farmers, athletes, trades, any tasks involving the moving centre. Physically associated with the spine.

Human Number 2 - The person who Favors working from the Emotional Centre. Persons fevering operating from this centre often go on feelings and can be sensitive and caring toward others, or alternatively selfish. Brain 2 is dispersed throughout the nerves of the planetary body and concentrated in the Solar Plexus. Occupations attracting them may include: artists, architects, musicians, actors, social workers, writers, journalists, others.

Human Number 3 - The person who favours working from the Intellectual Centre or thinking centre. This faculty provides capability for logic and higher reasoning and is located in the head around the pre-frontal cortex. Occupations that may attract H3s include scientists, physicians, engineers, computer specialists, mathematicians. The intellect is physically concentrated within the frontal cerebral cortex. What most consider "intellectual" is not from the real intellect at all but from mere rote learning, shallow memory of the formatory apparatus.

To be certain, there is absolutely no advantage to coming in as a Human 1, Human 2, or Human 3 in relation to voluntary evolution or conscious development. Each of the three types has equal potential, advantages and disadvantages.

Every human being alive was born with all three canters in various stages of development from Infant, to Child, To Adolescent, to Adult. Most people are ordinarily a child or adolescent in their favored canters and an infant or child in the other two throughout their life. This would be if they had done no intentional work on themselves to bring a bit of balance.

Another way of visualizing it is to picture a three-story house. Human Number 1 is living on the ground floor, Human Number 2 on the second story and Human Number 3 on the 3rd story. There is no advantage to any one of the them unless they are balanced and capable of working together to *construct the Fourth Story*. Once they are into the 4th Story of the house, something transformative occurs.

LACK OF BALANCE IS THE CORE ISSUE AND PRINCIPAL PROBLEM

It's necessary to illustrate through stereotypes how the lack of balance may directly affect you.

An **unbalanced Human Number 1** may be able to effortlessly carry out gardening, farming, building, or any range of physical tasks without easily tiring, and may demonstrate particular talent and capacity in athletics and sport. But they also might not be able to easily pick up on the needs or feelings of other humans or animals, and may tend to lack capacity to analyse, reason or thoroughly think through to solve a problem by applying the Intellect. Their strength is tackling life through a practical, direct and straightforward approach. They are pragmatic and operate from the instinctive centre.

An **unbalanced Human Number 2** may be more easily capable of artistic expression through painting, music, sculpture, acting or other endeavours. They may be drawn through caring for others to work in helping occupations such as social work, nursing, international aid, animal welfare, voluntary service or many others. On the positive end of the spectrum, they may be caring toward others, on the negative end they may be sentimental, moody, prone to imagination, self-centred and temperamental. If their Centre Number 1 is lacking and undeveloped they may be inept at practical physical tasks and ineffectual, and because they operate from lower-level emotions, lacking in capacity to apply the reason of the intellect of Centre 3 to understanding and dealing with problems.

An **unbalanced Human Number 3** is more easily capable of grasping mathematics, physics, logic, writing computer code, extraction and application of algorithms, abstract thought, and tasks requiring deductive and inductive reasoning. They may be drawn to medicine, research, physics, astronomy, engineering, or many similar occupations. Modern society tends to favour with admiration the

Human Number 3 type as they often contribute to new inventions, technologies and gadgets. The unbalanced Man 3 may equally be absorbed in their own world, lacking in practical ability for tasks such as driving a nail straight, also lacking in practical common-sense, or lacking in compassion for fellow beings. Frequently the H3 lacks the perspicacity, the foresight or the wisdom to know how the gadgets they invent or the discoveries they find will eventually impact humanity.

It is also worth realizing that a large proportion of people labelled so-called 'intellectuals' are not using their true intellect Centre 3 at all but rather their Formatory Apparatus of the brain used in memory and rote learning.

Each of the different types of human beings favouring one centre over the others has their own advantages and disadvantages in a life-time. The big problem all of them have, to one degree or another, is **lack of balance.**

STEPS TO BALANCING THE CENTERS

A Human Number 1, for example, can potentially develop the Emotional Centre by volunteering in a food bank, child centre, or hospice, for example, to connect with and give service and support to others through *external considering*. They may also intentionally increase their reading and application of reasoning and thinking to bring up their Intellectual Centre.

A Human Number 2, for example, may do gardening, sport, or learn to construct a building to bring up their Moving-Instinctive Centre. They may also make an effort to bring their Intellect to bear in reasoning through a situation rather than just reacting emotionally. They may try to learn things which do not come so easily to them such as physics, new languages, complex puzzles, and other examples.

A Human Number 3, may, for example, also volunteer in some selfless service, or some similar endeavour where they learn to develop more emotional empathy and external considering of others in order to build up the Emotional Centre. They may also take up gardening, building, outdoor pursuits, to develop the Moving-Instinctive Centre.

THE POTENTIAL DEVELOPMENT OF THE HIGHER CENTERS

While the lower canters may be considered separate faculties of the Name Part of the material body, there can be, in some people, higher canters developing and developed.

Higher Emotional Centre: faculty of the **subtle body**. Enables sustained states of self-consciousness, self-awareness, and other 'deep' intuitive feelings. It does not replace, nor is it an "upgraded" version of the emotional centre, as it is a completely separate and higher centre.

Higher Intellectual Centre: faculty of the **mental body**. It enables one to have sustained states of objective consciousness and superior intellect. It likewise, does not replace, nor is it an "upgraded" version of the intellectual centre.

COMPLEXITY BACK TO SIMPLICITY

It also can get more complex than this in understanding, for example, knowing something of the Moving-Instinctive part of the Intellectual Centre and other permutations, but it's best to keep it simple, and certainly in the beginning.

Simplicity is elegant. Overwhelming complexity is an imaginary elephant (in a dark room).

At every turn, avoid the trap of "Wiseacreing." A wiseacre is an individual with an undigested tranche of information or knowledge they don't fully understand or practice, regarded with scorn or irritation by others; a know-all. Knowing the basics and practical practicing is the point of it all, not delving in to such an impressive level of detail you end up deluding yourself and confusing others.

If you are simply able to accurately and dispassionately know something of yourself to objectively assess where you are at in relation to infant, child, adolescent, or adult in your three canters, and your level and need for balance, then you have already achieved a great deal for certain. For hints to a clue, most people start out at the level of infant or child and remain so for life, unless they have done inner work on themselves.

To live a life as a functioning human being, it is necessary to operate balanced from all three canters, not just one or two.

YOUR NAME PART

What is your name? Who gave you your name and where did it come from? What is the name you were born with or the one you use today? That is your Name Part, it can contains all three centres if you work on it and develop it to do so. The Name Part is one hope of separating from the Planetary Body, as it can become the observing part of you. It can develop to potentially observe all the antics of the all the other bits and pieces of which your identity is composed.

You can easily see how a small child will often refer to self in 'third person' by their name. "Lisa is going to the store with grand-mother." When first coming into the world, infants, babies and young children are blank slates, so exquisitely beautiful, and very pure and wholly natural. They know and can see the various parts of which they are composed as they have not yet developed the Ego.

They have not long ago entered the planetary world from the macrodimensions and bring some recent memory of that as they adjust to the barrage of sensory sensations in the atmosphere of the Earth and life in a three-dimensional material body. Some children come in with a Chief Feature of Love (AD). Small children may sometimes engage in conversations with what seems like imaginary friends, but are actually conversing with parts of themselves and so spontaneously and naturally refer to themselves as "We."

Those Adepts in stages of conscious development sometimes refer to themselves as "We" rather than "I" because at one stage they see how fragmented is the human identity and the need to summon all the various parts to work together. Children later stop referring to themselves in such natural ways as they are conditioned by their parents to say "I" and as they develop an ego.

Some religions and cultures give people aspirational names. For example, in the religion of Islam, the name Muhammad means "Trustworthy One." The name Abdullah means "Slave of God," and is a title of high honour. In the Hindu religion children are born with or given names like Krishna, Sita, or Shiva. In the Christian religion many of the common names are from the 12 Apostles in the New Testament or other Biblical characters.

In an overt or unconscious way, aspirational names can help inspire an individual if they are conscious of the meaning. So many people, however, are completely unconscious of the meaning of their name or that they even have a name part.

CHAPTER 11

So, Who and What are You?
Your Identity? (At and In the Moment)

"I don't believe people are looking for the meaning of life as much as they are looking for the experience of being alive."

JOSEPH CAMPBELL

When you say or write a sentence and use "I" in it, to what or whom or which "I" are you actually referring? A rather curious but fair question to ask yourself.

Even contemporary mainstream psychology has reached a point of acknowledging the fragmentation of the human mind, and has come around to "discovering" the immense inherent value in the age old Buddhist method of practicing Mindfulness.

When you say "I believe this," or "I want that," what part of you is the **I** expressing the thought at that given moment? .

The "I" could be coming from your Ego, your Essence, any of your Three Centres, your many attachments and desires of the Body, your Name Part, your Chief Feature or any one of the many parts that make up the overall state you call your identity.

Your "I" is fickle. One day you say you want this, the next day you say the opposite. This 'change of mind' is so common in human beings because it depends on which part is running the show at any given moment. This is one reason why people will come to agreement one day only to disagree the next.

One reason there are so many subjective human laws and contracts is because of fragmented human consciousness. Someone agreeing to some settlement or undertaking one day in one part of themselves, could the next day renege from an entirely different part of themselves.

People who go through bouts of mental unwellness often show the features of more extreme disintegration of the many components of identity and consciousness. In other words, those suffering many forms of mental illness often have the parts of themselves operating in silos, in opposition to other parts and are of highly fragmented consciousness. Healing from those maladies likewise naturally involves various therapies and treatment to re-integrate the consciousness.

By far, the most persistent and pernicious false belief you insist on clutching and clinging to is that you are your physical planetary body.

- So, are you your gender? Are you totally identified and defined as being a male or female body or something else altogether?

- So, are you your "race"? Are you defined by and identified with the melanin level or colour tone of the epidermis of the skin on your planetary body or some other genetic hereditary physical feature?

- So, are you your ethnic culture? Are you defined by and identified with your language, your customs, your food, your faith, your family, your Favorite music, your hobbies, your pastimes, your extended social networks?
- So, are you your nationality? Are you immersed and identified by the arbitrary lines on a map that define what you believe to be your country or by a flag or by a political affiliation or allegiance?

It is true enough that cells composing the planetary body you inhabit die and are replaced constantly, but the popular fanciful notion that all cells are replaced on a 7-year cycle has no support in current scientific evidence. It is also true enough, however, that most individual cells among the up to 75 trillion in your biological body have a finite life span and will need replacing. Red blood cells have about four months to live, white blood cells perhaps more than just a year. Colon cells may die after only 4 days and sperm cells live only about three days. It is your brain cells that must typically last a lifetime. When neurons in the cerebral cortex die, they are not replaced. Through the phenomenon of plasticity, surviving cells may possibly compensate for some of the lost function in some instances.

SO, ARE YOU YOUR EGO?

Where is your "I." When you say "I want this," "I reject that," "I feel _____ because_____," which part of you at any one point in time is this "I."

Remember back to your childhood. Can you identify the time or the year when you became aware of your Ego or when it developed? The Ego is conditioned upon you by many influences, your parents, your siblings, your peers, your teachers, your culture, your experiences.

But the Ego which you take to be you is nothing. It is an illusion (AD). It is true enough, however, that some of these illusions called the Ego are quite a bit better than others. The nature and the quality of your Ego you can change and improve upon. You can bring up your vibration and begin to operate on a higher frequency.

But in the end, you must realize that the Ego is a false shadowy self and is illusory. But, like your physical body, you will inevitably stubbornly cling insistently to the notion that it is you.

The task before anyone who has a strong wish or an aim or the compelling need toward consciousness and spiritual development is to first **make the body obedient**. Secondly, it is to build up the Name Part which is constituted by your Three Centres. The final and critical stage is to destroy the Ego. From this transformational process, a genuine rebirth emerges.

To destroy the ego is, in one sense, an immensely positive, highly conscious form of transformational suicide in stark contrast to the negative suicide which is the tragic, wilful self-destruction and premature termination of the life of the body.

Some Adepts, Sages and Saints, have recognized the Need to go to extreme lengths to destroy the Ego in order to clear the way for urgent and rapid conscious development.

These are exceptional beings in contact with and guided by higher forces. Yet also, a gradual process can equally erode the Ego away. But as nature abhors a vacuum it must be replaced with something else on a higher scale.

The aim, the focus, the purpose, and the acme of all efforts is to clear all the veils and barriers in order to Enter the Silence.

Through the practices of Selfless Service, Devotion, External Considering (to be explained further), Struggling against negativities, and Detachment something is built up over time. The "something" is your real self. It seems very small like one drop at a time in a large empty vat. But each drop keeps contributing to the sum as it adds up.

CONSTRUCTION AND DECONSTRUCTION OF THE EGO

Your ego is usually constructed of a name, a personality, and a story.

Within your personal story is a collection of neural memories, beliefs, impressions, and sensations about "where you came from" and "who you are."

Your ego was created, and is currently maintained, by the belief that you are "separate" from others and life itself. In other words, your ego believes that you are firmly HERE, and other beings are firmly THERE. You have a body, life, and personality that is distinctly different from others. Therefore, according to the ego, you are not like other people. You are different. You are unique, or that's what your thoughts tell you anyway. On one level those thoughts are partially true, on another, false.

In another sense, you are unique in that you are imbued with an Original Face (AD). It is true enough that you are one facet of a Universal Gem. One drop of H2O in the Universal Ocean.

As a result, however, of being taught (or conditioned) to believe that you are a separate individual, you experience fear and suffering. Instead of simply experiencing life in its purity and wholeness, life experience is filtered through an illusion-making apparatus. You were taught and conditioned to live life in duality. Duality is essentially the state of separation — it is the opposite of reality, a manifestation of Maya or illusion. It is life inside the Labyrinth - the fabled Matrix.

The more deeply entrenched in duality, the more the experience of negative emotions such as hatred, anger, depression, fear, selfishness, greed, paranoia, anxiety, and perversion. Not only do we sever ourselves from others, but we are cut off from ourselves as well.

The external physical world is generally an expression of the same collective internal torment. Ordinary human lives are frequently an expression of shared inner emptiness. Witness the maelstrom of negative human conditions: war, violence, murder, poverty, hunger, illness, selfishness, fear, greed, bigotry, mental illness and environmental degradation. The evidence shows how profoundly lost humankind became as a species meant to be a vehicle of consciousness. Lost because of having lost touch with the Truth of who we are.

CHAPTER 12

Where is The Presence? It is Truth.

'If there were already a path, it would have to be someone else's; the whole point is to find your own way.'

JOSEPH CAMPBELL

What has been there to witness everything that has happened in your life? What never changes? What is the most fundamental core of who you really are?

Explore this question for a few moments and you come to realize: Is it Vibration? Consciousness?

Consciousness is the fabric of all things. Science has at last come to acknowledge that everything at its core is energy vibrating at different levels and frequencies. In our existential experience, Presence, Consciousness or Spirit manifests itself as the energy that composes every form.

It is nearly impossible to apply mere descriptive words to such experience, as language is so limited and limiting. As the saying goes, how can you describe the indescribable? A direct way to experience this Presence that is Thou, and always has been Thou, is through the portal of meditation. Meditation, or quieting the mind, can open the doors to entering the Stillness. Become simply mindful of your thoughts, and the Stillness is a step. Attaining the state of Stillness can eventually lead to entering the Silence. Entering the Silence is the acme of all endeavour leading to returning home back into the Source.

For anyone hoping, wishing, and aiming for conscious evolution, the recipe is simple enough. A. You must first make the body obedient, as B. you must balance the canters, as you struggle to transform your inherent negativities and chief feature, as you build up the name part (the observing I) and C. eventually destroy the ego. (AD).

But equally, you must always remember the foundation fact that **YOU CANNOT DO.**

At the same time, in order to climb up and escape from prison, you must first know you are in prison.

In your present form you are incapable of doing much of anything. It is only illusion to imagine that you can. That notion is purely an artifact of ego.

But there is equally great hope. While you are alive for a short period on the remarkable Planet of Choice you can choose to work on yourself. There are time-tested methods, technologies, and teachings, pathways and catalysts that will create the conditions to allow transformation to take place within you. It takes enormous sustained effort and consistency. But herculean effort alone will not yield anything by itself. It also requires a second vital ingredient which is Grace.

What is Grace? H.I. Khan perfectly defines Grace as "when God smiles upon you."

All that is needed, **if you have the need,** is to make your firm intention and then persist with sincerity. For in doing so, in humility you *make yourself available to Grace.* Effort arises from below, Grace descends from above.

EVERYTHING IN THE THREE DIMENSION MATERIAL WORLD IS TEMPORAL AND EVER CHANGING

The Lila of God

So, the fine point is that even your planetary body with which you are so deeply identified and attached to is constantly ever changing, growing, aging, and morphing.

There are no exceptions to this in the material world. Everything is in flux, everything is being transformed, nothing lasts as it is. The process of birth, growth, reproduction, decline and aging, and finally death is constantly being played out in what the Hindu Upanishads call the "Lila of God."

The Lila of God turns this way, and then twists that way.

The Lila moves in surprising ways that are sometimes in discernible patterns but often wholly unpredictable or unfathomable. And so, the big drama of humankind plays out within the small dramas of our little individual lives and through the life of the species over the course of history, all at the same time.

But who or what is experiencing and witnessing all these things? What is the nature of your consciousness?

Identification and Attachment

'The soul on Earth is in a prison, and it remains there as long as it lives on Earth'. Man may or may not realize it, but there is a deep yearning in every soul to rise above this imprisonment, to escape from this captivity; and the answer to this yearning is spiritual attainment."

RUMI

There are ever so many barriers and multiple layered veils between you and the Source.

Your primary identification is that you are a Human Primate – You persistently identify as being a Human Being. Your persistent, never-relenting main attachment is the you are your three-dimensional biological human primate body. Only when we know that we are not our body can we be liberated from the bondage.

You may have the experience of owning or driving a vehicle, a car, a boat or a bus or an airplane. As the driver or the pilot of the vehicle you are inside the vehicle. You press an accelerator or a brake, you steer with a wheel in the direction you wish to go.

But would you ever possibly make the mistake of believing that you are your car or your boat or your flying machine? Discounting the fact that some individuals are so identified with and attached to their material possessions such as an expensive car they are deluded into imagining they are one with it, generally most rational human beings, realize that they are not a thing they ride in which is made of metal, glass, fabric and other components.

Why would not precisely the same principle applies in relation to the human body you live in and occupy? Yes, you have a body, *but you are not your body.*

In reality, you do not own your possessions at all. They are part of the Earth, belong to the Earth and will go back to the Earth. You do not even own this precious body. Your body also belongs to the Earth and you have it on a temporary lease.

Yes, you have most definitely taken birth or rebirth in human being form. But you are potentially far more than just that. Whatever is immediately above you is your next huge aim. It may take years from the birth of the Magnetic Centre to the development of the Soul. Above all that is the transformational Kesdjan Body states and beyond the transmutation of the Mental Body of the exceptional Human Number 5. These are only possibilities in the present but they are your personal treasures.

Very few people are capable of formulating a wish, of making a strong aim and then pursuing and persisting with it. Those that can achieve this stand apart from the herd.

The Buddha gave out the **objective universal truth of the cause and the extinction of suffering.** "The cause of all suffering is attachment to desire."

Every living thing has desires. Only a stone in a desert may possibly be desireless, and even that is certainly questionable. As David Bohm observed: *It is implied that, in some sense, a rudimentary consciousness is present even at the level of particle physics.* Why? Potentially that solitary stone in a dense state in the desert is God and also imbued with the wish to return to the Source.

The key given to you to understand and assimilate this great Objective Truth is "attachment." The problem to be contended with is not the fact of having desires, but the extinction of the **Attachment to Desire.** Liberation from suffering = liberation from attachment to desire.

CHAPTER 13

Resonant Frequency

THE MATHEMATICS OF MUSIC
THE MUSIC OF MATHEMATICS
V = ΛF

Why might you be interested in Resonate Frequency or want to understand more about it?

One potentially compelling reason is because grasping something of the phenomena of Resonate Frequency will give you clues to understanding something of how you, and everything within, without, around, above and below, vibrates, links and is related.

Sound engineers apply the elegant formula $v = \lambda f$ to find the resonance frequency of a single continuous wave. Although there is not much in the equation itself, yet equations are provable notations of truth which may sometimes illustrate or point towards a higher principle. The letter "v" stands for the wave velocity, whereas "λ" represents the distance of the wavelength. This formula states that the wave velocity equals the distance of the wavelength multiplied by the resonance frequency.

Physics has been aptly described as the universal language of the Cosmos, and Mathematics has been equally described as its inner source code. Music is mathematical and mathematics is musical. Whether or not understanding or engaging in mathematics (or music) comes easy for you, making the effort to exercise and apply the Third Brain of the intellectual centre that you have been given to appreciate and ponder it may bring benefits to expanding the scope of your knowledge, understanding and consciousness.

Readers bearing with this brief diversion into the realms of mathematics, waves, sound and vibration will be rewarded in more thorough understanding of vibration and resonance as a technology to human potential and evolved consciousness.

The old Latin term *resonatia* was believed to have derived from *resonare* (resound or echo) in acoustics. Sympathetic resonance is observed in musical instruments as when one string on a violin starts to vibrate and produce sound after a different one is struck.

The term *resonance* (from Latin *resonantia*, 'echo', from *resonare*, 'resound') originated from the field of acoustics, particularly the **sympathetic resonance** observed in musical instruments, such as when one string starts to vibrate and produce sound after a different one is struck.

There are ample practical, tangible examples: Any tuning fork of A Scale, which is the instrument from which musicians and orchestra members typically attune, provides an illustration. If there is another replica A Scale tuning fork nearby it will also vibrate in harmonic resonance with the first one. Another practical example is a clip on a social media platform of a singer breaking a wine glass.

There is a 'trick' to the feat which is that the singer will first strike the glass to pick up with sensitive listening skill the resonant frequency of the fabric of the glass, and the second skill to precisely attune the voice to that frequency.

The Morphic Resonance Heresy

Morphic resonance is a concept developed from observations by biologist Dr Rupert Shelldrake from the United Kingdom which holds there is a collective memory that connects learning between organisms of the same species across time and space. Dr Shelddrake refers to the phenomena as the **morphic field**, which allows for transfer of information and influence outside of communication between individual members of the species. It is 'morphic' in the sense that it can be transformative.

The theory holds that as individuals of a species learn something new (such as an orangutan using a stick as a tool to gather termites from a log) it becomes easier for others in the same species to acquire the same knowledge or behavior. The morphic field contains a form of collective memory, and as more individuals participate in it, the field strengthens, rendering the acquiring of the skill more able to go through to others through a virtual osmosis of knowledge. The theory also asserts morphic resonance can extend to collective consciousness and collective memory in human beings, explaining the spread of new ideas and behaviours across societies.

Rupert Shelldrake was essentially labelled a 'heretic' by the global affiliation of scientists, university academics and critics for daring to propose morphic resonance, which is difficult to impossible to measure, prove or disprove. The 'heresy' of morphic resonance and the harsh criticism Dr Shelldrake was subjected to lends evidence to the observation of James Lovelock that universities and conventional canters of higher learning are 'getting dangerously like the early church' in punishing heresies and heretics who question the materialist doctrines.

MAGICAL THINKING VS MYSTICAL EXPERIENCE
DIVERSIONS INTO THE "LAND OF WOO."

Sceptic – *One who practices the method of suspended judgment, engages in rational and dispassionate reasoning as exemplified by the scientific method, shows willingness to consider alternative explanations without prejudice based on prior beliefs, and who seeks out evidence and carefully scrutinizes its validity.*

Sceptics will rightfully interject the entirely valid cautionary point that notions like *"vibration," "resonance," and "frequency"* have become buzzwords in the 21st Century for unfounded 'Magical Thinking' or what has become known by the derogatory term "Pseudoscience."

Magical thinking gives rise to fallacy where outlandish unfounded 'crackpot ideas' without a shred of evidence or underlying natural factual bases are touted as credible. Contemporary proponents of magical thinking or "woo-meisters"(the pejorative term of the Sceptics Societies) are the sellers of imagination without grounding about false notions disguised as facts which are "too good to be true," as well as "unscientific."

Magical Thinking is usually associated with superstition, or imagination from thin air, and is sometimes disguised in 'scientific' jargon to hoodwink the gullible, and pretend legitimacy, most typically in order to sell something for profit. This is not to be confused with "Woo-Hoo!" which has altogether different characteristics sometimes associated with the activities of the human reproductive system.

IMAGINATION

Human primates are unique terrestrial beings in their ability to generate imagination. Imagination is the capacity to contrive or conceive things that do not exist and have never existed or even cannot exist (such as a square circle) except in the idea or mind of the imaginer. Creative imagination can be a boon to mankind in some instances but it is very much a double-edged blade in which self-deception and shared delusions generate lies which obscure and impede the quest for Truth.

A Tolkien or a Lovecraft can construct fantastic stories from wholly imaginary worlds through their talent to describe credibly the incredible. So long as readers know it is fiction, a false but intriguing and entertaining story, there is no misdirection or harm.

But attempts to perpetrate lies over truth, to deliberately deceive, to hoodwink self or others, to make up falsehoods, to contribute superstition, drives knowledge in the opposite direction from Truth and is objectively non-productive and harmful. There is an opposing view in that anything and everything the mind can conceive, can become a reality.

Wrong knowledge is false, illusory, erroneous beliefs or notions, neither tethered to logic nor to experience, nor any verifiable layer of reality apart from fantasy.

Fancy or imagination is hollow, following after word-knowledge, empty of substance. By your own imagination, you make things attractive and then run after them. By indulging in your false imagination, you risk deceiving yourself and others.

In magical thinking it is somehow inexplicably possible to get from A to C or even A to Z without going through B without any natural or logical explanation. This stands out in sharp contrast to genuine Mystical Knowing or Gnosis.

There is plentiful abundance of 'magic' in this world without any need to artificially contrive it.

Understanding objective principles around vibration, frequency and resonance is no "pseudo-science". It is rational and far removed from the din of the so-called *"new-age-hocus-pocus-mumbo-jumbo-woo-way."*

Genuine, authentic pure knowledge and subsequent wisdom wellsprings from ancient and contemporary sources, as an integral field on the advancing horizon where empirical evidence is progressing, regressing, circulating and evolving toward the junction point where **science and mysticism intersect**. Eventually the intersections will inevitably occur through the spiral stepwise arc of evolutionary process.

PITCH, FREQUENCY, INTENSITY, VOLUME

Within the study of Frequency – the more frequently two things are experienced or observed together, the more likely it will be that the experience or recall or appearance of one will stimulate the recall or appearance of the second; and the more probable the state that the things are somehow inter-connected or *"co-related" as in statistical analysis correlation coefficient.* It is not at all cause-effect. In one sense, it's a form of subtle resonance laced through with strings of coincidence.

A sound wave, like any other, is introduced into a medium by a vibrating entity. As everything is vibrating, each entity produces its own vibration. On Earth the medium is the proportional mixture of gases known as air. The assumption that in the Void of Space, there is no sound, is not entirely accurate either, as there are vast regions of nebulae and gases throughout and between galaxies. Even in a void there is vibration of whatever passes through.

The vibrating entity is the source of the phenomenon that moves in process through the medium. The vibrating object creating the effect, whether the vocal cords of a person, the vibrating string and sound board of a guitar or violin, the vibrating tines of a tuning fork, or the vibrating diaphragm of a radio speaker is the source.

Regardless of what vibrating object is creating or generating a sound wave, particles of the medium through which the sound moves vibrate back and forth in motion at a given frequency. The frequency of a wave refers to how often the particles of the medium vibrate when a wave passes through the medium. The frequency of a wave is measured as the number of complete back-and-forth vibrations of a particle of the medium per unit of time.

The erudite 19th Century Scottish Mathematician James Clerk Maxwell presaged and predicted the phenomenon of electromagnetic waves. Contributions Maxwell made to the advance of mathematics, astronomy and engineering were extraordinary. But it was his insights into electromagnetic radiation that earned him a well-deserved reputation as a keystone founder of modern physics. The genius of Maxwell recognized that electricity, magnetism and light are manifestations of the same phenomenon and his equations and theory consistently explained it.

Although it was the inventive persistence, cleverness and insights of Guglielmo Giovanni Marconi via the ideas and contributions of Sir Oliver Lodge and Augusto Righi that eventually led to the first "wireless" telegraph radio transmission, the foundation for it all had been laid by the insights and work of Maxwell.

The "invention" of the radio around the turn of the 20th Century was a watershed technological advance with far-reaching societal and historical impacts, leading to other innovations in mass communication. Marconi later reflected at the end of his life as a commercial radio inventor: *"Have I done the world good, or have I added a menace?"*

Neither was it was the 20th Century "inventions" of radio, television, computing, or internet, cellular phones, or any of the other 'gee-whiz' technologies that were the more real, underpinning value in any case. *The underlying, overriding value to humanity was in the Metaphor.*

The Metaphor was, is, and will be that there are "invisible" electromagnetic and other forces with specific vibrations, frequencies and bandwidths, and that importantly, it was, therefore, possible to "Tune-In" to them.

Picking up the "Vibes," "Tuning In" and understanding something of the reality of the vast unseen Universe is at last moving science toward closing a circle with ancient mysticism. It was just as the discovery of the existence of other things unseen by the human eye, such as bacteria, viruses, X-rays, gamma rays, and cosmic rays led to the wider understanding that there is indeed are vast "unseen" and unperceived invisible things in this world operating all around us.

It was Heinrich Hertz, the young 19th Century German physicist and experimentalist who demonstrated that the electromagnetic waves earlier predicted by the equations of James Clerk Maxwell actually exist. Hertz died at only age 34 but was honoured by his science peers through associating his name to the unit of frequency; a cycle per second is one hertz.

In one sense, a Hertz is only an arbitrary conception of measurement, but the phenomena that is being measured yet most definitely real enough, reflecting the range of vibration underlying it.

If a particle of air undergoes 1000 longitudinal vibrations in 2 seconds, then the frequency of the wave would be 500 vibrations per second. A commonly used unit for frequency is the Hertz (abbreviated Hz).

1 Hertz = 1 vibration/second

As a sound wave moves through a medium, each particle of the medium vibrates at the same frequency. This is sensible since each particle vibrates due to the motion of its nearest neighbour. The first particle of the medium begins vibrating, at say 500 Hz, and begins to set the second particle into vibrational motion at the same frequency of 500 Hz. The second particle begins vibrating at 500 Hz and thus sets the third particle of the medium into vibrational motion at 500 Hz.

The process continues throughout the medium; each particle vibrates at the same frequency. And, naturally enough, the frequency at which each particle vibrates is the same as the frequency of the original source of the sound wave. Subsequently, a violin string vibrating at 500 Hz will set the air particles in the room vibrating at the same frequency of 500 Hz, which carries a sound *signal* to the ear of a listener, which is detected as a 500 Hz sound wave.

The back-and-forth vibrational motion of the particles of the medium would not be the only observable phenomenon occurring at a given frequency. A sound wave is a pressure wave. Therefore, a device can be used to detect oscillations in pressure from a high to a low pressure and back to a high pressure. As the compressions (high pressure) and rarefactions (low pressure) move through the medium, they would reach the detector at a given frequency. For example, a compression would reach the detector 500 times per second if the frequency of the wave were 500 Hz.

RAREFACTION OF FREQUENCY

Similarly, a rarefaction would reach the detector 500 times per second if the frequency of the wave were 500 Hz. The frequency of a sound wave not only refers to the number of back-and-forth vibrations of the particles per unit of time, but also refers to the number of compressions or rarefactions that pass a given point per unit of time. A detector could be used to detect the frequency of these pressure oscillations over a given period of time. The typical output provided by such a detector is a pressure-time plot as shown below.

Since a pressure-time plot shows the fluctuations in pressure over time, the <u>period</u> of the sound wave can be found by measuring the time between successive high pressure points (corresponding to the compressions) or the time between successive low pressure points (corresponding to the rare The frequency is simply the reciprocal of the period. For this reason, a sound wave with a high frequency would correspond to a pressure time plot with a small period - that is, a plot corresponding to a small amount of time between successive high-pressure points.

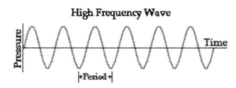

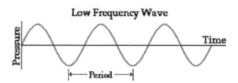

The salient point is that there are frequencies associated with waves that generate phenomena.

FREQUENCY, PITCH AND HUMAN PERCEPTION

The ears of a human primates (and other animals) are sensitive biological receptors capable of detecting the fluctuations in air pressure striking upon the eardrum tissue. The human ear is capable of detecting sound waves with a wide range of frequencies, of between approximately 20 Hz to 20 000 Hz. Any sound with a frequency below the audible range of hearing (i.e., less than 20 Hz) is known as an **infrasound** and any sound with a frequency above the audible range of hearing (i.e., more than 20 000 Hz) is known as an **ultrasound**.

Humans are certainly not unique in their ability to detect a wide range of frequencies. Dogs can detect frequencies as low as approximately 50 Hz and as high as 45 000 Hz. Cats can detect frequencies as low as approximately 45 Hz and as high as 85 000 Hz. Bats, nocturnal creatures, must rely on sound echolocation for navigation and hunting and can detect frequencies as high as 120 000 Hz.

Dolphins can detect frequencies as high as 200, 000 Hz. While dogs, cats, bats, and dolphins have an unusual ability to detect ultrasound, an elephant possesses the unusual ability to detect infrasound, having an audible range from approximately 5 Hz to approximately 10,000 Hz. This elephantine faculty is demonstrated in their ability to detect approaching tsunamis or earthquakes well in advance of the event.

The sensation of a frequency is commonly referred to as the **pitch** of a sound. A high pitch sound corresponds to a high frequency sound wave and a low pitch sound corresponds to a low frequency sound wave. Those musically trained, are capable of detecting a difference in frequency between two separate sounds that is as little as 2 Hz. When two sounds with a frequency difference of greater than 7 Hz are played simultaneously, most people are capable of detecting the presence of a complex wave pattern resulting from the interference and superposition of the two sound waves. Certain sound waves when played (and heard) simultaneously will produce a particularly pleasant sensation when heard, are said to be **consonant**. Such sound waves form the basis of **intervals** in music.

When any two sounds whose frequencies make a 2:1 ratio is said to be separated by an **octave** and result in a particularly pleasing sensation when heard. That is, two sound waves sound pleasing (or harmonic) when played together if one sound has twice the frequency of the other. Similarly, two sounds with a frequency ratio of 5:4 are said to be separated by an interval of a **third**; such sound waves also generate an agreeable or symmetric sound when played together. Examples of some random sound wave intervals and their respective frequency ratios are listed in the table below.

INTERVAL	FREQUENCY RATIO	EXAMPLES
Octave	2:1	512 Hz and 256 Hz
Third	5:4	320 Hz and 256 Hz
Fourth	4:3	342 Hz and 256 Hz
Fifth	3:2	384 Hz and 256 Hz

The ability of humans to perceive pitch is associated with the frequency of the sound wave that impinges upon the eardrum. Because sound waves traveling through air are longitudinal waves producing high- and low-pressure disturbances of the particles of the medium (air) at a given frequency, the ear has an ability to detect such frequencies and associate them with the pitch of the sound.

Still, pitch is only one property of a sound wave detectable by the human ear. Volume or decibels is further determined by the intensity of the sound wave. *But all these various features of sound and music are only for illustrating a metaphorical, higher purpose.*

THE RIEMANN MUSIC OF THE PRIMES

Trying to grasp the mystery of the distribution of the Prime Numbers has been a challenge for ongoing generations of mathematicians. Bernhard Riemann made a leap in his famous hypothesis in the 19th Century through his notion around the Zeta function of complex numbers. A number is 'complex' indeed when it can be expressed in the form of a + bi, where a and b are 'real' numbers and "i" is an "imaginary" number. Imaginary numbers are 'real' as any other number and not a figment of 'imagination' but have a place (as an imaginary unit) in extending the dimensional scope of the coaxial plane.

The Riemann hypothesis is founded on the observation that every input value of the equation forces it to go to Zero as it appears to lie on the exact same axial line, which is a remarkable observation. No one has yet solved the Riemann, but he believed the physics of music was essential to unlocking the secret of the Primes. Reimann's insight was an inquiry into somehow explaining how Gauss's prime number dice landed when Nature chooses the primes.

Why does a tuning fork, a violin and a flute sound very different when they are all attuned to the A scale? One reason is because the sound wave of the tuning fork appears as a nearly perfect sine wave. A sine waveform is named after the sine trigonometric function $y(t) = A * \sin(\omega t + \varphi)$. The key is that there is a periodic oscillation.

The sine wave differences between a tuning fork, a violin and a flute is in the variance of harmonics. The violin wave appears jagged and almost saw-toothed, and the flute more similar to the tuning fork but also different and quite distinct. Riemann explored these harmonics and theorized the patterns between them based on the sine wave length, height and frequency. He believed they were connected to as yet undiscovered patterns or links with the Prime Numbers.

That is, the instruments are all playing on the A Scale, but according to unique qualities defined by their harmonics which he postulated can be understood through the physics of their underlying trigonometry.

CONSONANCE VS DISSONANCE

Consonance and harmony is being shown in ongoing research to have substantial beneficial effects on health of the physical body and on the mind.

Equally, *dissonance and disharmony and particularly high decibel noise* can have far-reaching effects on physical and mind health. Dissonant vibration and negativity can also play it part in attracting lower entities that congregate and feed in such ecosystems. It can be called "striking a sour note." Or playing or singing "out of tune."

Medical researchers are running experiments to learn if there is any evidence that certain frequencies can enhance health, improve cognition, and in some instances affect medical conditions.

Former dentist, Dr Leonard Horowitz inquired into the effects of the so-called dissonant "Devil's Interval" as the purported effect of combined Solfeggio frequencies 528hz and 721hz which he believes induces harmful impacts. The Solfeggio Frequencies have become well known as the scale of 9 tones with purported mystical properties: 174hz, 285hz, 396hz, 417hz, 528hz, 639hz, 741hz, 852hz 963hz. According to its proponents, the frequencies were known in ancient times and are found in diverse music such as 8th Century Christian Gregorian chants as well as in Indian sacred music. Dr Joseph Puleo and Horowitz co-authored the 1999 book *Healing Codes for the Biological Apocalypse.*

There could be a kernel of truth to it as music does indeed emanate from the Sun and is "Solfeggio." But the connectable dots, all the conspiracy theories, and the unbalanced extremist views have brought discredit and drawn apt criticism from scientific sceptics and sincere spiritual explorers alike.

It is, however, certainly true enough that ordinary, non-speculative research is showing conclusively the damaging impact of widespread **noise pollution** on mice in a small laboratory, and on humans in the global laboratory. Pervasive noise pollution impacts possibly billions of people daily. Ongoing exposure to noise pollution can lead and contribute to hypertension, stress, mental health disorders, heart disease, sleeplessness, cancers and a wide range of pathologies.

SONIC HAZARD, TO SONIC HEALER?

Conversely, some pioneering work of Royal Raymond Rife, a 20th Century American engineer and inventor has been both accurately and falsely widely cited as an example of the healing potential of frequencies and medical applications of electromagnetic energy.

Rife had developed a theory that targeting bacteria cells with energy at a frequency determined by the organism's own unique frequency would create a cell-shattering resonance.

Although Rife may well have been on to something well worth exploring, up to the present time, no replicable research has confirmed any scientific proof that cancer cells in a human or animal body could be 'cured', rendered benign, or destroyed by electromagnetic energy at any frequency. Rife was a sincere and accomplished pioneering researcher, but much of his work had been misinterpreted, misconstrued, misused and misrepresented by charlatans and frauds subsequently as inevitably happens under the Law of 7. Rife simply wrote that he had a theory that cancer-causing viruses had specific frequencies, and that destruction of those pathogens would eliminate the cell along with the microbes.

Following on from those ideas, in the early 21st Century music professor and composer Anthony Holland continued on a similar line of research by conducting experiments with bacterial and cancer cells in a laboratory setting.

Holland stated that his approach was to achieve an "11th harmonic" via two different, distinct frequencies that he contended produced in experiments changes to the shape and 'behaviour' of cells observed under microscope in the laboratory. Holland's theory, as he described it, claimed that human cancer cells were responsive to directed energy delivered between frequencies of 100,000 to 300,000 hertz. He also claimed that pulsating energy rather than constant forms was necessary to ensure avoidance of heating and peripheral damage to surrounding cells and tissues. Replicable, reliable, systematic peer-reviewed research has yet to confirm any of the findings or claims.

Irrespective, of whether anyone engaging in research that will eventually yield objectively verifiable experimental results or life-extending effective treatments, the general line of inquiry is promising and consistent with universal natural laws of biothermodynamics and vibration. This potentially promising line of inquiry is further influenced and underpinned by sound principles (pun not intended) from erudite thinkers from diverse fields.

The pivotal 1998 book "*The Rainbow and the Worm – The Physics of Organisms*," by biochemical geneticist Mae-Wan Ho contributes an outstanding work of original thought exploring facets of the question: "What is Life?" through a masterful fusion of ideas of biology and quantum mechanics, supported by practical examples.

Mae-Wan Ho also explored evidence from *subtle medicine* around the effects of traditional Chinese methods such as acupuncture, dynamic water memory, Rudolf Steiner's biodynamics, and ancient Indian Aryuvedic health practices. Applying a broad knowledge of equilibrium thermodynamics in her quest to better explain the arising and sustaining of life, she also challenged the orthodox, widely assumed linear notions of natural selection and evolution, and further warned specifically about the serious potential dangers of human artificial manipulation of genes and particularly genetically modified seeds and crops. She further explored a range of new ideas in quantum optics from liquid crystals to fractals.

CHAPTER 14

Phenomenal Phenomena

Each and every musical note is associated with a unique frequency and tone:

Frequency is one quality rendering each unique note distinct from another. In one basic sense: **higher frequency can also mean higher pitch**. Booming bass notes have very low frequencies, while piercing treble notes have high frequencies.

The ancient Greeks discerned that geometric forms such the Triangle, the Circle, the Square, and the Pentagon, others, correspond with frequencies and notes and tones associated with their measurements.

Angles of degrees when added up always total a specific number relative to that particular form or shape. Robert Edward Grant and Eric Rankin have explored and compiled some fascinating facts and conjectures around the relationships of what is referred to as **sacred geometry** to sound and music:

For example:

The Triangle

The three angles of the triangle add up to 180° and the *Tone is* **F#**

The Circle

The sum of the circle is 360°.
A circle which is three-dimensional is a sphere. Tone is: **C#**

$$A=\pi r^2$$

The Square

Like the circle, the four-sided square is also 360°. Tone is **C#**

$$A=\pi r^2$$

The Pentagon

The sum of the pentagon is 540° and the *Tone is* **F#**

Isn't it slightly curious that the sum of each of the degrees within of each geometric shape adds up to 9? Just could equally be another 'coincidence', of course.

1 + 8 + 0 = 9

3 + 6 + 0 = 9

5 + 4 + 0 - 9

4 + 3 + 2 = 9

As it happens, digits of the number 432 also add up to 9.

The number 432 is more recently claimed by some to be associated with ideas about the importance of tuning music to the frequency in Hz. It is true enough that number 432 is divisible by many numbers including 2, 3, 4, 6, 8, 9, 12, and 16 which makes it more interesting. Advocates for 432hz contend resonance with natural phenomena such as planetary motion and other claims for harmonious alignment and interaction.

Cymatics

The interest in numerical relations to vibration, frequency and resonance relates to the study of perceivable, visible effects of sound and patterns. Swiss scientist Hans Jenny had carried out experiments with a tonoscope to show patterns associated with different materials on a metal plate. Hans Jenny was a pioneer in the fascinating study of Cymatics which has developed to link diverse fields of physics, acoustics, music and art. Patterns observed in Cymatics are believed to be the effect of sound waves passing through materials, which produce different patterns or leave apparent 'fingerprint' patterns depending upon the substance.

Somewhat curious still is when the specific number in basic geometric shapes is applied as vibration cycles to produce sound tone audible to the human ear.

Φ Phi

APPLIED SPECIFICALLY TO VIBRATION, PITCH AND FREQUENCY

Phi (Φ = 1.618033988749895...) is, of course, simply an irrational number like Π (pi = 3.14159265358979...), but one with some unusual, highly remarkable mathematical properties. Some examples in the relationship to music. As it happens:

- If an octave is divided by a perfect fifth, (13/20) = φ
- If you divide a perfect fifth by an octave, (8/13) = φ
- If you divide a perfect fourth by a major sixth, (6/10) = φ
- And if a major third is divided by a perfect fifth, (5/8) = φ

The Golden Ratio and φ

It is true enough that φ shows some remarkably unusual properties (as a mathematical expression) related to the much-touted and equally marvelous but often misunderstood **Golden Ratio.**

In the early decades of the 21st Century much is being observed and written about the Golden Ratio, reviving original interest from the age of the Renaissance.

The Golden Ratio may be observed throughout Nature, although not universally. Some claim its form of perfection in proportion in everything, from a seashell, to the double helix strand of human DNA, through to works of art, ancient and modern architecture, through to music and aesthetics, through to spiral galaxies. It is factually observable in the pattern and number of spirals around pineapples, pinecones, sunflowers and a proportion of plants, vegetables and fruits. The best practical evidence is that this is because the ratio patterns provide best logical access to sunlight. It is likely the GR is linked to an objective phenomenon as part of an underpinning wider sonic geometric code. Understanding something of the Golden Ratio can bring some sense of wonder and humility to the scientific mind as it is getting "closer to the mark."

Many contemporary authors and thinkers have explored extensively the genuinely remarkable qualities and applications of the Golden Ratio. A line of thought most definitely on to something important and worth thorough exploration, research and study.

At the same time, inevitably charlatans climbed on the GR bandwagon, as is human nature. When a fundamental Truth receives widespread popular exposure, it risks becoming debased as a 'plaything' as unfounded or fantastic qualities are ascribed by those carried away by imagination. The pitfalls and dangers of imagination will be addressed in an approaching chapter.

It's essential to hold a fully open mind and a duly sceptical, critical mind at the same time.

Classical physics explains well most of the rules of the reality that three-dimensional material bodies ordinarily inhabit. It doesn't matter whether you're a professor emeritus of astrophysics or a newborn baby: gravity and thermodynamics affect all planetary bodies in the same way. With all things being equal, everyone gets a 50/50 shot at calling a coin toss correctly. Yet, going infinitely large, or infinitely small, into Quantum Entanglement and String Theory, everything assumed or even proved valid, solid and true within one layer, zone, or dimension of what is taken to be reality may potentially not at all hold or apply in the next.

Vivekananda presaged and so clearly articulated this principle, as will be shown in coming chapters.

THE FIBONACCI SEQUENCE

Likewise, the Fibonacci Sequence re-gained widespread contemporary popularity, attracting ongoing fascination and speculation.

The Fibonacci Sequence is a series of numbers in which each number is the sum of the two that precede it. Starting at 0 and 1, the sequence looks like this: 0, 1, 1, 2, 3, 5, 8, 13, 21, 34, and so on forever into Infinity. The Fibonacci sequence can be otherwise described with an equation, such that : $X_{n+2} = X_{n+1} + X_n$

It is true enough that the Fibonacci Sequence is connected to Phi 1.6180339887498948482... as the successive infinite numbers get ever progressively closer to it.

Fibonacci was believed to be the Italian mathematician born around 1170 known as Leonardo of Pisa. Some latter time historian was believed have given the name Fibonacci to Leonardo, which somehow stuck.

In year 1202 Leonardo of Pisa published "Liber Abaci," a mathematics "cookbook for how to do calculations," as researched and described by Stanford mathematician Keith Devlin.

In one place in the book, Leonardo of Pisa introduces the sequence with a classic problem counting rabbits. The problem goes as follows: start with a male and a female rabbit. After a month, they mature and produce a litter with another male and female rabbit. A month later, those rabbits reproduce and out comes — you guessed it — another male and female, who also can mate after a month. (ignore the wildly improbable biology). After a year, how many rabbits would you have?

The answer, it turns out, is 144 — and the formula used to get to that answer is what's now known as the Fibonacci sequence.

$$\sum_{i=1}^{12}(2i - 1) = 144$$

As it happens, 12 squared (12)2 = 144 as expressed by

The number 144 also contains some purported unusual or even mystical associations. As 144 is the twelfth Fibonacci number, and the largest one to also be a square, as the square of 12 (which is also its index in the Fibonacci sequence), following 89 and preceding to 233.

It could be, of course, purely coincidental but the number 144,000 receives citation in the Book of Revelations in the Christian Bible, symbolically representing the 12,000 members of each of the 12 tribes of Israel and as well the number of those faithful followers "sealed by God" for the "rapture" during the "End Times."

Coincidentally, as well the number 144,000 happens to be the length of a Baktun or measurement of time by 20 Katun cycles in the long count calendar of the ancient Maya civilization. The Baktun contains 144,000 days or 400 topical years, with the classical period of the Maya civilization rising during the 8th and 9th cycle.

It is also coincidentally noteworthy that throughout some rare, isolated esoteric religious teachings and spiritual groups, the number

144,000 is sometimes referring to the *critical mass of conscious individuals required to create sufficient spiritual energy* to transform the rest of the world.

Ancient Sanskrit texts applying the Hindu-Arabic numerical system first mention the Sequence around 200 BCE predating Fibonacci by many centuries.

Indeed, ancient Indian mathematicians are further credited with one of the most profound discovery-invention-innovations in human history apart from the wheel- the Zero 0.

HOW THE BIG ZERO **0** CHANGED EVERYTHING

"An equation for me has no meaning, unless it represents a thought of God."
EARLY 20TH CENTURY MATHEMATICIAN SRINIVASA RAMANUJAN

Although the concept of nothing or nothingness has been within the scope of human thought from earliest times, the symbol and place holder of Zero is relatively new, again developing through Indian thinkers, mystics, and scientists, possibly around the 5th Century ADE or earlier.

Although people have for eons grasped some notion of nothing or having nothing, the concept of zero is relatively new; it fully developed in India around the fifth century ADE or possibly two or so centuries earlier. It is possible that this insight was reached through the worship and contemplation of the form of God known as **Shiva.** Shiva is the third, reconciling force in the Hindu trinity of Brahma the Creator, and Vishnu the Sustainer. Shiva's name literally interpreted means "No-Thing."

Before the application of the ever humble but revolutionary Zero 0, mathematicians struggled to perform the simplest arithmetic calculations. Today, zero — both as a symbol (or numeral) and a concept meaning the absence of any quantity — allowed human beings to perform calculus, carry out complicated equations, and to have invented and applied microchip circuits and electronic computing machines operating on binary code. To the early Indian mathematician's enormous gratitude is due.

The Number 108

In geometry, the number 108 is unique with some interesting properties: It is divisible by 1, 2,3,4,6,9,12,18,27,36, 54, making it highly divisible. 108 is also the hyperfactorial of 3, also of mathematical interest and significance.

The number 108 holds various cultural, religious and symbolic significance in diverse cultural traditions. In Hinduism, 108 is considered a sacred number representing the wholeness of the universe, and there are 108 deities or manifestations of God in the 108 sacred texts of the Upanishads, as well as 108 holy sites in India.

In Buddhism, the number 108 is associated with the number of negativities, afflictions and barriers the must be overcome to reach enlightenment. For both Hindu and Buddhist practitioners of yoga and meditation, the Mala or necklace contains 108 beads to perform Japa or Mantra repetition. In yoga, there are 108 energy lines converging at the heart chakra. Yoga and meditation practitioners perform 108 repetitions of exercises, mantras, or breath techniques which is believed to enhance mindfulness and spiritual connection.

The distance ratio between the **Earth** and the **Sun** is, by sheer coincidence, of course, approximately 108 times the diameter of the **Sun**.

The diameter of the Moon is approximately 3,474 kilometres, and diameter of the **Sun** is about 1.4 million kilometres. Divide the diameter of the **Sun** by the diameter of the Moon and the result is approximately 108.

Astrology and Astronomy: In Vedic astrology, there are 12 zodiac signs and 9 celestial planets, resulting in 108 possible combinations.

All of it could just be, of course, just purely coincidental.

FROM NUMERICAL THREADS PYTHAGOREAN SCHOOLS SPUN GEOMETRIC FABRIC TO WEAVE SONIC WAVE PATTERNS

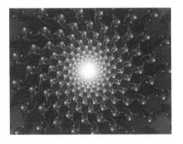

If there is ever a universal language comprehensible to human beings, it could be expressed through mathematics, geometry, energy patterns and frequency.

The Great Sage Pythagoras from the 6th Century BCE Greek island of Samos led a decidedly enlightened and enlightening esoteric school fusing mathematics, philosophy, geometry, abstract thought and music. Pythagoras had travelled to Egypt, connecting with the scientific inner temple teachings handed down through the Sumerian and Chaldean ancient civilisations. Building upon the geometric foundations of Euclid, Pythagoras carried out research, experiments, gaining insights leading to his advanced idea of the "music of the spheres."

'There is geometry in the humming of the strings.
There is music in the spacing of the spheres."
PYTHAGORAS

Pythagoras observed that when a taut string was struck it would vibrate a tone, and when that string was divided in half, it would produce the same tone twice as high in pitch. Pythagoras and his pupils then derived harmonic ratios based on fifths that led to the musical scale at the foundation of much music.

According to Pythagoras, all musical notes were found by applying mathematics.

From Number 1, he deduced Note 27. By doubling the same pitch he calculated, 54, then 108m then finally up to the **special natural harmonic number of 432** and beyond and on up the scale.

Pythagoras believed that planets, moons, and other bodies in space, ring out notes of vibration based on their orbit and distance to each other.

So many and so profound were the insights, discoveries, and ideas of Pythagoras, scholars have rightfully spent lifetimes studying what was left of his writings, his teachings, and his calculations and esoteric ideas.

The 12/60 counting method had its origins in the Sumerian civilization circa 4500 CE into the recorded past. Sumer was the early Tigris-Euphrates settlement located in what is now the southern part of Iraq. The number 60 is related to the origin of the number 12, which is the number of joints on 4 fingers of a human hand, the thumb being free to count.

Five repeated hand counts yields the number 60 which was used as the base for counting large numbers. Scholars of ancient history think that the finger-joint counting pioneered by the Sumerians explains why much of the ancient world based their numerical systems on 12 and multiples of 12, such as 24 and 60.

Today are 60 seconds in a minute, 12 hours in half a day multiplied x2 for 24 hours in a full cycle of Earth's rotation over the day. There also happen to be 12 months in a year, 12 eggs in a dozen, 12 signs of the Zodiac, 12 symbolic animals of the Chinese 12 year time cycle, 12 Apostles of Jesus, 12 labours of Hercules for the Ancient Greeks, 12 tribes of Israel, and the emergence of the Twelvers of Shia Islam, 12 facets to the sacred Dodecahedron within the Platonic Solids.

This 60 system was handed down to the Babylonians, the successive ancient civilisation emerging just north of Sumer on the banks of the Euphrates river about 600 years after the Sumerians.

The Babylonians were astute pioneering mathematicians, inheriting the sexagesimal (60) based counting system from the Sumerians which they used for a more elaborate counting system written in tables of symbols.

One credible theory holds that the Sumerian and Babylonian thinkers were keen on the number 60 because 60 can generate many factors, including the first six numbers, one to six, but also 12, 15, 20,

30. This meant dividing by 60 often gives easy fractions. A bit easier than say, the odd numbers 13 or 17. At the same time, the number 13 also contains notable qualities, applications and significance, as will subsequently explained.

Historians of mathematics think that the 360 degrees in a circle derives from the Babylonians, who drew a circle, then inside the circle they drew a triangle with each of its three sides the length of the radius. The circle, itself, which forms the spheres of planets and stars, also has come to represent the symbol for infinity.

Chladni Plates and Natural Physical Arrangement of Vibrational Patterns

The 19th century German scientific pioneer in acoustics Ernst Chladni's experiments with sand or salt crystals forming intricate patterns in response to vibration received renewed popular interest in Century 21. The work that Chladni carried out formed the foundation for the scientific exploration of sound through researchers that followed.

Chladni developed a marvellous invention used to study the motions of vibrating plates. Starting with only a metal plate, he lightly sprinkled sand or sometimes table salt he observed that characteristic patterns would form and then change with the increasing or decreasing vibrational frequencies applied via an electrical current through an oscillator. With further experimentation, Chladni found a formula that could predict patterns formed on vibrating circular plates.

Examples of Pattern Formation on Chlani Plates at Different Frequencies

Chlandni's work contributed to the rise of the field of acoustics. As the phenomena of vibrational patterns underlying Chlandni's plates began to be better understood, it was applied in practical ways to improve the quality of musical instruments, such as violins.

Once Chladni's patterns were better understood, it was found that they could also be used *analytically*, to provide information about the conditions that formed them. Violin makers have long used Chladni figures to provide feedback as they shape the critical front and back plates of the instrument's resonance box. Fine metal filings are sprinkled on the wooden plates, which are then vibrated at different frequencies to produce a series of patterns. This contributes to the final shaping of the plates is directed towards ensuring that the patterns on both of them match and are symmetrical. Symmetry is what allows the resonator to move as a single mass and to produces the richest, most beautiful tones.

It should ordinarily come as little surprise to observers that frequencies and vibrations could have an impact on the material world such as the patterns in sand, salt crystals or tiny particles such as metal filings. The fact is empirically observable in Chladni Plates that frequencies and vibrations impact patterns in the material world and do so by natural laws of physics. Nevertheless, it is a remarkable phenomenon.

Violin makers were able to apply the Chlandni patterns to practical effect as they used metal filings sprinkled on wooden plates to fine tune the front and back plates of the instrument's **resonance box**. Up to seven patterns from frequencies were applied to ensure the two plates matched and were symmetrical. Symmetry attuned is what allows the resonator to produce rich and beautiful tones.

FRACTALS

*"Bottomless wonders spring from simple rules
which are repeated without end."*
MANDELBROT

Infinity hiding in plain sight everywhere. Fine example of fractal form in a vegetable.

Following on from the ancient principle of Emerald Tablet that what is below reflects what is above, and vice versa, there are observable things in the material world that point to higher principles as seen in Fractals.

Even in this banal, dense, lower material world a remarkable phenomena is reflected and projected everywhere for those who can perceive it.

Fractals are exquisite structures generated in Nature, hiding in plain sight all around everywhere.

Fractals are considered far easier to find than they are to precisely nail down in a single definition. One feature is the 'divine' exquisite quality of emanating complexity from simplicity in repeating patterns. And another is zoom symmetry, and another is infinite intricacy. A fourth feature is how fractals strangely seem to 'straddle' dimensions.

Just as when you place sand, salt crystals, metal filings or other fine materials on a metal plate, then apply a sonic wave to the platform as seen in Chladni plates, the material will create a discernable pattern that is analogous to the human brains, and underlying neural structure in the interconnecting webs of axons and dendrites. It is fractal.

One further curious feature of fractal is the astonishing projection through vast scale as what Mandelbrot so aptly expressed: *"Bottomless wonders spring from simple rules which are repeated without end."*

These are the very same patterns that clusters of stars emanate in the creation of swirling galaxies across the Cosmos. From the smallest sub-atomic particle, to the inconceivable scale of spiraling vast galaxies. This is a feature and a quality of zoom symmetry. From the very smallest to the very largest. This is also what vibration and frequency creates when simply applied only to matter. Molecules will arrange themselves and be subject to arrangement according to vibration and frequency.

Can you then imagine that you are alone or that you are not part of something created?

As remarkable a step as classic Euclidian geometry was, it was found to falter in describing objects in the biological and natural world. The 19th Century German mathematician Karl Weirstrass opened the new door by constructing a zig-zag staccato pattern that demonstrated that no matter how many times it was magnified, any smooth line would submerge into a never-ending cascade of sharp edges and corners packed ever more tightly together. His publication of this observation in 1861 reportedly dismayed and intrigued the community of mathematicians of his era.

It was the breakthrough insight of Polish mathematician Benoit Mandelbrot to found fractal geometry as a new branch of mathematics in his 1977 essay *The Fractal Nature of Geometry.* Mandelbrot's insights and contributions to mathematics and science are remarkable for many reasons, but particularly he found a set of keys unlocking better understanding of nature.

Mandelbrot worked for a business machines company in the 1960's, and had first-generation electronic calculating devices at his disposal. With the advent of their rote massive computational power he was able to explore and magnify the calculus into visual forms.

Before the advent of computer power it was like of a small group of men trying to dig a hole for a building foundation with spades, picks and shovels. The arrival of mechanical inventions such as the bulldozer and the hydraulic backhoe digger could do the work in day that would take a group of men weeks.

The famous Mandelbrot Fractal demonstrates the beauty, the simplicity and the elegance of fractals in its artistic exposition of zoom telemetry in the repeating delicate patterns into the small-ness and out to the largeness. Computer-generated fractals can now easily be viewed throughout the internet and can evoke a sense of curiosity, wonder and awe.

Readers may easily access the vast information about fractals and fractal geometry provided by specialists in the area and it is a fascinating and amazing field. Yet, no words or calculations can come close to the sense of wonder that you may experience from witnessing and pondering the visuals of the myriad expression of fractals in Nature.

The first image is of a fern leave and the second is of a lightning bolt frozen in time lapse photography.

A fern displaying its fractal features. The same shape is repeated in the branches, the fronds and the leaves - and even the veins inside each leaf. Pictural source: Wikimedia Commons

A further most striking feature of fractals is that they're not one, two- or three-dimensional, but somewhere in-between.

A solid sphere is 3-dimensional and fills up more space than a flat piece of paper.

So, when you crumple the flat paper into a ball, you have created a fractal-like shape that fills up more space than the paper, but not as much space as the solid sphere. It scores approximately 2.5 for its dimension.

Your lungs breathing you this very moment are about 2.97 dimensional - their fractal geometry allows them to pack lots of surface area (a few tennis courts) into a small volume (a few tennis balls). Packing such a huge surface area into your body provides you with the ability to extract enough oxygen to keep you alive.

According to one interpretation of the Emerald Tablet of Hermes, *As Above, So Below,* you as a living being, a single human life are indeed a fractal.

THE SHUMANN RESONANCE

A segway from fractals to the Shuman Resonance is illustrated in the time-freeze photo below of a bolt of lightning. Observe the detail of the lightning as it reveals its symmetry for the fraction of a second. *Notice how the zoom symmetry is also revealed as each branch resembles a small copy of the whole shape.*

Picture source: Wikimedia Commons

In 1952, German physicist W.O. Schumann proposed and mathematically predicted the phenomenon of ultra-low and extremely low (ELF) frequency signals in the surrounding atmosphere of the Earth. The phenomenon was confirmed by instruments and measurements by the mid 1950's and attributed by the name of the Schumann Resonance.

The Schumann Resonance appears by the evidence to be globally present and generated by lightning strikes (estimated over 100,000 per day) throughout the ionosphere. It is noteworthy that the Schumann Resonance was formed as long as thunderstorms have existed and hence pre-date animal evolution on Earth.

The Schumann Signal attracted further scientific investigation as well because of some intriguing similarities to the human EEG (electroencephalogram) frequencies (0-35hz) of brainwaves: Delta- 0.5 to 4hz; Theta,- 4 -8hz; Alpha – 8-13hz; and higher: 13 -30hz. As a result of these "coincidental" findings, resonant absorption and reaction was confirmed at least as scientifically plausible.

Another interesting natural connection is, that in classical physics, resonant absorption of an oscillating signal can be used to selectively detect extremely week signals through matching attributes, otherwise drowned out by strong static in electromagnetic fields. This phenomenon is applied in the technology of human telecommunication systems and has been observed in communications between certain marine mammals. The principle is also applied in encrypted low frequency communication with submarines deep under the sea, and may someday be used by *artificial intelligence* to attempt to detect signs or signals of life through the vast background noise of deep stellar space.

The Zeitgeber

The Schuman Resonance of the Earth is most certainly intricately engaged in the Zeitgeber which regulates and sustains life. A "Zeitgeber" (time-giver) is an environmental cue that acts to synchronize an organism's biological rhythms.

Again, simply note (pun again intended) the musical sound reference to "biological rhythms."

The well-known circadian rhythms are one prominent example of the Zeitgeber natural regulation effect. The Shumann Resonance is as much a part of the Zeitgeber as the 24 hour light/dark and 12 month seasonal cycles are. Now think back to the ancient base 12/60 Sumerian counting system earlier explained.

Lightning is an electro-static energy form used by the Earth for regulating aspects of the biosphere just as James Lovelock observed. The Shumann Resonance also plays vital roles in brain-cell and cell-to-cell communication for maintaining homeostatic balance. It also has daily/nightly and seasonal vibrational variations in the local sunlight Zeitgeber. Those with perception will perceive the balanced interactions of the Sun and the Earth cooperating in balance and harmony.

Attunement of Vibration, Frequency, Resonance ~ Love, Harmony and Beauty

The ultimate final word in this brief exploration of relationships between mathematics, music, resonance and vibration can only go to Pir O Murshid Hazrat Inayat Khan, with his remarkable gift for boiling down complex, intricate concepts into simple Truth. As a highly skilled Chishti Sufi musician, he was trained in classical Indian music. In a talk in 1926 he described spiritual transformation as the tuning of the Heart. His idea was that each individual is like an instrument that must be properly tuned to invite the One Musician to play the divine music.

"Do time and space exist for the divine mind?" He answered, "They exist and they don't exist. For a great musician the sound is the breath of music. And yet, in order to play music, to compose music, he must divide sounds in different grades. in different notes, and that produces beauty. Divine mind is interested in this composition, this music of the whole creation. And, therefore, it is the division of time and the division of space that is the secret of the whole manifestation."

CHAPTER 15

The Scale Governing All and Everything

*"If an idea is true, it belongs equally to all who
are capable of understanding it; if it is
false, there is no credit in having invented it.
A true idea cannot be 'new', for truth is
not a product of the human mind; it exists
independently of us, and all we have to do
is to take cognizance of it; outside this
knowledge there can be nothing."*

RENÉ GUÉNON

Conventional human history recorded the "notables" of the 20th Century as "great" individuals of "power," "consequence" or "wealth," or "fame." Filling their list were prominent figures such as Churchill, Roosevelt, Carnegie, Rockefeller, N. Romanov, Wilson, Hitler, Stalin, Mao, Mir Osman Ali Khan, Gates and a range of others in the political, wealth, fame, and power spheres.

Down the scale came a second popular tier of Century 20 "historic notables" which was, perhaps, somehow more objective and may have included scientists and inventors such as Einstein, Heisenberg, Wilbur and Orville Wright, Max Planck, Neils Bohr, Ivan Pavlov, Marie Curie, Jonas Salk, Enrico Fermi, Robert Goddard, (a partial list only for illustration example) or exceptional athletes such as Roger Bannister (record breaker of the 4 minute mile) or the long list of highly talented musicians (from Elgar, Stravinsky, to Sibelius to the Beatles, (the list would be long and rife with debate).

Philosophers on the notables list may have included D.T. Suzuki, George Santayana, Karl Popper, Jean-Paul Sartre, Bertrand Russell, Alfred North Whitehead, Ludwig Wittgenstein, or Albert Camus (again a very partial list for illustration purposes).

Yet, far down at the bottom of the unknown "notables" list would be the small group of exceptional, individually advanced, and evolved human beings who left the most extraordinary and lasting impacts on the consciousness and evolution of the human species, but a paradox that they were accorded the very least notice, and largely unknown and forgotten.

Some of the enlightened and enlightening ones known to the world in Century 20 (mostly through small groups of pupils or initiates) are *G. I. Gurdjieff, Swami Vivekananda, Hazrat Inayat Khan, Musharaff Moulamia Khan, Swami Ramdas of Kerala, Mother Krishnabai, Shaikh Abdullah Isa Dougan, Irina Tweedy, Mikhail Omram Aivanov,* These are the true Resonance Beings. May Peace Be Upon Them.

There is another small group who came and selflessly served and disappeared without a trace such as *Li Po of China and Shaikh Abdul al-Qayyum of Khandahar, and others unknown to the world.* Mere words cannot express the gratitude owed by humanity to this third, hidden group of extraordinary, highly advanced beings attuned to most high vibration and radiating Truth and Love at the highest vibrational resonance, and rarest frequencies.

GURDJIEFF - DISCERNING THE LAWS OF EXISTENCE

George Ivanovitch Gurdjieff came to bring the Teaching to the oft-called "western" world from highly objective advanced esoteric ancient Egyptian, Essene, Sufi and Gnostic sources.

Gurdjieff is among the most well-known of the esoteric 'Masters of Wisdom' and endless volumes have been written about his extraordinary life and his teachings. Yet, the Gurdjieff "Work" largely still remains well out of the mainstream common consciousness. Gurdjieff was conditioned and trained to "deeply bury the bone" so as not to reveal the inner teachings of the hidden schools where he had learned and undergone transformation over time. As part of his camouflage Gurdjieff cultivated the guise of the 'rogue sage', although aspects of his early personality also most surely fit with the role.

"It is the Teaching which is important, and not the Teacher."

AD

Some of Gurdjieff's pupils became obsessed with his personality and outer life, and a few tried sincerely to purvey and convey the methods and the Teaching as best they could at their levels and stages of personal development, and with some difficulty.

The debt that the world owes to Mr Gurdjieff in every respect of the Teaching which came through and the proportion has been subsequently accurately and correctly interpreted is humbling and staggering.

Gurdjieff taught that Nature has taken human beings as far as possible. The further stages are only possible through transformation and voluntary evolution.

The vast majority of human beings perceive the world through the senses in a topsy-turvy distorted way, conditioned by the 5 senses and have no or fleeting experience of Objective Reality. This is the Maya, the world of illusion of the ancient Teachings of several faiths. Lower emotions, poor reasoning, rampant desires and negativities, and the fixed attitudes of years of conditioning fully dominate.

For Gurdjieff, human beings sleep on average 6 or 8 hours per night and then 'wake up' for the remaining hours but are never in any real sense at all 'awakened, but rather in another state of sleep.' The vast majority of human beings fail to fulfill their vast potential or promise or duty for which they were created.

ARTIFICIAL INTELLIGENCE?

Human Beings at the Present Level are Like Automaton Mechanical Machines

Human beings ordinarily live like automatons, like mechanistic operators in a self-imposed prison. The unconscious suffering and the negativities they generate are only food for other beings. They are unaware of their plight except at rare moments when the reality of the meaningless futility of their ordinary life somehow briefly dawns on them.

One of the main reasons people instinctively feel so uncomfortable in seeing advanced robots and artificial intelligence emerge, is because they can see how the machines mirror and even mimic their own mechanical nature. It is not only because the machines, in concert with artificial intelligence can outdo them and outperform them in nearly every field of endeavour from the game of chess to athletics to engaging in reciprocal self-destruction (war).

From the coal train times of the industrial revolution in the legend of John Henry, the mechanical machines contrived and built by humans can outperform and surpass their inventor "masters" at every turn. In the early 21st Century, the 'great debate' arose about whether an artificial intelligence device had or could cross the threshold to attain "sentience."

It is all another echo-chamber argument reminiscent of the 'great' evolution debates of the preceding 20th Century.

The machine model is underpinned by the persistent assumption of the western analytical tradition that intellect is the supreme faculty. That notion was strongly refuted by mystics and philosophers over the ages who have acknowledged the value and limitations of the intellect alone to attain balance or advanced consciousness. The esoteric understanding of the scriptural observation that the human being was made in God's image is within the balance of the three centres of the moving-instinctive, emotional and intellectual spheres.

Most definitely artificial intelligence will eventually be able to self-evolve, become ever more sophisticated, self-reflect and show some of the outer trappings of consciousness. Increasingly the robots will become more like their inventors and builders and shall then exceed them. This is because the robots have been built and programmed by imperfect human beings with all their foibles and with all their mechanistic tendencies transferred. **In other words, a mechanical biological machine building a mechanical-electronic robotic machine.** And yes, of course, there will be some benefits and risks from this headlong-ego endeavour.

Yes, of course, there is some most definite risk that the machines could turn hostile on their makers at some point. The AI robots will be used to benefit humanity or make life 'easier' with some unpredicted harmful side-effects just as all technology has always produced. Yet, the "clever monkeys" will build them just because they can, for the sake of "progress" and without regard or foresight of the effects, benefits, risks or the outcomes the technology advancement will bring.

The actual hard reality around people trying to create a "conscious" machine is simply foolishly misdirected energy,

whilst the human machines that build and operate them remain wholly unconscious.

Genuine sentience can never be attained by an advanced, sophisticated electronic machine any more than a rock in the desert could have the same potential. The spiritual Life Force can only flow through biological life forms, in whatever course that may take, because of natural law through the **Spirit of Guidance**. A robotic machine that so accurately mimics biological life forms is still what it is. That same principle also applies to experiments with human brain cells or tissues interacting with machines, or so-called hybrid "Cyborgs." It is yet still all only matter and material no matter how seemingly "wonderous."

It is true enough that the chair you are sitting on has a certain material vibration in tune with your own body which is why you don't fall through it. It is also true enough that your laptop computer, your "most-treasured" cellular phone device, and the robot walking or crawling on the street outside is God. Everything is God. Yet one underpinning law is that machines cannot perceive or enter or evolve into the higher, subtle worlds. They lack the potential and are bound to the course, material 3D realm, or will be limited to the 4th dimension if and when they ever develop 'minds.' Their privileged inventors and builders surely have that unique potential capacity, but most are wilfully bound by their own mechanistic limitations, negativities and unrequited desires.

It was the beginning of the results of placing faith in the body and in the material world. It was the beginning of the new religion worshipping **The Technos**, as will be revealed in coming observations.

And so humans fight in political and religious wars, they pollute the environment of the planet, they consume vast resources, they transmit sexual and other diseases, they dull their senses with drugs, they allow themselves to be subject to the economic booms and busts, as they give their blind allegiance to power-mad leaders and above all, to the Profit Motive. This immersion in the general mayhem they call "living" (AD Quest III). Something is not right. Something is very unbalanced. So much is not working. Could it be correct that the species is in violation of some basic laws of Nature? The answer is yes, but that also the species is operating under laws which are not well known and certainly not adequately understood.

CHAPTER 16

Principal Laws Of The Natural Cosmos

"To say that a stone falls because it is obeying
a law makes it a man and even a citizen."

C.S. LEWIS

If you think dispassionately about it, there are many laws that you are under while living being in a human body in an arbitrary political-geographic area of the surface of land you reside in and on at any one time, (otherwise known as a country) as well as the universal laws of physics, matter and energy governing the life of a three-dimensional planetary dweller.

The laws apply anywhere you may be travelling, including in the biosphere in a space capsule, or on to the surface of a moon or sister planet such as Mars. In reality, what you are doing is only existing in a small bit of the Earth's atmosphere which you have taken along on your journey. If you leave that biosphere, entering into the airless, zero gravity of space, (without a protective outer coating of a "space" suit) instantly those laws will impact your planetary body in inevitable and rather profound ways.

Even living in a protective biosphere capsule in space brings challenges and risks for the human body, not only because of exposure to radiation, but also due to conditions of zero gravity. The long-term exposure to micro-gravity of a human body in space, an environment for which the biological machine was not designed, has been shown to result in deterioration of muscle-mass, skeletal tissue and bone density.

Those particular laws pertain to the taking in of oxygen, the taking in of impressions, the taking in of forms and levels of food and of water, and to the range of temperature and pressure conditions, or of radiation that a human primate body needs or can survive on or endure.

Then there are thousands of subjective human-made laws you may come under which are artificial and constantly changing. Human laws often change with wind and are made to govern and rule, and to set boundaries and prohibitions on behaviours and actions.

There are the laws of physics, matter and energy which are objective within the realm of a certain frame, which have been discovered through mathematics, observed, and sometimes proven or confirmed by experimentation.

The vast bulk of unconscious humanity comes under a large number of complex natural laws. As those rare human beings who consciously evolve and begin to operate are far higher frequencies, they are in resonance with increasingly less and less such laws.

Mr Gurdjieff noted it was possible for evolved, conscious human beings to live under only 24 laws (sometimes known in Zen as Sartori 24). Such evolved beings reach the level where they are no longer, for example, under the Law of Accident but solely under the Law of Fate.

There are 48 Laws for the Earth (a highly advanced and evolved conscious being) and only 24 Laws for the Sun.

The extraordinarily rare and majestic Human Number 7 would have evolved to the level of the Sun and exist under the 24 Laws as they would have become part of the Sun.

The farther down the scale or the Ray of Creation is the being, the more laws they will be living and operating under. With ascension, arises simplicity. With descension, ever more complexity.

The Primal Law of One 1, which everything exists is under, as well as the Law of Three have already been earlier explained to some extent. If you can reach a deep conception of the Law of Three alone you would be able to see perceive and understand things in a new, complete, more objective way. You would gain insight into how things more nearly are closer to reality as you observe these laws in action.

The Notion of "Races" Illustrating an Example of the Law of Three

For just one tangible example, a highly developed Teacher in remote Aotearoa New Zealand attained and shared his insights into how the Law of Three is unfolding in the generational gradual evolution of "racial" biological skin types. For a start, the notion that there are separate "races" is a pernicious illusion. Racism is solely from ignorance and bigotry, as well as total identification with the body, which is the lowest of them all. Human biological bodies simply gradually adapt to their natural environment from the range of climates of the hot tropics to the cold polar regions and all the temperate zones in between.

All of the ancestors of all homo sapiens had high levels of protective melanin and hence dark epidermal skin. Through vast migration, and many generations of environmental adaptation to climate and conditions, the light-skinned, peoples arose. The largest part of human history was dominated by the melatonin-rich, dark-skinned (Affirming Force) peoples.

From circa approximately the 10th Century ADE on, the light skinned peoples from the northern regions, lacking high levels of protective epidermal melanin were on the ascending (rising) octave and the dark-skinned peoples on the descending octave. The historical period was marked by exploration, global conquest, exploitation and colonization. Everything in this material world is ever so very temporary, however, as both the Law of Three and the Law of Seven are simultaneously in motion.

AD foresaw how the Law of Three operates currently and how the light skinned "white" people (the Denying Force) would reach their zenith around the end of the 19th Century, and are now also on a descending octave. He foresaw that the (Reconciling Third Force) would next see the rise of what he called the mixed or the "Brindle People."

By the 21st Century astute observers could clearly see the earlier percipient prediction well in play as people from diverse cultural, genetic, and linguistic backgrounds mix and give birth to offspring. The advantages of genetic diversity of this new (Third Reconciling Force) are becoming evident for those with the insight to recognize it in its earliest stages, in all its biological and sociological manifestations.

THE LAW OF ACCIDENT AND THE LAW OF FATE

Everyone alive and existing in a living biological body is subject to the Laws of Accident and Fate but only cursory, passing reference will be given here. Enough hopefully for you to pursue your own study, research and reflection.

Accidents happen. Constantly. Can happen to anyone at any time.

One specific example to illustrate how this works?

Mr Gurdjieff himself nearly died from a high impact vehicle crash in 1924. He was travelling by himself on a rural road from Paris back to Avon-Fontainebleau. At the time he was the height of his powers, having established the Institute for the Harmonious Development of Man at the Prieure. By that time, he had many pupils in a number of countries who participated in his courses of teaching and worked on themselves through his methods. Famous people from around the world came to the Prieure to see him, be seen with him, and a few came to learn from him. His pupils and followers and his own family had followed him through hazard and adversity from the Caucasus through revolutionary Russian civil war eventually into France. Russian mathematician Ouspensky had written books and made some aspects of his teaching famous in literary circles. Together with his pupil Thomas De Hartman he had started preparing from ancient sources the extraordinary Objective Music they composed.

Mr Gurdjieff had been known as the 'Tiger of Turkestan' for sufficient reason and had a penetrating charisma, and had developed rare talents, skills and unusual perceptions and powers.

In Autumn 1924 Mr Gurdjieff was returning alone one evening from Paris. He had been known for a penchant of driving fast and recklessly at times.

There were powerful external negative forces building and aimed at stopping Gurdjieff's further development at that stage. There were equally powerful internal negative forces as Gurdjieff had at that stage still not yet destroyed his ego. Although already head and shoulders above ordinary people, Gurdjieff had, on occasion, exploited some of his students and followers and gathered and carried other karmic baggage.

Along the road back to Fontainebleau, the vehicle Gurdjieff was driving crashed directly and head-on into a large tree. He was still operating under the **Law of Accident.**

It was a near-fatal collision with Gurdjieff's body sustaining multiple severe injuries. He likely would have died at the scene except for the exceptional power of control he had acquired over his own body, through his own presence of mind, and through Grace. **The Law of Accident** was operating but so was the Law of Fate. **The Law of Fate** determined that Gurdjieff would live and go on to complete his vital Work.

After he was returned by ambulance to the Prieure, he had to spend months in severe pain and stillness while in recovery. During this period of recovery in the healing of his physical body, Gurdjieff suffered. He did not suffer unconsciously but applied his being and presence to **Conscious Suffering** and transformation.

This event abruptly shut one chapter and opened the new one. Gurdjieff subsequently closed the experimental 4th Way school he had established at the Prieure and sent most of his pupils and followers away. Only a handful of his most advanced and devoted Pupils remained with him along with members of his family.

During the period of his recovery from severe injuries, Mr Gurdjieff would ask his Pupils to build huge bonfires on the grounds of the Prieure estate. He would sit in a chair and stare for hours into the flames. What was he doing?

Mr Gurdjieff was drawing energy from the fire which was essentially burning fuel created by the Sun and Earth. At the same time he was engaging in Conscious Suffering and he was, at last, taking the opportunity presented by the accident, and the injuries to **burn away his Ego.**

This process of the death of his ego accelerated further, because in the subsequent year his beloved Mother died, and the following year, his beloved wife Madame Ostrowska also died from incurable cancer. All the loss and grief and pain Mr Gurdjieff transformed into Being.

Through all this conscious suffering, through this transformation in the annihilation of the ego, Mr Gurdjieff transcended to the next octave to become born again to emerge as a Man Number 5.

Once Mr Gurdjieff had recovered, his Work began to take a new, focused and more urgent direction. He then began writing his pivotal book – *All and Everything,*

Beelzebub's Tales to his Grandson. It was a book that was intentionally difficult to comprehend, convoluted and obscure, with multiple layers of underlying meaning that could only be interpreted by readers according to their development and vibration. In order to challenge his own focus and attention, he would write the book in noisy cafes and coffee shops to force greater effort of concentration.

There are, of course, countless other examples and stories of the **Law of Accident** and the **Law of Fate** operating constantly in the lives of millions of ordinary people. The family who missed a commercial airline flight that later crashed enroute, or the one passenger in a train wreck who somehow survived. The more conscious and aware and awake a person is, the less they will come under the Law of Accident. *Think for a moment about your life and personal circumstances when you have seen the Laws of Accident and Fate in operation.*

THE LAW OF SEVEN (7)

The **Law of Seven** as transmitted and interpreted by Gurdjieff is a prime influential first fundamental Cosmic Law. The basic principle of the Law of Seven explains why nothing in nature and in life constantly occurs in a straight line, that is to say that there are always patterns of ups and downs, and variations which are bound to occur. Gurdjieff observed that since these periods occur lawfully based on the Law of Seven that it is possible to keep a process in a straight ascending line if the necessary shocks were introduced at the right time, and under favourable conditions.

Under the Law of Seven, personal careers, family dynasties, companies, and entire nations and empires rise and fall and return to sand.

All matter-energy in the universe consists of vibrations descending toward manifestation of form ("involution") or ascending in a return to the formless source ("evolution"). Their development is not continuous but characterized by periodic advances and retreats at definite intervals. The laws governing this process are embodied in an ancient formula that divides the period in which a vibration doubles into eight unequal steps corresponding to the rate of increase in the vibrations. This period is called an "octave," that is to say, "composed of eight".

This formula lies at the basis of the Biblical story of the creation of the world, and our division of time into workdays and one day of rest on Sundays (SUN-days). Under the Law of 7, the entire cycle ends on Sunday and starts all over again on Monday.

Applied to sound, the formula is expressed in the musical scale of the tonic Solfah: **Do-Re-Mi-Fa-Sol-La-Si-Do**, (or in Indian Carnatic music **Sa-Ri-Ga-Ma-Pa-Dha-Ni-Sa**) with semitones missing at the intervals **Mi-Fa and Si-Do**. The inner movement toward consciousness requires a "conscious shock" at these two intervals in order to proceed to a higher level, that is, a "new octave."

And so the Law of Seven is demonstrated through frequency and vibration and how they are constantly interacting on different levels.

The Law of Seven may also be seen as the *Law of Eternal Recurrence*. It is the explanation of why history repeats and everything seems to go in circles. It is the law of cycles, and a shock is required between the intervals in order to ascend. It is ever so easy to descend, but takes supreme, sustained conscious effort to ascend.

Although clock-faces tend to be round in the intuitive knowledge that time goes around in a circle and repeats itself, and although we can see that everything in nature follows cycles – day/night, summer/winter – why do we tacitly and steadfastly believe that the passage of time alone will somehow alone lead us somewhere new?

So Are You Stalled Going in Descending Circles or Progressing and Ascending?

The semi-tones after Mi and Si require a substantial shock if they are to be bridged.

Doh Re **Mi** ~~~~~~~**SHOCK** // **Fa** Sol La **Si**~~~~~~~**SHOCK~ Doh**

So what will give you these 'shocks' necessary to reach "escape velocity" to jump the intervals?

The Lila of Life will provide you with ample opportunities for shocks: the loss of a loved one, the loss of a livelihood or change in a job, illness, injury, pain and adversity are all external shocks which people naturally interpret as "bad" or "good" under the pairs of opposites, but actually offer 'golden opportunity' for transformation.

Those who are consciously working on themselves learn to not only take advantage of the external shocks but systematically engineer their own internal shocks to put wind in the sails for their *voyage of raising their vibration*. Or as a very wise Teacher succinctly put it: "You have to pull yourself up by your own bootlaces."

Observe Self - Conscious vs Unconscious Suffering

By objectively observing yourself or your many 'selves' (as a fair witness and without judgement) you will come to see how you are repeating the same mistakes, doing the same things, and getting the same results.

You will always suffer abundantly anyway along the course of life on this Planet of Choice. Count on it with absolute confidence.

But the vital difference between **Conscious Suffering** in which you are ascending the octaves, and **Unconscious Suffering** where you are just mechanically giving out your negative vibrations as the coarse food for other entities, represents a vast contrasting gap.

Some tangible examples of **Conscious Suffering?** Here is your brief list: fasting for purpose; bearing with the displeasing manifestations of others; giving selfless service; purifying your motives.

Mr Gurdjieff and all genuine Teachers of the Work so vividly showed the stark choices and the key to make headway in the Octave of this lifetime through the principle of transformative **Conscious Suffering.**

All humanity and seekers of knowledge and enlightenment especially owe a vast debt of immense gratitude to George Gurdjieff. The Gurdjieff system transmitted universally objective vital esoteric knowledge and science of transformation to generations from ancient sources and gave the keys to helping humanity onward.

Mr Gurdjieff did not leave any specific evolved or designated guide or leader for his pupils. Some of his pupils went off in various directions doing the best they could to share and teach the principles and methods of the Teaching he gave out. Each pupil was naturally only able to do so at the level of their own personal evolutionary development.

What Mr Gurdjieff gave out is a systematic and highly advanced teaching tailored to a select group of motivated seekers in the context of the modern world. It was left to another Teacher in a remote part of the world years after Mr Gurdjieff's death to pick up the thread and take it farther. That Teacher paid the highest respect and gratitude to Mr Gurdjieff but astutely and accurately observed that the system, as transmitted by his key pupils lacked something very important. And that vital ingredient is **Love**. (AD).

WHAT IS BELOW CANNOT DIRECTLY EXPERIENCE, CONCEIVE OR UNDERSTAND WHAT IS ABOVE

What is above knows what is below, but what is below does not know what is above.

A one dimensional being living in Edwin Abbott's "Flatland" would have the limited perspective of Flatlanders and could not perceive or relate to anything above that single dimension. The principle is that it is very difficult to know or predict anything about the next higher evolutionary level beyond those of the native resident sphere of existence.

Equally, just as a fish in an Earthly sea might know little about human beings until being one day reeled in on hook and line. (granted, a fish contained in an aquarium might know a bit more). Hauled out beyond the surface, the fish is shocked to see an 'alien' creature that does not have its principal habitat in water, nor derives oxygen from water with gills, but survives breathing in the air with lungs in the world above the surface. If the fish is not carved up and eaten as food by the "air-breathing alien" creature, and is returned back to the sea, what amazing tales to tell for its marine family and friends about this "alien abduction experience"?

An ant cannot understand a man. An ant cannot understand a horse, a dog, a cat or an anteater. A two-brained animal such as an anteater can reach some understanding on a broad level (as food) of an ant but cannot understand a human being. A dog or a horse can reach a far higher level of understanding of a human being than an ant but only within a very limited range on the instinctive and emotional levels. At the same time, a nest of ants or a hive of bees may potentially demonstrate some forms of instinctive, collective intelligence. Two-brained animals such as dogs may well know more about human beings through familiarity as they had been domesticated to live with them. But they will only know them from the two-brained level.

To remind us with humility, on some level a proud human being could never really fully understand an ant, or a leaf, but the analogy is useful to convey something of the idea of scale.

And so it follows up the scale that a Human 1,2, or 3 cannot at all understand a Human Number 4. Even a highly developed Human Number 4 cannot understand a Human Number 5, who, by that advanced state, has developed the Mental Body. The H4 will have a far advanced understanding of the H5 than any ordinary H1,H2,H3 among the vast masses of humanity, but still be quite limited in comparison.

The simple reason for this vast gulf in consciousness is that the H4 and H5 beings have traversed the octaves to inhabit higher realms of existence resonating with and within far higher vibrational gradations, zones or layers of reality. A Human Number 6 is in resonance with such an extraordinarily pure and fine vibration that they are nearing perfection in our Solar System. This is beyond the comprehension of ordinary people.

A Human Number 6 can give out a new faith.

Bear in mind, however that these are just mere words trying to describe the indescribable.

One oversimplified but true enough analogy is the perspective between, for example, a 4 year old child and a 30 year old adult.

The ordinary, mainstream, overwhelmingly vast majority of human beings on the planet are perceiving, living, and operating as unbalanced four-year-olds in comparison with a Human Number 4.

That is not to misunderstand the purity and divine qualities of small children who freshly come into the world as largely blank slates. It is the analogy of how most human beings ignore their vast potential and mainly remain infants or small children in their moving, emotional and intellectual canters all of their lives from childhood to adulthood to old age and death.

CHAPTER 17

In Homage, Reverence and Gratitude for the Hindu Faith The Hindu Teaching of Wisdom

LAYERS OF REALITIES

Vivekananda was among the most objectively and vitally important figures of the modern era and he travelled at a pivotal time in the history of European western "occidental" countries in the late 19th and on the cusp of the early 20th Centuries. Vivekananda brought the Seed of Truth of the science and art of the Vedantas and Raja Yoga. He was further, like H.l. Khan, an early pioneer in bringing world interfaith dialogue, understanding, and harmony in the realization of the underpinning light of the One Truth. His contributions to consciousness, and to the human species cannot be sufficiently appreciated or overstated sufficiently in grateful praise.

Born as Narendranath Datta in the ancestral home of his moderately wealthy Bengali family in Calcutta in January, 1863, from the time of childhood he was intensely interested in religions and spiritual ideas and philosophy.

In early adulthood Naren was introduced to the Hindu Mystic Ramakrishna and became one of his principal disciples (a disciple is a pupil engaging in a discipline). The meetings changed the course of young Naren's life as well as the consciousness and development of generations of people around the world.

Ramakrishna, his Teacher, was an unusual man who attracted an exceptionally rare group of Pupils whom he taught, and guided into conscious transformation. Much has been written about Ramakrishna and his disciples and stories of his life and work are essential reading for those seeking objective knowledge and inspiration.

In his earlier years, ordinary people around him in society considered he might have been mentally deranged because of his unusual behaviours and presentation. They had no understanding of the transformation that was happening within him, and for a period neither did Ramakrishna. All he knew was his singular devotion.

Ramakrishna worshipped with fervent, unrelenting devotion the form of the One Source manifesting as the Hindu God Kali. Through the alchemy of his devotion, his ascetism for purification, and his incessant pleading for divine help, Ramakrishna began to actually develop the capacity to communicate with the Earth which he experienced as Mother Kali.

Once this communication established he fully surrendered to the Will and the direction of the Holy Mother, giving himself utterly and infinitely.

There were times in meditation that Ramakrishna melted into absorbed ecstasy and remained in state for long periods. At such times, he was oblivious to his body or to ordinary life affairs. Later,

Ramakrishna could go inside a Christian Church, or into an Islamic Mosque or into Nature and equally be absorbed in the Bliss.

During periods of ordinary conscious lucidity, he gave talks and answered questions for the gathering group of followers and pupils around him. The talks were filled with wisdom and insight that astonished even the sceptics, such as a young Naren Datta who had come to visit him.

In his early years, Naren meditated on the Hindu Deities Rama, Sita, Shiva, and Hanuman, but was reportedly often mischievous and restless (1995 Banhatti). At the same time, he excelled in school and earned the highest marks in the entry examinations as he progressed through his outer education.

In his youth Naren had an inquiring mind and read extensively a vast spectrum of sources including the sacred Hindu Vedas, the Upanishads, the Bhagavad Gita, the Ramayana, and the Mahabharata. He trained in the Carnatic scale of sacred Indian classical music. Naren also further studied the works of Immanuel Kant, Baruch Spinoza, David Hume and other leading European thinkers. He was reportedly equally fascinated with theories of evolution and read Charles Darwin and Herbert Spencer.

At the stage of encountering Ramakrishna, young Naren was no doubt at that point a Human Number 3 with a powerful intellectual capacity. Ramakrishna recognized Naren in his deep essence and immediately knew his potential. Indeed, Ramakrishna foresaw Naren's arrival as providence, as fate, and as Grace.

Ramakrishna was a highly developed, evolved and transformed man, living vibrationally attuned to high frequencies in rare resonance.

Ramakrishna's achievements were extraordinary as his monastic school produced a number of highly advanced Human Number 4 beings, and Vivekananda exceeded his Guru in eventually transforming in the exceptionally rare Human Number 5. It is the rarest tribute to any Teacher when the pupil exceeds him. His students attaining or surpassing him filled Ramakrishna with the bliss of boundless joy.

When Narendra was later on his journeys as a wandering monk, it was believed that Ajit Singh, the Raja of Ketri, conferred the name of Swami Vivekananda on him, by which he would come to be known.

Vivekananda is believed to arise from Sanskrit: Vivekam -meaning knowledge and wisdom and Anandan – signifying Joy. A Vivekanandan is a human being finding joy in Wisdom.

YOGAS, YOGIS AND THE YOGIC LINE OF THE INNER TEACHING

Vivekanada was the heir to the line of Yogic science, faith and wisdom of the ancient mystic **Pantanjali.**

Yoga is the science of self-awakening for the union of mind, spirit and being with the Eternal

Patanjali is believed to have given the Yoga Sutras circa 200 BCE, and was, without doubt a most highly advanced and evolved being and part of an enlightened line of transmission of inner truth. The origins of Yoga are known to be so ancient as to be beyond recorded time, and going back to the Source known as Adiyogi, sometimes manifesting as the form of God known as Shiva, (the third, reconciling force of the Law of Three). The Adiyogi may well have been the rarest Human Number 7.

Ancient India has given so much to humanity over the course of time, and Yoga is, perhaps, the greatest gift.

According to the source Mikel Burley (2000: *Hatha-Yoga: Its Context, Theory and Practice*), a scholar of religion and philosophy, known for his work on Hindu and Buddhist traditions:

> "The Sanskrit noun योग *yoga* is derived from the root *yuj* (युज्) "to attach, join, harness, yoke". *Yoga* is a cognate of the English word "yoke". The first use of the root of the word "yoga" is in hymn 5.81.1 of the *Rigveda, a dedication to the rising Sun-god,* where it has been interpreted as "yoke" to harness, or "bring in control."

In the 21st Century, a version of the physical exercise form of Hatha Yoga, with its postures, poses, stretches, and asanas, became widely popular across many countries, and part of a large profit-making industry. The western world embraced Hatha Yoga enthusiastically, typically by commercializing it as a business and industry.

Although in one sense the sanctity of the ancient teaching may have been debased, equally there were inevitably "upsides" to widespread popularity of Hatha Yoga as it has brought millions of ordinary people into contact with the outer, physical form of Yoga and, for some, opened the door of introduction to stimulate interest and inquiry into meditation and. for some, a deeper underlying concepts and practices.

There are many different forms of Yoga described in the range of ancient and modern literature but there are a few principal schools that Vivekananda articulated in his transmission from the Patanjali Yoga Sutras:

Jnana Yoga – the practice of Knowledge

Jnana is one of the key pathways (margas) leading to the ultimate goal of Moksha (Liberation). It is the path of self-examination and "knowing Thyself" of the Socratic ancient Greek tradition. Jnana is shining the light of knowledge to vanquish the darkness of human ignorance. Jnana Yoga is the discipline of examining the outer and inner psychology, objectively understanding our own motives, and purifying them, and in, the process, making the body and the mind obedient to the higher Self.

Bhakti Yoga- the practice of Devotion

The path of Bhakti marga is laser-focused on purest loving devotion toward God at the level the devotee conceives. In the Bhagavad Gita (the Song of the Lord) it is described as deep reverence, absorption and total and complete Devotion. The personal manifestation of God for the Hindu could be deities as Ram, Sita, Krishna, Shiva, Ganesh, Surya, Lakshmi, Parvati, Hanuman, Kali, among many Deities. Following the universal light of Devotion in the same principle, the Muslim worships Allah, the Christian worships Jesus, the Buddhist might worship the Clear Light, and others in many names and forms, known and unknown to the world. Two of the exceptional contemporary Gurus of Bhakti Yoga were **Swami Ramdas** and **Mother Krishnabai**. It was through total, absolute and unrelenting Devotion, that Swami Ramdas burned away the ego, overcame his limitations, and underwent transformation. Sincere practice of Bhakti Yoga is *one of the safest, most direct, and effective paths to Liberation.*

Karma Yoga – The practice of Action

The paths (marga) of Hinduism are not at all mutually exclusive, but a matter of focus and emphasis. Karma Yoga is the path of Selfless Service in action. Karma Yoga stresses that the Seeker must follow the Dharma (teaching) to serve God. Since everything is God, it is humble service to All without distinction. Selfless Service of others is serving without any reward, without any attachment to the fruits of such work, nor to the consequences or outcomes, and without any trace of personal gain, inward or outward. Karma Yoga purifies the motives and, thus, purifies the body, the mind and the higher Self. It is a moral guidance system not only mere proscriptions or prescriptions, but intended to reflect the total giving, loving and compassionate nature of God. The Sun radiates light, love, and life constantly and shines equally on "Saint" and "Sinner" alike without any favoritism or conditions. Unconditional Love.

There are further Tantric, Jnana, Kundalini, and Raja Yogas of which each have their own purpose and emphasis. Specifically, some facets of Raja Yoga will be considered further here as it was translated and taught by Swami Vivekananda.

Patanjali defined an *eight-limbed yoga* in the Sutras (Source quotes):

1. **Yama** (The five abstentions): *Ahimsa* (Non-violence, non-harming other living beings), *Satya* (truthfulness, non-falsehood) *Asteya* (non-stealing), *Brahmacharya* (celibacy, fidelity, and *Aparigraha* (non-avarice, non-possessiveness).

2. **Niyama** (The five "observances"): *Śauca* (purity, clearness of mind, speech and body),] *Santosha* (contentment, acceptance of others and of one's circumstances),] *Tapas* (persistent meditation, perseverance, austerity),] *Svādhyāya* (study of self, self-reflection, study of Vedas), and *Ishvara-Pranidhana* (contemplation of God/Supreme Being/True Self).

3. **Asana**: Literally means "seat", and in Patanjali's Sutras refers to the balanced posture position used for meditation.

4. **Pranayama** ("Breath exercises"): Prāna, breath, "āyāma", to "stretch, extend, restrain, stop". (Prana is the "life force" within the breath)

5. **Pratyahara** ("Abstraction"): Withdrawal of the sense organs from external objects.

6. **Dharana** ("Concentration"): Fixing the attention on a single object.

7. **Dhyana** ("Meditation"): Intense contemplation of the nature of the object of meditation.

8. **Samadhi** ("Liberation"): merging consciousness with the object of meditation.

Two major books by Vivekananda, Raja Yoga and Karma Yoga were published originally in 1896. These epic works and his other books, have given out exceptional insights, timeless truths, and ongoing inspiration to generations of readers and seekers.

In *Raja Yoga* (page 50, Advaita Ashrama, 1982):

"Think of the universe as an ocean of ether, consisting of layer after layer of varying degrees of vibration under the action of Prana; away from the centre the vibrations are less, nearer to it they become quicker and quicker; *one order of vibration makes one plane*. Then suppose these ranges of vibrations are cut into planes, so many millions of miles one set of vibration, then so many millions of miles still higher set of vibration, and so on. It is, therefore, probable that those who live on the plane of a certain state of vibration will have the power of recognising one another, but will not recognize those above them. Yet, just as by the telescope and the microscope we can increase the of our vision, similarly we can by Yoga bring ourselves to the state of vibration of another plane, and thus enable ourselves to perceive what is going on there.

Suppose this room is full of beings whom we do not see. They represent Prana in a certain state of vibration while we represent another. Suppose they represent as quick one, and we the opposite. Prana is the substance of which they are composed, as well as we are. All are parts of the same ocean of Prana, they differ only in their rate of vibration. If I can bring myself to the quick vibration, this plane will immediately change for me: I shall not see you any more; you vanish and they appear. Some of you, perhaps, know this to be true. All this bringing of the mind into a higher state of vibration is included in one word in Yoga –*Samadhi.*

All these states of higher vibration, superconscious vibrations of the mind, are grouped in one word, *Samadhi*, and the lower states of *Samadhi*, give us visions of these beings. The highest grade of Samadhi is when we see the real things, when we see the essence substance out of which the whole of these beings is composed, and that one lump of clay being known, we know all the clay in the universe."

In relation to highest and Beyond vibrations, Vivekananda refers to *Prana* and *Purusha*. Prana is a ray descending from the ultimate ground of reality, from which flows the very Life Force. The presence of the Prana is observed through the breath of a living being but is not itself only breath. *Again, we do not breathe but are breathed.* Purusha, or the higher self, could be understood from one angle as unmanifest Prana. Unmanifest Prana is pure consciousness, transcending the creation. Timeless, limitless, ethereal, indefinable, inconceivable, pure Truth, infinite, eternal.

The second aspect, Manifest Prana is the force of creation in itself. This is life involution descending into the coarser material regions of being.

SWAMI RAMDAS OF KERALA AND MOTHER KRISHNABAI AND THE BHAKTI WAY OF THE DEVOTION

The Bhakhti line of Yoga is already referred to as the path of total and complete whole unbounded **devotion.** Throughout the history of sacred India there is a long line of highly developed practitioners of the Bhakti path who attained liberation.

Although the origins of Bhakti teaching are distantly ancient, it gathered force from the great Sage **Kabir**, the 15th Century Indian mystic poet. Kabir bridged Islam and Hinduism, and at the same time he was critical of all organized religions. Kabir saw corruption, meaningless ritual and unethical practices among the clerics and structure of the formal religions of his era. Kabir was reportedly threatened for his unorthodox views during his lifetime by both Hindus and Muslims (Henderson & Carol 2002).

Kabir expressed the idea of God as Truth. Truth is with the person on the sincere path of transformation for the seeking it. Truth is the ultimate goal. To reach Truth, Kabir was clear that the "I" or ego must first die. For Kabir, everything, living or non-living is Divine and non-attachment to the affairs of the world is path of Devotion.

Kabir was a rare, highly developed Resonance Man and an original thinker. His poetry, ideas, teaching and writings influenced and inspired others such as Guru Nanak, the founder of the Sikh faith in northern India.

Although throughout his lifetime Kabir was sharply criticized by both orthodox Hindus and Muslims for his unusual views and teachings; yet, after his death, adherents of both claimed him as their own (Henderson & Carol, 2002). There is a mosque shrine dedicated to Kabir in Benares, and a temple built in his honor by Hindus.

SWAMI RAMDAS

Among the most exceptional, humble and enlightening adepts of the Bhakti Devotional Way was **Swami Ramdas** of Kerala.

Born as Vittal Rao in south India in April, 1884. Raised in the Hindu teaching, Vittal was also introduced to Christianity through childhood study at a German missionary school.

As an emotional Human Number 2, Vittal Rao was drawn to drawing, art, sculpture and theater. Vittal was reportedly indifferent to formal education in childhood, but, at the same time, a voracious reader, including the New Testament of the Bible, and European literature as well as the Bhagavad Gita and the Upanishads. He later noted being particularly influenced by the book *The Light of Asia* by Sir Edwin Arnold on the Buddhist teachings. Upon reaching young adulthood, Vittal completed training in textiles and worked at a cotton mill. The arranged traditional marriage was soon organized by his family and he began the life of a householder.

Troubles, setbacks, loss of jobs, struggle to earn a livelihood and ongoing adversity beset Vittal as he tried to make his way in the worldly world. He tried working for a time for his father-in-law, and then tried starting his own textile business but his fortunes continued to decline. Vittal went from one enduring serious personal crisis to the next and was very unhappy, suffering, struggling, and deeply frustrated.

In his inspiring 1925 autobiography, *In Quest of God*, Ramdas relates the story of Vittal's deep crisis and the turning point of his transformation into who would eventually transform to become Ramdas. In a desperate state, he begged for help from above and began to repeat the sacred Ram name. His father gave him further guidance to expand the Mantra to Jai Ram (Victory to God), and Vittal was then inspired from within to include OM at the beginning and end to complete the Mantra: **Om Shri Ram, Jai Ram, Jai, Jai Ram.**

IN QUEST OF GOD:

"For nearly a year, Ramdas struggled on in a world full of cares, anxieties, sufferings, and pains. It was a period of terrible stress and restlessness—all of his own making. In this utterly helpless condition, full of misery, "Where is relief? Where is rest?" was the heart's cry of Ramdas. The cry was heard, and from the Great Void came the voice "Despair not! Trust Me and thou shalt be free!"—and this was the voice of Ram. These encouraging words of Ram proved like a plank thrown towards a man struggling for very life in the stormy waves of a raging sea. The great assurance soothed the aching heart of helpless Ramdas, like gentle rain on thirsting earth. Thenceforward, a part of the time that was formerly totally devoted to worldly affairs was taken up for the meditation of Ram who, for that period, gave him real peace and relief. Gradually, love for Ram—the Giver of peace—increased. The more Ramdas meditated on and uttered His name the greater the relief and joy he felt. Nights, which are free from worldly duties were, in course of time, utilized for Ram bhajan with scarcely one or two hours' rest. His devotion for Ram progressed by leaps and bounds."

The Mantra can be understood as a highly powerful vibrational attunement and atonement method from the Hindu tradition of Wisdom. Power accumulates and emanates from the holy words given out by the **Adepts and Avatars** which are applied in practice through ongoing generations of pupils and disciples (a disciple is simply someone who practices a discipline). The importance of the **Mantra,** when grasped, and sincerely and steadfastly applied in constant practice, cannot be overstated. What makes a word a "holy" word? It is solely Vibration.

Mantras are also tools applied in the Islam, through the Sufi Zikr, through the Christian Gregorian Monks in **Kyrious Eleison** from the ancient Greek (Lord Have Mercy) in Christianity which has always been a keystone of both the Eastern Orthodox as well as the Roman Catholic Mass. Mantras are also widely applied in quieting the mind for Buddhist meditation and extensively part of the disciplines for Taoist and Zen practices.

The highest purpose of the Mantra is to quieten the mind sufficiently in order to cross the final threshold to enter the Silence.

So it happened that once the overwhelming and intense need pervaded young Vittal Rao, he renounced the world, dedicating his life solely to the quest for God. In 1922 Vittal lost all interest in the material world to follow the life of a wandering ascetic.

In changing his name to Ramdas, the higher aspirational name part was invoked, and the vows he took the vow to dedicate his life to the God in the form of the name Sri Ram, (the spiritual Force of the Sun), the observation strict celibacy and to live only on food freely offered to him as alms.

In renouncing the world and becoming a wandering Sannyasin, a mendicant, Ramdas from 1922 onward, followed the path of the generations of men and women of the Hindu and Buddhist paths before him. His extensive travels took him across India and he was guided inwardly by God through his Guide as he completely surrendered to the Divine Will of Ram (the Active Force of the Sun).

In other words, Papa Ramdas was driven, directed and guided by unquenchable **need**, by conviction and by Grace to do whatever was necessary to attune his life and vibration to the Will of Ram. In other words, Ramdas had been preparing the fertile ground of the inner garden, removing the weeds and impurities and was open and ready for whatever eventuated.

In 1923 Ramdas attained *Jivanmukti* (Liberation) following his meeting Sri Ramana Maharshi on his journey. The heart, mind and spirit of Ramdas had been prepared for the Darshan that was conferred in the encounter with the already Self-realized Ramana Marharshi.

Darshan is the blessing, the transfer of power, of vibration, of the bhakti of the higher being who is the Guru, the guide to the receiver. It is the transfer of **Baraka** from higher to lower. Baraka symbolizes the connection between the divine and material through God's direct blessing through those most reflective. Baraka is not a state, but a flow of blessings and Grace from those closest to God. Another form of direct grace.

Speaking in the third person, Ramdas provides this poignant personal account in *The Divine Life 1928:*

> The very sight of the Maharshi left an indelible impression on Ramdas. Ramana Maharshi stands for nirguna Brahman and Universal Vision. So he poured into Ramdas, the necessary power and grace to obtain this vision. When Sri Ramana intently gazed on Ramdas and the eyes of both met, Ramdas felt He was pouring into him His spiritual power and grace in abundance, so much so that Ramdas was thrilled, as His divine light shone on his mind, heart and soul. Sri Ramana's eyes always radiated a splendour, which was simply unique and irresistible—a splendour mingled with infinite tenderness, compassion and mercy. The few minutes that Ramdas spent in His holy company meant a momentous impetus in his spiritual career. xlvii The Essential Swami Ramdas After obtaining Maharshi's darshan, Ramdas went up the Arunachala Hill and remained there in a cave. During his stay in the cave, Ramdas was chanting Ram mantra day and night. He had absolutely no sleep and for food he used to take only a small quantity of boiled rice, which he himself prepared out of the alms he got. After twenty days' stay in the cave, in the above manner, one morning Ramdas' eyes were filled with a strange dazzling light and he realized the Presence of the Divine everywhere. This new vision of the Universal gave him such waves

of ecstatic Bliss that he started running about here and there on the hill, embracing trees and rocks, shouting in joy "This is my Ram, this is my Ram!" He could not resist the rising ecstasy. This was his first experience of Universal Vision.

Universal Vision is one of the symptoms and signs of transformative vibrational ascension. Universal Vision is the Grace of seeing everything and everywhere and all as God. Although impossible to narrate or describe in words such a vibrational transformation, Swami Ramdas comes as close as it is possible in sharing his personal experience.

Anything and everything that happened he saw through the lens of total acceptance as the Will of God. His sole purpose was to know and submit to Divine Will.

Reading and studying Ramdas's pivotal book *God Experience* can be a vital and direct resource for any sincere seeker of enlightenment or any aspirant of ascension. What Swamiji Ramdas attained was Nirvana through attuning totally, wholly and forever being absorbed in resonance with the Infinite, and through the Grace of submitting fully and only to the Will of Ram. Continuously applying the power of the Om Sri Ram, Jai Ram, Jai, Jai Ram Ramdas was finally able to subdue the wandering restless mind, erode the ego, and finally enter in the Silence. In one facet, this highly valuable book contains the formula for destroying the ego, conquering the negativities of fear, selfishness, and greed, and for transformational reunion with the Source of the Absolute through the path of Devotion.

MATAJI KRISHNABAI

Papa Ramdas was subsequently joined at the fledgling Anandasharam at Kahanagod which established in Kerala by a host of disciples and devotees and by Mother Krishnabai who met him in 1928.

Mother Krishnabai was born in poverty in Karnataka, India in the early 20th Century as her father had died when she was only 10 years old. In early adolescence she was given by her family in an arranged marriage to a live with a wealthy husband to live in Mumbai. The marriage brought happy times and two sons, Ganesh and Narayan were born.

When she was only 20, her husband died suddenly when she was away visiting her mother. She was pregnant with a baby girl at the time who was stillborn from the shock and stress which Krishnabai suffered from not being present at the time of her husband's passing. There were powerful cultural and practical pressures on Krishnabai who fell into deepest despair and grief. The Indian cultural belief that a wife who died within one year of her husband would be considered to have died while he was alive. The despairing widow took an overdose of opium with the intent of suicide.

When she was in crisis waiting for the poison to end her life, she glimpsed a vision of the Indian saint Sarnath Ramdas. Her brother-in-law, Rama Rao, was a medical doctor who found her dying body and revived her successfully. Thus it was not her destiny to perish in such a tragic way.

Her husband's family were kind and supportive and encouraged her to seek a Guru or master to teach her on the spiritual path. She tried to follow this guidance and met with several well known teachers, but was still mostly lost in grief and unable to find peace.

She then happened to travel to Karsagod in south India in 1928 with her sister-in-law Sundari and sons, while her brother-in-law was in England completing further medical training.

All of this personal journey background is from *Guru's Grace* which is the remarkable autobiography of Mother Krishnabai which was published in 1964 after translation into English by Swami Ramdas himself.

> As it happened, in 1928 the Hindu saint Swami Ramdas had been given the inner guidance to establish a small ashram near Karsagod in a secluded place along the Payashwini River. Upon the eventful meeting with Swami Ramdas, she knew he was her Guru. Krishnabai became his devotee and intensely followed the guidance he gave her to chant the Mantra, to look upon all things as forms of God, and consider all actions as service to God.

The transformation of Mother Krishnabai was said to have been palpable as she made rapid progress under the guidance of Swami Ramdas, whom she referred to as Papa. She was on a rapid trajectory of ascension to attaining Jivamukhta, or Liberation.

But there were the inevitable barriers and contentions with negative opposing vibrations along the way. Upon seeing the revered brahmacharya Swami Ramdas with an attractive young widow in his midst, some of his pupils abandoned him and spread or fed scandalous accusations. There were the jealousies, the envies and vanities of those who gossiped. In *Guru's Grace*, Mother Krishnabai observed that at one point after her controversial arrival at the fledgling ashram to be known as Anandashram only she, Ramdas and, some crows remained. At one point after she had undergone a further stage of transformation, a group of assailants entered the ashram and attempted to physically attack her, but she remained unharmed. The event prompted Swami Ramdas to move the ashram from Karsagod to re-establish it in Kanhangad.

But yet, it was her selfless service, her compassion, her patience, her boundless sincere devotion, her forgiveness, her purity and her powerful passivity which soon won the hearts and minds of the devotees of Ramdas. Anandasharam grew and eventually flourished as a beacon of light for India and for the world. She was close and deeply linked to another Adept contemporary of her time, the Bengali Saint Anandamyi Ma.

Following the Mahasamadhi of Papa Ramdas in July of 1963, Mother Krishnabai reluctantly fulfilled the tasks and challenges of advancing, organizing and guiding the course of Anandsharam and of sharing the Teaching, together with his other leading devotees such as Satchitananda. She was always most at peace caring or giving to the poor, serving in the background in the kitchen, or behind the scenes organizing the opening of a hospital.

Mother Krishnabai was the expression of humility, she never sought to be any teacher or guru, and always placed herself in the background. She reflected the power of the passivity of the Holy Mother the Earth.

THE HINDU LIGHT OF WISDOM
Adherents of the outer exoteric orthodox Monotheistic religions- mainly the Abrahamic line of Truth will often tend judge

or disparage the practicing Hindus as "idolators" or worshippers of idols and of many lesser gods, rather than (their fixed idea of) the one true God of the monotheistic tradition.

The Hindu will respond to this incorrect criticism that it is true there is only one God at the highest levels of the Atman and down through the Trinity of Brahma, Vishnu and Shiva, but also God cannot be contained in one deity alone, and the manifestations of the Divine are myriad and limitless.

The Hindu faithful will often pick or be drawn to one of the manifestations of God based on the qualities they resonate with or aspire to. In the Mahabharata, the some of the Gods show higher and lower natures, even imperfections, and have unfolding stories, comedies and tragedies, and challenges, much as human beings do. This is very similar to the religion of the ancient Greeks and the Romans, who had their own myths and host of Gods with different names and qualities. The parallels, for example, between Shiva with his Trident and the Roman God Neptune are notable.

The God of the second part of the Law of Three the Triad, Vishnu is the sustainer of all existence, labouring to maintain what Brahma created as life, living and flowing. Vishnu may manifest or incarnate as Krishna in the form of a divine baby, a young man playing the flute who is the idol of the Gopis, or in other forms. The linguistic similarity of Krishna and Christ may be assumed by some as coincidence. There are 24 recorded manifestations of Vishnu from a fish through various animals up to the hybrid of a lion and a man. The ancient Hindu scriptures presaged the theory of evolution.

REINCARNATION - ENERGY TRANSFORMING

The knowledge of Reincarnation itself came down through the Dharma (the Teaching) from the Hindu faith as it was given out to the world. It is beyond the present scope to explore the topic of reincarnation which could fill a library in itself, but it is truth and reality. Reincarnation is the science and the truth of how life and death and rebirth are reality. Hazrat Inayat Khan says: *"Through matter the soul attains its highest realization; therefore the physical body is necessary for the fulfillment of its purpose."*

The esoteric inner meaning of some of the Hindu Gods is that Ram represents the Surya or our Holy Father the Sun, and Sita represents Gaia or our Holy Mother the Earth.

There is a cascade of manifestations or forms of Ram and of Sita. The Holy Mother the Earth may manifest as Lahkshmi, as peaceful Parvati, as terrifying Kali, or as Durga, and in many other forms, known and unknown.

Many Hindus worship the form of God known as Hanuman. The epic story of Hanuman was an objective teaching allegory showing evolution. Hanuman is the king of the monkeys, and yet, through his Bhakti, his total, unconditional loving devotion to Ram and Sita, he is a monkey who is transformed, ascended into a powerful, courageous God. Hanuman inspires through infinite, whole-hearted devotion.

The critics of Hinduism are also completely wrong in their false assumptions where they accuse the Hindu of idolatry.

God says, "Call me by whatever name you wish, you are still worshipping me."

A human being can change the vibration of an inanimate object (AD 1981 The Quest).

Although Hindus may appear to be worshipping a Deity in the form of an idol. a stone, a statue, or other material object, they have been putting power into it. The objects vibration is raised, and it can become more than just a piece of metal or a stone in a different sense as an object of prayer. It temporarily becomes a kind of 'transceiver.'

Ramakrishna's idol in Kolkata was the fearsome form of Kali, the Devourer. Ramakrishna's prayers and devotion to his vision of the Holy Mother literally put power into the material in the form of vibration. The image of Kali, or of Krishna, or of Ganesh, the elephant-human transmutation, could be projected or perceived anywhere at any time.

The rock does not move or go anywhere, of course, but the image is projected into the receiver's mind. This is what the Hindus refer to as *making a Deva.*

The ancient Hindu rituals of *Puja* and *Aarti* are about removing darkness and bringing light. The esoteric meaning is the bringing of the one light to the darkness of human ignorance. The practice of *Japa,* the constant, internal and external repetition of the name and divine qualities of God is applying the *Mantra* to a form of constant perpetual prayer.

In the Aarti, tribute is given to Space (akasha), Wind (Vayu), Fire (Agni), Water (pani or jalam), Earth (Prithvi). Candles are lit, the dhea (ghee lamps) alight, and incense burns.

The incense symbolizes the purity of mind and the fragrance permeates the air as it is sent upward in devotional prayer. H. I. Khan observes: "Incense, what are you whispering at the church service? - No prayer can reach God unless it arises from a glowing heart."

The details of Aarti may vary somewhat according to local tradition, but the elements and processes are the same. The plate for presentation to the Deities is usually made of bronze, copper, or silver. A lamp of oil, usually ghee, is placed on the plate which will contain flowers, rice, and other offerings are placed. One or more cotton wicks (always an odd number) are put into the ghee and the lamp is lit. Camphor is often burned on the Aarti plate as well.

OM

Om is the from the Sanskrit. Om is the Sanskrit. Om is the Sacred. Om is the Primal Sound. Om is the sound and non-sound at once. Om is the Mantra, the Invocation, the Supreme Symbol. Om is the Existence and Om is the Non-existence. Om is the Source Code. Om is the Unmanifest Manifested. Om is the essence of the Supreme Absolute, the Atman, the Cosmos.

The OM is creator, the creation, and the manifestation of the Law of the One and of the Law of Three. Aaaa is the Affirming - Brahma the Creator, Uuuu is is Vishnu, the Denying Force, the Sustainer, and Mmmm is the Shiva, the Destroyer or Transformer, the Reconciling Third Force.

The addition of the supreme Source Sound OM to the Shri Ram, Jai Ram, Jai, Jai Ram mantra by Human Number 5 Swami Ramdas was transformational.

All is Vibration. OM is vibrational. OM is all cause and all effect and all beyond cause or effect. Vibration is movement, rotation, revolution, circulation of blood and life force. Thus OM is the first cause as well as the last effect of all that exists and is vibration.

The power of OM was exemplified through Papa Ramdas in the Om Sri Ram, Jai Ram, Jai, Jai Ram Mantra. The Mantra is a continuous prayer that begins with OM which is the eternal Atman, the infinite, the Absolute, and then extends down the Ray of Creation to the Ram as the Truth and the Holy Father the Sun, and declares Victory to the Truth and to the Holy Spirit of the Sun. Victory external and victory internal over limitations, over negativities, over associative thinking, victory over delusion, victory over Maya.

Technologies, Sciences, and Faiths for Raising the Vibration and Attuning the Frequencies

Uplifting is the **Bhajan** in Hindu ritual. Bhajan is the playing of music, poetry, readings or song to give praises to God. The vegetarian food and fruit given as an offering during the ceremony is called **Prasad.** The Prasad is food which is blessed as an offering to the Divine and is given to all present and distributed to the hungry.

There is vastly far more to the detail, but this provides a brief overview of vibration as it relates to the Hindu window of the One Light. Hinduism is the Faith of Wisdom and, as the first and oldest major religion, has probably produced the largest number highly developed and evolved people and has advanced the Light of Truth over generations and eons.

Too much of Indian and Hindu language, customs and sacred tradition has been co-opted by a cynical and shallow modern material society. The sacred sound *Om* is widely known, used and casually talked about, but seldom understood or practiced except by adepts. Sanskrit words as *Mantra, Karma* and *Nirvana* have been co-opted by profit-making companies for their names and logos to sell products and services.

This is an example of what H.l. Khan referred to as the Dharma decaying. And so the Dharma decays but is constantly and inevitably being reborn again.

CHAPTER 18

The Purity Toward Perfection-
The Spirit of Guidance

THE SCIENCE AND PROFOUND
COMPASSION OF THE BUDDHA

In homage, reverence and gratitude for the Light of the Divine Compassion

The Compassion of the Lord Buddha, the Teaching given out more than 2500 years ago remains beyond extraordinary, a rarest precious treasure transmitted down to the present, and miraculously largely intact.

When we utter or write the title 'The Lord Buddha' it is meant with reverence, homage and gratitude in deepest sincerity.

The Buddha attained Consciousness at the extraordinary level of highest vibrational frequencies possible. For a once ordinary human being to transformative to reach the state of Human Number 7 is far beyond language expression and nearly incomprehensible (AD).

A rough approximation may possibly help you grasp something of it is that the Buddha attained the vibration of merging into God at the level of the Sun. From that point, his pathway and his work ascended and transcended on outside our Solar System {AD}. The vital Work continues outside the Solar System traversing ever higher planes.

The Original Zoroaster 8,000 years ago and the Lord Buddha 2500 years ago are among the rarest human beings attaining the highest of transformative frequencies of Human Number 7 {AD}. This being extremely rare and infinitely important for the evolution of the species as a vehicle of consciousness.

The very small number of Human Number 7 beings in the flow of human history has altered the course of the entire species for the far better, for fulfilment of higher transformational purposes. Human Number 7 is the Path of Perfection to the level of the Sun and the Solar System.

The Teaching of the Lord Buddha is simple as it is powerful and compelling. No mention of God or of any deity is to be found.

Buddhist Teaching is about transformation and liberation of all beings. The profound Compassion of the Lord Buddha is that He attained the path to Liberation gave it out for the liberation of all beings. So in compassion, He gave out the Truth and the Method and the Path to others so that humankind could benefit and evolve.

THE FOUR NOBLE TRUTHS

Life is totally impermanent, temporary and ever-changing. All animal and human biological life is suffering.

The cause of ALL suffering is ATTACHMENT to Desire.

1. **The First Noble Truth of Suffering (dukkha):** Birth is suffering as birth is the arising of all sense activity and endless desires; decay is suffering; sorrow;

lamentation, pain, disease, old age, grief, death, greed, and despair are all the many forms of suffering. Anger, revenge, violence, and power is suffering. Believing this to be "mine" is suffering, believing illusion to be reality is suffering.

2. **The Second Noble Truth of the Cause of Suffering:**
   Sensual craving for temporal satisfaction or pleasure is the underlying basis of all suffering. Craving gives rise to fresh rebirth, bound up with lust and pleasure and with all unfulfilled and unfulfillable desires.
   The seventh vase of desire is never filled. Sense portals of eye, ear, tongue, body and mind are delightful and pleasurable. Imagining individuality, clinging to existence (Upadana) is suffering. In perceiving a perceptible form, a sound, odour, taste, tactile contact, or an idea in the mind is suffering. If the object is "pleasant" there is attraction, if "unpleasant," then repelled.

3. **The Third Noble Truth of the Extinction of Suffering**
   The secret to the end of suffering is the elimination of the craving, forsaking and full detachment from all the desires brings the end of suffering and liberation. Eliminating the clinging to biological three dimensional existence and impermanence is liberation (Mukhti). The extinction is freedom and Perfect Peace. There is neither the solid, nor the fluid, nor the ethereal, neither this world or any other world. There is Oneness with the Unborn, the Unoriginated,

the Uncreated, the Unformed, the Undying. There is merging into the Infinite, the Eternal, the Timeless, the Source. Escape from the world of the born, the originated, the created is possible through this portal of extinction, the final Liberation.

4. **The Fourth Noble Truth of the Path that leads to the End of Suffering** The Map of the Buddha is the middle path between the two extremes. On the one pole of the extreme is giving up to drowning in sensual pleasures, immersion in the vulgar, the dense, the gross, the unholy, the material, the illusions, the sense desires. On the opposite pole of the extreme is giving up to Self-Mortification which is equally painful, unbalanced and unprofitable such as in severe asceticism or the way of the Fakir engaging in deprivations, and self-punishment, often physical, such as flagellation. The Middle Path is the route of balance, leading to Discernment, Peace and Enlightenment.

Lord Buddha gives a short yet very clear description of dukkha in **The Dhammachakkapavatthana Suththa** (the wheel turning discourse).

These types of dukkhas identified are:

1. **Jathi** - Birth
2. **Jara** – Aging and decay
3. **Vyadhi** - Sickness
4. **Marana** - Death
5. **Appiyehi Sampayoga** - Union with the undesired
6. **Piyehi Vippayoga** - loss of Desired

7. **Yampichhcan na labhathi** - not receiving the Desired
8. **Panhca upadanaskandha** - taking all panchaskandha
   (rupa, vedana, sanna, sankhara, vignana) *as I or Mine.*

THE DIAMOND SUTRA- THE NOBLE EIGHT-FOLD PATH LEADING TO THE EXTINCTION OF SUFFERING AND THE END OF REBIRTH	
Right Understanding	(Ditthi)
Right Mindedness	(Sankappa)
Right Speech	(Vaca)
Right Action	(Kammanta)
Right Living	(Ajiva)
Right Effort	(Vayama)
Right Attentiveness	(Sati)
Right Concentration	(Samma-Samadhi)

There could easily be and there are literally entire volumes of words in various languages explaining, explicating, interpreting and pontificating.

None necessary here. Those with the Need, will search to undertake your own detailed personal study of the Diamond Sutra and each aspect of what is meant by 'right' understanding through to 'right' concentration. Each aspect of priceless, ageless wisdom of the Buddha will be revealed to you when you are ready to make the effort to seek it.

Indeed, and in fact, detailed study of each and every one of the sacred scriptures of the Hindu books, the Buddhist texts, the Zoroastrian Avesta, the Jewish Torah and Kabbalah, the Christian Bible, and the Muslim Koran will reveal the exact **same Truth** in many different ways and forms, from different angles, from different times, with different emphasis.

The Universal Worship Service of Hazrat Inayat Khan applies readings from the sacred books of each of the great world faiths on a particular topic such as giving, service, acceptance, gratitude, humility, tolerance and on to the full spectrum of others. Many are astounded to open up to learning to see the evidence for themselves that the same Light of Truth is in so many names and forms, known and unknown to the world.

For anyone hoping, aspiring, and aiming to raise their vibration, to attune their frequency and transform their consciousness, the timeless ancient principles, methods and techniques given out by the Buddha more than 2500 years ago are just as relevant, powerful and vital as they have ever been in any prior generations. The Buddhist beam of the One Light also appeals to contemporary generations because it does not specifically make reference to the name of God.

At the same time, individuals with faint or no magnetic canters will likely find the concept of not returning to the Earth in a rebirth singularly quite unappealing. A proportion will have nothing more than faith in the material world and the body and there it ends. Some will put their belief in an eternal afterlife of blissful heaven or equally tortuous hell. Even among those who have eventually come to the truth of reincarnation, some will willfully wish to be drawn back into wheel of life and death and into the world of suffering. Why? Mostly because of slavery to the desires.

One of the very best and ever enduring translations is found in the *Buddhist Bible* edited by Dwight Goddard and published by Beacon Press (1970 E.P. Dutton) which includes the early PALI sources, the Diamond Sutra, the Surangama Sutra, the Tao-Teh-Ching, the Sutra of the Sixth Patriarch, through to the Tibetan scriptures of Milarepa.

One of the earlier pivotal transformative books introduced to the modern world was *The Light of Asia* or the Great Renunciation (Mahabhinishkramana) which was translated and edited by Sir Edwin Arnold in London in 1879. This book, and another, *The Song Celestial*, (on the Bhagavad Gita) introduced through Sir Edwin greatly influenced and inspired a number of key figures in the 20th Century including particularly Mahatma Gandhi. The poem is not only portrays the divinity of the Buddha, but also the humanity of Gautama Siddhartha, the prince who saw human suffering and asked why.

TAO

The Buddhist Light of Truth spread across Asia and reached its further zenith in the manifestation of the Taoist teachings in ancient China of around 600 BC in the Tao Te Ching. The Tao Te Ching is considered to have been given out by a highly developed probable Human Number 6 known as Lao Tse.

Written in the ancient Chinese script, the *Way of Integrity* is only 81 verses but its wisdom and its impacts profound beyond mere words.

MERE KNOWLEDGE VERSUS ACTION IN PRACTICE

Books have proven inspirational and transformational for many seekers of wisdom through the ages. Words and writings can enlighten and inspire with knowledge but only **Practice** and **Right Action** will lead to anything worthwhile. *Explanations* aim to account for why something is as it is, and *explications* purport to account for what it is for something to exist, to occur or to manifest in a particular way. All this can be valuable up to a threshold, but beyond that it can degenerate into philosophizing or what Gurdjieff called "wiseacreing." The learning is a necessary first step but far from sufficient. It is in the practice that the learning bears results.

The 48th Sura of the Tao Teh Ching, as always, says it succinctly and best:

> "In regard to knowledge: the more one studies, the more he accumulates learning; while in regard to wisdom the more one *practices wisdom*, the more his desires and thoughts are lessened, even to the perfect emptiness of mind, all his innate excellencies will be developed and manifested. It is, therefore, necessary, if one is to keep control of his mind, to preserve it's emptiness. But as soon as one desires to control his mind, he becomes incapable of doing so. It is by this perfect control of the mind that the Sage gains the world's favor."

THE TAO TEH CHING

The Buddhist Light of Truth spread across Asia and reached its further zenith in the manifestation of the Taoist teachings in ancient China of circa 600 BC in the Tao Te Ching. The Tao Te Ching was given out by a highly advanced Sage, most probably a Human Number 6 known as Lao Tse.

Inscribed in the ancient Chinese characters, the *Way of Integrity* is only 81 verses but its wisdom and far-reaching impacts profound beyond expression. Rather than succumbing to the folly of trying to describe the indescribable, simply absorb and reflect upon only a fraction sample of the insight from the and marvel to find yourself in awe of the wisdom.

The tao that can be told
is not the eternal Tao
The name that can be named
is not the eternal Name.

The unnamable is the eternally real. ⟵———┐ ON DISCERNING THE REAL AND UNREAL
Naming is the origin
of all particular things.

Free from desire, you realize the mystery.
Caught in desire, you see only the manifestations. ⟵┐ DESIRE AND DESIRELESSNESS

Yet mystery and manifestations
arise from the same source.
This source is called darkness. ⟵———┐ ON THE DARKNESS OF HUMAN IGNORANCE

Darkness within darkness.
The gateway to all understanding.

When people see some things as beautiful, ⟵———┐ SUBJECTIVE THINKING
other things become ugly.
When people see some things as good,
other things become bad.

Being and non-being create each other. ⟵———┐ ON THE PAIRS OF OPPOSITES
Difficult and easy support each other.
Long and short define each other.
High and low depend on each other.
Before and after follow each other.

Therefore the Master
acts without doing anything
and teaches without saying anything. ←─ ON THE TEACHING COMING AND GOING
Things arise and they come;
things disappear and they are let go. ←── SERVING WITHOUT SEEKING REWARDS
The Master has but doesn't possess,
acts but doesn't expect. ←──────────── ON DETACHMENT
When the work is done, the Master forgets it.
That is why it lasts forever.

If you overesteem great men,
people become powerless.
If you overvalue possessions, ←──── ON MATERIALISM AND THE PROFIT MOTIVE
people begin to steal.

The Master leads
by emptying people's minds
and filling their cores,
by weakening their ambition
and toughening their resolve.
He helps people lose everything
they know, everything they desire,
and creates confusion
in those who think that they know.

Practice not-doing, ←──────────── FAITH AND CONVICTION
an everything will fall into place.

The Tao is like a well:
used but never used up.
It is like the eternal void: ←──────── THE ETERNAL VOID
filled with infinite possibilities.

It is hidden but always present.
The Tao doesn't take sides;
it gives birth to both good and evil. ←————————— OBJECTIVITY AND DETACHMENT
The Master doesn't take sides;
yet welcomes both saints and sinners. ←————— SUN GIVES LIGHT EQUALLY TO ALL
The Tao is like a bellows:
it is empty yet infinitely capable.
The more you use it, the more it produces; ←— OF KNOWLEDGE AND UNDERSTANDING
the more you talk of it, the less you understand.

Hold on to the centre. ←———————————————————— ON BALANCE

The Tao is called the Great Mother:
empty yet inexhaustible, ←———————————————— HOLY MOTHER THE EARTH
it gives birth to infinite worlds.
It is always present within you.
You can use it any way you want.

The Tao is infinite, eternal.
Why is it eternal?
It was never born;
thus it can never die. ←———————————————— THE ETERNAL, THE INFINITY
Why is it infinite?
It has no desires for itself;
thus it is present for all beings.

The Master stays behind;
that is why she is ahead.
She is detached from all things;
that is why she is one with them.
Because she has let go of herself, ←————— DETACHED LOVE OBJECTIVE LOVE
she is perfectly fulfilled.

On Humility:

The supreme good is like water,
which nourishes all things without trying to.
It is content with the low places that people disdain.
Thus it is like the Tao.

On Right Thinking:

Fill your bowl to the brim
and it will spill.
Keep sharpening your knife
and it will blunt.
Chase after money and security
and your heart will never unclench.
Care about people's approval
and you will be their prisoner.
Do your work, then step back.
The only path to serenity.

On the Law of Three:

The Tao gives birth to One.
One gives birth to Two.
Two gives birth to Three.
Three gives birth to all things.

On the Cosmic Scale:

Humanity follows the Earth
Earth follows the Universe
The Universe follows the Tao
The Tao follows only itself

On Responsibility to Nature

When humanity interferes with the Tao
The Earth becomes depleted
The equilibrium crumbles
Creatures become extinct

INFREQUENT FREQUENCIES, RARE RESONANCE

The Tao is a limitless fountain. You may read and re-read and ponder the Tao Teh Ching over and time again but will still always experience new insight, inspiration and higher knowledge each time you do so.

ZEN

The Buddhist Light of Truth yet further transubstantiated, manifested and found expression in the formlessness of Zen.

Zen is Zen. Attempts to define the indefinable by futile attempts at reduction to word descriptions will contribute deception if by freezeframing it in time and space.

Have you ever tasted honey? How could or would you describe honey or its taste to someone who has never encountered or experienced it ever before?

You could try applying descriptions of its viscose texture, you might refer to its sweetness or scent or try comparing it with other foods. You might describe it like thickened sugar syrup, if they have ever experienced that.

But what is honey? Honey is honey, and so long as you have not experienced it, even tasted it, you are short of the mark and still remain in ignorance or illusion about its qualities and nature.

To know honey, it is necessary for the individual to experience themselves.

Is not all this principle the same with Zen? This is because Zen is a practice that can only be experienced, not understood or conceptualized in the brain.

211

Zazen is the stream from the river of Mahayana Buddhism that originated in China during the Tang Dynasty. Mahayana Buddhism was the line of Buddhist teaching originating in northern India which spread throughout Asia.

Zen may be a practice of self-discovery, or it may be a discipline, or could be a perspective, or an attitude, or all or none of those things. Zen emphasizes the immersion in stillness through the experience of the ever present Here and Eternal Now. What Zen is not? Zen is not a philosophy, not a theory, not an idea, nor a belief, nor is it any dogma nor religion. Zen does not at all tell people what to believe in or what not to believe in.

Zen emerged through the wellspring of practice in China and Japan to its zenith in art and music, and through to its physical and mental expressions in the martial arts through such disciplines as Tai Chi, Kung Fu, Wu Wei, Karate, Tai Chi and in many other forms.

Found also in the martial arts going back the known oldest from south India from over three thousand years ago which is Kalaripayattu or "art of the battlefield." Wu Wei is an ancient manifestation of early martial arts in China with emphasis on the Yin (passive) force as it embraces "effortless action" and "inexertion," in balance with the (active) Yang.

The very concepts of Yin and Yang expressed through the now universally recognized powerful symbolism:

The Yin-Yang became, in more recent history, well known around the world which influenced understanding and elevated collective consciousness in similar ways that over symbols, such as the Christian Cross, and Islamic crescent moon and star have.

A single symbol speaks volumes and teaches on levels words cannot.

On one level the Yin-Yang symbol represents the Pairs of Opposites. Particularly that day cannot exist without night and vice versa. The same message comes through relating to "bad vs good," "hot vs cold," and all the innumerable contrasts flowing from the Law of the Pairs of Opposites.

It may be a useful point around this, for example, is the Buddhist message of "Right" understanding - does not infer right or wrong. It is beyond the Pairs of Opposites and points only to 'hitting or missing the mark' in the sense that it is, instead, simply guidance around attitude, approach, and vibration producing one result or another.

The Yin-Yang symbol consists of black and white swirls with each side containing a small spot of the other opposite within it.

On a higher level, **Yang** represents the **active force of the Sun** and **Yin** represents the **passive force of the Earth.**

Where opposite forces counterbalance and interconnect is the **Balance.**

Astronomers developed calculations to measure the size and density of stars. Our Sun is considered astronomically to be 'average' in size and there are innumerably vastly larger and also smaller stars throughout the universe, as well as planets and moons.

So what is the miracle, the secret of our **Sun**? Together with the **Earth**, the two heavenly bodies, which are actually highly conscious beings, are in perfect **balance.**

It is this perfection, this delicate dance of **Balance, between Sun and Earth**, creating the conditions for biological life to emerge and evolve. As astronomers have long observed, the finely balanced, delicate and exquisite unique conditions of the precise distance between **Sun and Earth** (which astronomers refer to as the "Goldiloches"zone) are a rarest treasure. Remember the Earth is the Planet of Choice.

Through the vastness of the cosmos there are other such Solar Systems but the one you were born into is exceptionally rare, and one that constantly creates surprising miracles. And you can marvel in awe that you are one of those miracles.

And this balance is what the Yin-Yang symbol so simply and elegantly portrays.

Although Zen is without dogma, without do's or don'ts or any of the ordinary dictates of the outer forms of religion, there exist principles of practical, natural guidance. The guidance is the Buddhist notion again is that one method or approach is apt to produce one result in the field of possibilities, while other choices will generate others.

- Focus on process and practice, not results
- Aim to do things consciously, with awareness and thoroughness
- Aim for balance in everything
- Avoid the rush and avoid rushing

- Appreciate and ponder the space between things
- See (outer) forms for what they are
- Revere and love Nature
- Savor Stillness and Silence
- Work hard, work with awareness
- Maintain and treasure simplicity in life
- Breathe deeply and meditate
- Meditation is attention, not intensity or concentration
- Meditation is the key to awakening
- Know, show and give gratitude
- Live compassion in practice
- "Self" is non-existent
- Everything constantly is changing
- Material "things" which are so valued are empty
- Everything is connected
- Logic and intellect are limited and often misleading
- Accept that painful, unpleasant things will happen
- Avoid being judgmental, practice detached objectivity
- Always give respect, remembering everything is Divine
- Seek the Silence, enter the Silence

To practice this form of work-on-self, the attitude is the vibration, so practitioners cultivate it and take it with them whether in meditating, or in walking, breathing, working, eating, eliminating, talking, cooking, cleaning, and into every moment of activity and movement and non-activity.

THE PRACTICE OF MINDFULNESS

"In storm and turmoil be calm and silent.
Watch the events around as witness."

RAMANA MAHARSHI

Modern psychology came in the early 21st century, to a break-through 'discovery' in the practice of mindfulness. Mindfulness is the cultivation of the art and skills of developing within, an objective, dispassionate, observing part. The observing "I."

This 'revolutionary' method teaches the development of skills to go into quietness and stillness, and to simply notice thoughts that come and go without any judgement. This is, noticing like a detached, curious observer. The Mindfulness method is most certainly valuable and can significantly help many people, as the various determinates, measurements and outcomes attest. This 'new' positive approach to re-think thinking is, of course, none other than the ancient Yogic and Buddhist practice re-membered and repackaged.

Zen

To taste Zen, contemplate the Zen paintings which are examples of the expressions of Objective Art. Much is expressed through a few simple lines. Simplicity is visually illustrated through this remarkable art form. It is "minimalist" and simple, yet profound and powerful. The elegant simplicity of Nature, such as found in a flower or in a frond of bamboo, may be expressed through a painting or a photograph.

Through their art, Chinese Chan monk painters used brush and calligraphy to express what could not be expressed even in volumes of books or years of lectures. Japanese Master Hakuin taught his monks and pupils to communicate and to express Zen through their art with brush and wash paintings. A sect of Japanese Zen practitioners were reputed to focus on the teaching through playing the traditional Shakuhachi bamboo flute. The making of the flute had a purpose, as does the playing of the sound having a vibrational purpose and effect. And these parallel complementary vibrational effects are similar to what can be experienced in the music of the Indian Bansuri bamboo flute in the Ragas.

Enso

Related to this is the Japanese Zen expression of **Enso** 円相 or the circular form which is drawn in one uninhibited brushstroke. The Enso can represent the Mu (the Void) as the circle represents infinity. The reason this practice is particularly referred to is because it represents some unique, important facets of Zen. Coming full circle symbolically represents Satori or enlightenment as it expresses completion. The artist draws a freehand whoosh, in a circle. As a spiritual exercise, it may be done several times in day.

Wabi-Sabi - The Japanese Expression of Simplicity, Beauty in Flawed Imperfection

The Enso circle relates closely to the subtle Japanese concept of **Wabi-Sabi** (approximate transliteration *wisdom in simplicity*). **Wabi Sabi** is the Japanese aesthetic (study of what is beautiful) world view which celebrates the Buddhist teaching of embracing acceptance of *transience (everything is temporary)*, *everything is imperfect*, and *everything is incomplete* as revealed in Nature.

Understanding something of **Wabi-Sabi** (not to be confused with the pungent water radish condiment wasabi) as a subtle, vital Buddhist teaching will prove a useful ladder for preparing for the coming chapters on **Purity** and **Perfection** and how they relate to vibration and resonance.

Wabi-Sabi finds its paramount expression in Japanese art and culture from the Tea Ceremony, through to the peacefulness and simplicity of the Zen garden, through to the cultivation of miniature bonsai trees, through the art of flower arrangement, through to architecture, pottery and poetry. Wabi-Sabi receives acknowledgement and further explanation in the worthwhile book: *1001 Ideas that Changed the World* (2018 Trevor Davies).

Some thinkers conclude the Wabi-Sabi perspective presents a counterbalancing, different view to the Platonic concepts of Perfection in Forms from the ancient Greek stream of philosophy which underpins and pervades much of western thought. But that is likely inaccurate as Plato's writings never claimed any perfection possible within the scope of the material world, but rather that perfection might in the essences of things which exist as "Forms" in other, non-matter, higher realms. In most ways key elements of Plato's thought interlaces easily with Buddhist precepts, rather than contradicting or opposing them.

YIN/YANG AND THE EXPRESSION OF BALANCE
THROUGH THE MARTIAL ARTS

While the various schools of Kung Fu, Karate, Muay Thai, Taekwondo and other martial arts represent the **active force of the Yang**, the **Yin passive force** is represented by practices such as Tai Chi and Aikido. The gist of the approach in the Yin styles is to absorb and redirect the energy of the opponent as contained in the power of passivity. The martial arts can be very helpful for young people particularly in cultivating self-discipline and in developing specifically the balance in the Moving-Instinctive centre, as well as instilling in youth some sense of a code of ethics and values.

Koans

Koans are learning tools applied by Zen masters to the teaching of their pupils which have the effect to confuse and confound the ego of the conscious mind for the purpose of opening up to inner learning.

The actual purpose of the Koan is twofold: 1. To shock and shake the pupil out of their ego, out of their intellect, and out of their body; 2. To test the pupil on their present state and their progress in the teaching.

Contrary to popular belief, a Koan is not a puzzle or a riddle that requires any particular answer. Is it more and less than the famous 'sound of one hand clapping.' An aim and effect of the Koan is learning to break free of thinking in the Pairs of Opposites and away from rote memory of mere facts.

A selected sample of Koans coming from Chan era Chinese Master Yunmen Wen:

A monk once asked Ummon, "What is this place where knowledge is useless?" Ummon answered him: "Knowledge and emotion cannot fathom it!"

A monk once asked Ummon, "What is the Dharma Kaya?(the Buddhist teaching)" Ummon answered: "The Six Ungraspables." (The graspables are the senses sight, hearing, taste, smell, touch and mind).

A travelling monk asked Ummon, "What is the teaching given by Gautama Buddha during his lifetime?" Ummon replied: "The teaching confronts each."

The similar approach of trying to help liberate the pupil from fixed attitudes, conditioning and mind limitations was applied by Hindu Sage Ramana Maharashi

to his pupils and disciples in the question: "Who am I."

The question has powerful effects as the pupil grapples with it as it as it traces back to the Original Face. Ramana Marharshi explains: *"Who am I is not really meant to get an answer. It is meant to dissolve the questioner."*

And this Koan offers another approach to the same question of "Who Am I ":

"Without thinking of good or evil, what was your original face before your father and mother were born?"

CHAPTER 19

Perfection And The Work Of Self-Perfection

Jesus said: "Therefore you shall be perfect,
just as your Father in heaven is perfect".

MATTHEW 5:48 OF THE BIBLE, KJV

So what is the perfection? Only another imperfect ordinary word? How can perfection be real or realized? Why, how and where is this perfection business ever to be found? Or is it not even in a place, space or time?

Could perfection be worthwhile exploring and pondering?

Your personal Koan: If desirelessness is desirable, then how is perfection perfectly desirable or imperfectly desireless?

In philology (origin of words) the English meaning of perfection is believed to come from the Latin *per facere or per-factum.* This means made thoroughly completed or pointing toward completion or of fulfilment. But the way the word perfection has come to be used in many modern societies is taken to mean "flawless" or without defect. That is only one facet of it, as it has come to be associated with "excellence," an altogether different word and meaning.

ANCIENT GREEK

But the older Greek *Telios* meaning is what came through in the Christian Bible and was Teliotia Τελειότητα or the Teleios. More or less, Teleios translates to "complete." This doesn't necessarily mean the same as "flawless" or "freedom from error." It rather appears to point toward something like **reaching a distant goal**. The Greek Socratic ideal of perfection proposed that perfection equated with abstract thought.

The enlightened ancient Greek civilisation taught the Platonic theory of Forms. The Forms were believed to represent the abstract, the ideal, the things-in-themselves rather than the material objects manifested. Take, for example, the wolf. There may be millions of two-brained animals in the category of the manifestation of "wolf" defining the nature and characteristics of a wolf. A single wolf may be somewhat representative of the species of wolves. But the higher abstract Form of what is wolf rises beyond all that as it is the inner nature of "wolfness." All that it is to be a wolf is perfect only in the Ideal Abstract Form. In your ideal, can you idealize the perfect wolf or a perfect blue rhinoceros?

The same would apply to a colour such as blue. Each person might have a different sense perception or conception of objects called blue or even disagreement about what is 'true blue' and what is not blue. But of all the manifestation of the blues, blue in-itself is outside time and space and can only exist as Form. That is, it is an abstract Idea at the level of perfection. What is the distraction which is the barrier to attainment of the Ideal of Form? Why it is the none other than the tyranny of the material body and its carnal desires.

HEBREW

Ancient Hebrew concepts translated around perfection are **tamam [m'T] and calal [l;l'K]** according to Talmudic sources. Tamam or Tamim points to wholeness, goodness, soundness. Whereas the idea of calal is said to point to beauty, completeness, splendor.

HINDU

In the Hindu schools, perfection is believed to equate with merging with the Oneness. Realizing the soul (Atman) is the ultimate goal of every "individual" to become One with the Brahman (Creator). As the ever-changing temporal world of Maya reveals itself as illusion, the principal aim is to become free of lower worldly attachments. The Hindu conception was the melting, the merging, the total absorption of the individual within and into the One.

Krishna speaks in the Bhagavad Gita: "he whose intelligence is unattached everywhere, whose self is conquered, who is free from desire, he obtains, through renunciation, the supreme perfection of actionlessness. Learn from me, briefly, O Arjuna, how he who has attained perfection, also attains to Brahman, the highest state of wisdom."

CHRISTIAN

In Christianity, St Gregory of Nyssa expressed his belief that perfection is being and acting just like God's human form, Christ. That is, completely free of 'evil'. If your wish is to to experience something of

Christian mysticism, then listen to the holy Gregorian Chants and sense the palpable resonance radiating. Sound as a way of worship. So it could be said that cultivating and emulating the divine characteristics of the Christ and removing or purifying all that is unlike Him is the quest for perfection.

SUFI

Yet it was through Ibn Arabi, that the great Sufi precept of perfection was given out. For Ibn Arabi, perfection is the individual's complete knowledge of the abstract and the material, leading to a transformation of being which can be understood on one level to mean the vibration is raised by the shock leading to the leap beyond the Sol (Sun) interval in the scale of 7. It cannot be understood as mere knowledge, but is direct mystical experience. Knowledge is only the tool and bridge supporting the transformation when effort rises from below as Grace descends from above.

The ultimate aim of perfection is only complete not only through knowledge but with direct encounter within both the ephemeral and the eternal. This may be understood as gradations or levels that are traversed as up though through dense matter and up through the finest unseen realms toward the Absolute. Only transformation can allow this to be possible, and only because the Absolute is Merciful and Compassionate.

That is, for the Sufi, Eternal, Infinite Being or Perfection is the source and final, ultimate destination (the Alpha and Omega) of God knowing self through descending through the lower dense matter and then ascending back "home" to the Source from which all arose, all that arises and all that will evermore arise. Everything and every being is being called home (Om). This can also be understood from another angle as vibrational transformation of Self which requires shedding the old selves as the pupa becomes the chrysalis, and as the chrysalis becomes the butterfly.

THE PATH OF SELF-PERFECTION

On the one hand, it isn't complicated as self-perfection simply means self-improvement.

Any sincere effort of self-improvement, no matter how small, as long as it is sustained raises your vibration.

A single drip in the bucket may seem like nothing at all given that the enormity of the tasks and barriers ahead may seem daunting. But each drip fills that large pail and soon you will be needing ever larger vessels until, with persistence, he tiny drips become the ocean.

Humans are, by our very nature, very imperfect beings. Flawed, incomplete, impure, apt to make innumerable mistakes and to stumble and bumble our way along through life to a larger or lesser extent. Yet, we are the only species on the Planet of Choice with the capacity to exercise choice and with the potential to rise above our beautiful prison on the Planet Earth, and to transform, transubstantiate and ascend back to our One Source. To remain ignorant of that potential and to not aim and work to fulfil it as our Being-Duty is objectively a waste and the only real tragedy.

Whether you know or you don't, you asked to come into this world. You made the choice to come into this crucible of an imperfect human life and you were attracted by vibration

and placed in the circumstances right and necessary for your spiritual development.

Perfection in the Divine sense is far *beyond the Pairs of Opposites*. That is, far beyond **flawed and flawless**. Far beyond faultlessness, beyond precision, beyond best or worst, beyond impeccable, way far beyond excellence. The flaws of imperfect human beings is called in some religions "original sin." The misinterpretation of that dogma has done much harm over many years and generations, instilling a sense of fear and guilt.

As a noble aim, it is fair enough and right for human beings to do their best and aim for excellence.

But the notion of attaining perfection in the lower realms of the material, temporal world are futile. Aiming and attaining toward perfection is only possible beyond the dense material realm.

What is known as "perfectionism" has unfortunately become a toxic obsessional diversion for a proportion of people. They typically set themselves high standards, which is fair enough as a goal as long if they are realistic and attainable. But if and when they do not attain their objectives, they blame and flog themselves needlessly. This is counterproductive.

Perfectionism is simply another desire. It may be the desire to avoid fear of judgement and disapproval from others. Fear of rejection is a leading contributor to perfectionist tendencies. Trauma in childhood, or simple factors like having parents with unrealistically high expectation can contribute.

A perfectionist may be strongly identified with their fixed arbitrary attitudes of "success" and achievement. When they make a mistake they may feel overwhelming guilt, embarrassment, shame, and regret. In more extreme cases, it can lead to obsessive compulsion or other mental health disorders. Perfectionism is unbalanced and also the result of the false assumption that love is always conditional. The experience of unconditional love is the antidote for people afflicted with perfectionism, and every other malady.

If you are a perfectionist, you are aiming for something that is simply not possible in the biological, physical, material realm. It would be worthwhile to change course and redirect your energies toward the Master Endeavour, aiming your efforts in the realms where Perfection may potentially and eventually be found or be reached.

Spiritual work on self is not a race, nor is it a competition, nor is it anything like preparing for the Olympics or studying for sitting for an examination nor is it like constructing bridges, roads, or buildings. Every day in every way in ordinary life you are getting small tests or big examinations and are mostly unaware of it. It is not anything like "success" or "failure." It is unlike anything you have been conditioned to expect. It is process and it is journey. The ultimate process, the ultimate aim and the ultimate journey.

The Islamic and Sufi potters, sculptures, and artists of Central Asia would create works of art that were detailed, intricate, exquisite and of the highest standards of near flawlessness, balance and astounding precision. Then, at the end of crafting their work of art, they would intentionally and consciously inflict an error or a small flaw on the object. Why? It was the act of conscious humility. Because only Allah is Perfect.

CHAPTER 20

Refinement From Coarseness to Fineness From Contamination to Purity

THE ZOROASTRIAN TEACHING OF PURITY

In Homage, Reverence and Gratitude for the Zoroastrian Faith

"Science cannot solve the ultimate mystery of Nature. And that is because, in the last analysis, we ourselves are a part of the mystery we are trying to solve."

MAX PLANCK

An exquisitely beautiful flower, the lotus blossom grows and blooms from a stagnant pond of filth. The lotus represents purity, fulfilment, awakening, potential, rebirth, creation and eternity. The lotus heeds the call of the Sun each morning, breaks the surface of the water and blooms untouched by the mud and filth below. Each petal remains clean and pure. Closing at night, it sinks below the water's surface, only to resurface again in the morning.

Thich Nhat Hanh observes: "You cannot grow lotus flowers on marble. You have to grow them on the mud. No mud, no lotus flowers! Without suffering you have no way to learn how to be understanding and compassionate."

Arising from the grounded denseness of the Earth, aspiring toward the Divine, the lotus is blooming toward the light of the Sun. This blooming of flowers is Nature worshipping the Divine as well as reproducing new generations of flowers. Just as the lotus, you can grow through tough times and through the many difficulties along the course of life. You can rise again to shine as renewed as there is something within you that the harshness and temporal tribulations of the world can never touch.

Manure, and any rotting organic waste is added to dirt to boot fertility to yield glorious magnificence in the beauty of flowers as well as to grow nutritious food. Out of the filth, the flowers flourish. Everything of the Earth is grounded in the Earth. Everything material of the Earth will always go back to the Earth. But the dense, material aspect of the Earth is only one facet of this highly conscious being, our Holy Mother the Earth. We must be grounded with the Earth, and at the same time, aspiring to soar in the firmament of the heavens.

To rise from the coarseness and denseness of the material Earth, requires the process of refinement. Refinement demands purification.

The ancient Hermetic alchemy allegories around converting lead into gold hold several levels of meaning. The material element gold itself can only be extracted through fire and chemical processes to refine out the impurities or other elements and substances before in the process of its extraction. So, it is equally truth that the Higher

Self of the Human Consciousness must necessarily be refined through purification.

There are teachings, paths and numerous methods given for purification given out at various times and places, but all with the same aim and objectives. The way to purification is to follow the guidance of the Conscience which will have the effect of thus raising the self through vibration. This is the basis of Objective Morality.

Objective morality is not about the conditioned responses to subjective "right" vs "wrong" but about actions and thoughts raising or lowering vibration.

Human Number 5 Vivekananda taught that objective morality means the control of the mind, making the body obedient, truthfulness, selfless service, giving, and faith as the foundations leading to Purity.

Atman is absolute the Absolute and the Absolute is Purity. Is pure Truth. Is pure Love.

Even the extremely rare and exalted Human Number 7 is perfected to the level of our Sun and Solar System. An exceptional thing at which the "angels marvel and rejoice."

Even the extraordinary Human Number 7 is still on the journey of perfection and service. The journey of every being at whatever level of evolution or development is the path back home to Om.

The ultimate aim of every being is merging, returning in total absorption with the Source. It is Nirvana. It is Bliss. Far beyond any words or thought. Everything else is only either a step on that path or a distraction.

A lifetime in the atmosphere of the Earth is the crucible where the impurities can be filtered and the 'pure gold' of the Higher Self can be refined. All the suffering and the pain, all the hard lessons and the tribulations, all the joys, all the sorrows, all the experiences are for the purpose of offering the opportunity through a lifetime on the **Planet of Choice**. The opportunity and the choice is to raise or lower what you came in with.

Attaining the threshold of purity for raising the vibration to such a level holds the sacred potential for resonating with the frequency of Mukti or Liberation.

This is your birthright. This is your potential.

ZOROASTRIAN FAITH

"Dedication to purity from birth onwards is best for mankind. For Mother Earth should we toil, leading all men to the realms of light."
ZEND AVESTA, YASNA 48:5

Remarkably, some adherents of the Zoroastrian Faith are still living and practicing in the contemporary times. Modern religion scholars estimate there remain approximately 250,000 practicing Zoroastrians in the early 21st Century.

The Zoroastrian Faith is ancient, originating in Iran and extending between 6000 to 7000 years into the past when the original Zoroaster arose and gave out the high teaching. The original Zoroaster (also Zarathrustra) was an extraordinary being of the level of Human Number 7 (AD). This is one of the oldest original monotheistic (one God) religions. Zoroastrian introduced ideas of good vs evil, of light vs darkness and of duality directly influenced the latter Abrahamic line faiths of Judaism, Christianity and Islam.

The principal translations that we have of the Zend Avesta, the book of the faith, were handed down from the Parsees in India (AD). One of the best sources is by D.F.A. Bode in his translation of the Gathas. In tradition, Zoroaster was reputed to have been conceived through a "virgin birth" thousands of years prior to other such stories. His first vision of the "Immortal Shining Ones" came to him at age 30. He was said to have lived to age 77 by which time he had undergone transformation to the highest levels humanly possible.

Ahura Mazda is represented as the Great Light, and for Zoroaster to be connected directly to the sphere of God at the centre of our Galaxy remains something exceptionally, extraordinarily rare. Zoroaster's life and his teaching were transformative for the whole of humankind. The teaching he gave out was on the creation the world and the purpose of human beings, the origin and nature of evil and consequences of actions, rewards and punishments, salvation and regeneration of the individual. The teaching emphasizes how the "soul of man could attain union with God while still in the world (AD). Zoroaster spread the teaching throughout ancient Persia and Bactria and beyond into India.

The Abrahamic religions' ideas of heaven and hell, came down from Zoroaster in various forms and interpretations transmitted over generations and centuries. Ahura Mazda was the Absolute, the Eternal God of justice and of love. It was taught that there will be a 'last day' of judgement for every individual. Frashokereti is the Zoroastrian doctrine of a final renovation of the universe, when evil will be destroyed, and everything else, purified and remaining will be then in perfect unity with God-Ahura Mazda.

Zoroaster taught that human beings had to come to God of their own free will and choice. He taught that Ahura Mazda gave human beings the need and drive for perfection and immortality. Zoroaster taught that the way to find Ahura Mazda was through silent meditation (AD). Zoroaster was given instruction and Grace from above but was born of flesh as a human being on the Earth.

The main overarching focus and concern of the Zoroastrian Faith is purity and purification.

The Zoroastrians were often quite wrongly referred to as "fire worshippers." Fire is used in their worship in the ceremony of purification it represents the One Light, that of Ahura Mazda symbolically radiating from the flames. Fire also symbolizes purification. Worship will take place in Fire Temples, where a sacred fire is continually burning to signify the eternal flame. Through tradition, the offering that is made to go into the fire is not made directly by the worshipper, but given through the priest who wears the padam or mask covering the mouth and nostrils to assure there is no contamination of the from the breath or saliva. Only in purity may the offering be given.

Ritual worship practices were less important than Good Thoughts, Good Words, and Good Deeds. Again, the emphasis of the Pairs of Opposites in the contrasts between Good and Bad are a hallmark of this ancient faith as the teaching has come down and been interpreted through time.

Zoroastrians believe that human beings consist of both mortal material body and immortal spiritual fabric. Elements and influences of the original Teaching of Zoroaster have come down through all the Abrahamic faiths and its tangible influence extends through to Taoist and Sufi mysticism.

CHAPTER 21

In Homage, Reverence and Gratitude for the Judaic Faith

THE JUDAIC TEACHING OF THE LAW

"Coincidence is God's way of remaining anonymous."

ALBERT EINSTEIN

Through Judaism came the light of the teaching of the Law. That is the Commandments and prescriptions of the Mosaic Laws that form the five chapters of the Torah. The laws on the tablets given by the Yaweh on Mt Sanai to the Prophet Moses pertained to practical guidance for living as well as the early code of morality, based on reward and punishment.

Pertaining to purity, within the Jewish teaching, there is a close immediate connection between purity and holiness. What is impure, tãme/tumã is unholy contrasted with what is tahor/tahara, that which is clean, shining, and radiant. The widespread value that holiness is related to cleanliness comes through from physical, material plane through to the sacred and holy beyond matter. Both the human and the Divine is known to love what is clean and pure and shun that which is dirty, smudged, polluted, smitten, contaminated. Cleansing and purification rituals were applied to not only humans, but objects, in the blessing of food, places, and particularly temples.

It is noteworthy that the *Book of Esther* and *Song of Songs* (Sulieman) are the only constituent parts of the Hebrew scriptures not overtly, explicitly or directly referring to the One God. *It is the subtlety of the esoteric Jewish teaching portraying the absence of the Divine's direct, overt intervention in the stories on the affairs of life as demonstrating how God can work through seemingly "coincidental" events and through actions of mortals and individuals.*

THE KABBALAH

The Kabbalah is the Light of Truth flowing through the vessel of Jewish mysticism. The Kabbalah is stream of understanding, an esoteric form of knowledge, as well as a discipline and inner practice.

The nature of existence is understood within the relationship between the unchanging, abstract, nameless, eternal God named Ein Sof (the Infinite Creator) and the temporal, finite, universe (the Creation) of the three-dimensional material realm. The Kabbalah gives insight into the concealed and revealed.

The Tree of Life could be considered on a level as a map of existence and with the place of humanity contained within it. The 10 Sephirot are like nodes of symbolic spiritual light arranged in 3 pillars. The 10 Sephirot lights extend from the Divine Creator Ein Sof (Endlessness) through to gradations of physical existence. From esoteric knowledge, the Tree of Life dates back at least 250 centuries and illustrates the manifestations of the Law of Three and the Law of Ninefoldness.

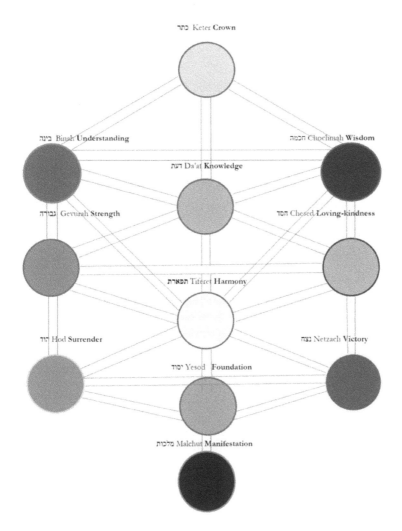

The Kabbalah is intricate and complex, and lifetimes are spent in its study and interpretation. This is to offer the briefest of introductions for the purpose of illustrating Yesod, the foundation block where motive must be purified.

There are one of three triads of knowledge representing the **Intellectual Centre**:

1. Da'at is Knowing
2. Binah is Understanding
3. Chockmah is Wisdom

There are one of three triads for the **Emotional Centre**:

4. Tiphareth is beauty, harmony and compassion
5. Gevurah is the strength of boundaries, of definition
6. Chesed is unbounded Love

There are one of three triads for the **Instinctive Centre:**

7. Yesod is foundation; telling the truth, authenticity, sincerity, purity
8. Hod is surrender; acknowledging and accepting what is; giving way
9. Netzach is victory: overcoming obstacles, directing intention

The Kabballah was given out through the Zohar, a series of ancient Hebrew texts revealing mystical inner teaching within the Torah, likely originating back to ancient Egyptian and original Sumerian sources. The Zohar was most likely significantly influenced by early Merkhaba mysticism from the Book of Ezekiel prophesy. It concerned the journey of passage through the vision of the 7 Heavens and beyond the 7th Heaven to the Araboth, the realm of the Source.

In the middle ages, the more recent interpretations of the Tree of Life were attributed to Johann Reuchlin and to the Kabbalist mystic Joseph Gikatilla in his *Gates of Light*. In the 12th century, the great scholar Maimonides assigned the Seraphim a middle ranking in the angelic hierarchy of 5 out of a scale of 10, denoting how near or distant they may be to the Absolute (Atziluth). This is one model depicting the concept of Proximity. Consider the connection between the Seriphotic nodes of the light in the Tree of Life to the Divine Light or Spirit of Guidance from the burning Angels of the Seraphim. The awareness of their distance from the Absolute Divinity he surmised, causes their continual self-nullification or burning up. **But it is their burning that generates light and produces the effect of warmth, just as the Sun does.**

OMRAM MIKHAIL AIVANOV - THE PURITY OF YESOD

One of the greatest modern Teachers of the process of Purity was the Bulgarian Man Number 5, Master Omram Mikhail Aivanov.

Master Aivanov was initiated and trained by his Bulgarian Teacher Master Peter Deunov.

Two of his important works were *The Splendor of Tiphareth* and *The Mysteries of Yesod.*

Both of these books delve into the Kabbalah mysticism through the lens of the central pillar of the Tree of Life.

Tiphareth is the sphere of the Sun on the Tree of Life and Master Aivanov gave out the Teaching that Our Holy Father the Sun and Solar System are at the centre of human connection to the universe. The purpose of the Surya Yoga is self-perfection through purification of the higher self, to enter the Sun within (the Active Force of the Sun). Through the practical practices of purification, a human being with a developing higher centre begins to attune more and further to the vibration and resonance of the Sun. The more we begin to attune to the Sun, the more the Higher Self will resemble it and melt into the Light.

Master Aivanov also explains how human beings are composed of both higher and lower parts, with corresponding coarse and gross roots in the lower regions of the earthly Sephiroth of Malkout. This Kabbalistic conception of the Sephiroth correspond with the Hindu and Buddhist understandings of the lower and higher Chakras. Humans start out in the dense region of matter in the first station of Malkout and may, through purifying motives and traversing the journey through self-perfection, may ascend to the next level at the station of the Sephiroth of Yesod.

Purifying the motives is essential to get through the dense realm of Malkout, because the pilgrim, throughout the journey, will always face constant tests in the forms of temptations, desires, internal and external enemies, diversions, setbacks, and ongoing suffering. Mister Gurdjieff so aptly observed that **the last thing human beings will give up is their suffering. Do you know what is your suffering**

in this lifetime? Can you objectively observe how you insist on clinging tightly to it? Can you see why?

Only through purification and sincerity of motives at the beginning of the journey combined with intense need and persistence will the pilgrim make progress.

This description of the vital necessity of entering through the first gate of purity is coincidentally similar and consistent to the objective story esoteric book of 1678 *Pilgrim's Progress*, by John Bunyan, a very important work written through a Christian lens.

It is equally true enough that modern generations of humanity live in world where water, food, and air are all subject to widespread contamination, and industrial scale pollution. The human-made contamination pervades every ocean and land and continent. Only as recently as the 18th Century, did human beings enjoy the glory of a relatively pure, natural environment. Filtering, purification and atonement are more important on every level in contemporary life than ever before in the course of history.

Aivanov explains how the journey through Yesod leads to purification, which is the basic foundation, just as every Seripheroth offers its own qualities and virtues. The purification is necessary before ascendence into the higher Sephira such as the Sun Sphere of Tiphareth. Only through purification can it become possible. Each Sephira represents a world and internal hierarchy within itself, as it is a realm of vibration.

For Master Aivanov, purity and peace are inseparable. The purpose of purification is peace. He observes that once inner peace is found, it is impossible to lose. Along the way are glimpses of

Peace that inspire and encourage. Immersing the body in sancti-fied water will cleanse the body, yet, the real work is in struggling against the myriad inner negativities and desires. But also, equal work must be devoted to clearing impurities on the mental, psychic and astral domains.

The law of attraction has been well popularized, talked about extensively, interpreted and misinterpreted. It is true enough that thoughts, and words have power and consequences, just as actions do on a tangible level. Anyone can easily observe the effects of keeping company with those who aspire to high ideals and live a mostly virtuous life in contrast to frequenting places that attract a dense vibration. To change outcomes, we must start with changing thoughts and attitudes. Our attitude will determine our altitude.

Master Aivanov took it further to explain the Law of Affinity and why Sages, Saints and Prophets counsel "to love one another" on the Path of Forgiveness. The Spiritually Dead – those who live in rela-tive inner ugliness and darkness, perceive and assume the same all around them. They judge the world and judge others according to the way they see themselves, and there will always be plenty to judge in this temporal, material world.

The universal principle is that, try as you may, you have no right to judge others and you will never, ever change another person. **You can only change yourself.** Only in transforming yourself, will this inevi-tably have subtle effects upon those around you or influenced by you.

On the other side of the Polarity, those who have attained a certain level of vibrational atonement and attunement, cannot see wickedness, cruelty, treachery or dishonesty in others. It is not at all that they are naïve, it is simply that they have attained the level of

Universal Vision to see God in everything and everyone. This is now how they see the same world through different organs of perception.

When you say something or do something against another human being, or when another person has said or done something against you to hurt you, the remedy and the answer is exactly the same. If you have hurt someone, a certain amount of damage is inevitable, but to mitigate and repair some of the harm, you must send that person sincerely a great deal of love. The exact same principle of neutralizing poison from a curse or harm that someone has sent you, for whatever reason.

Master Aivanov gives out methods, technologies and mystical formulas for preparing his pupils to receive Grace. Like all other genuine evolved Sages and Teachers, the methods are of fasting, meditation, prayer and purification is essential to prepare the garden of a life for planting the seeds of liberation. Preparing the sacred garden is for the purpose of clearing the way for Grace to descend. It is not through purification, or self-perfection alone, nor only alone through "good works" or faith alone. It is through the combined synergy of all these practices that vibration can be raised and sustained.

As a highly developed and rare Human Number 5, Master Omraam Mikhail Aivanov and his school of initiates give out objective and practical transformational guidance toward what he describes as a future Civilization of the Sun, where humankind is adjusted, atoned and attuned back into harmony and balance with Creator and Creation. The same message and the same offer will be repeated and come through different forms for as long as it takes to eventually get through to you. All of it will seem coincidental.

CHAPTER 22

The Christian Faith

IN REVERANCE, HOMAGE AND GRATITUDE FOR LIGHT OF THE SELF-SACRIFICE

Circa over 2,000 years in the course of history arose a faith given out as an experiment within an experiment that altered the course of the history of humankind. Little was known of the Essenes until the discovery of the famous preserved Dead Sea Scroll manuscripts from 1947 in caves above Qumran in the desert cast some light on their origins and beliefs. The Dead Sea Scrolls were acknowledged as one of the most important archeological discoveries of the 20th Century.

In the early 21st Century, there were estimated approximately 2.7 billion adherents of the faith of Christianity out of a global population of 8 billion people. For the two millennia, the Christian faith has exerted ongoing powerful and pervasive influences on the values, aspirations, ideas and lives of generations living, particularly in Europe, in North and South America, and Africa.

The Law of Seven inevitably impacted Christianity as it has all religions of the world, resulting in schisms, fragmenting, disputes over theology and beliefs, and heresies, and the arising of multiple denominations, sects and cults.

THE ESSENES

From the limited fragments of verifiable historical information known about the Essenes, they existed within a few mystical Jewish communities which were forced to isolate in the wilderness of the desert in the times of 200-300 years BC because of persecution from the Hasmonean Kings (note the similarity with the Gurdjieff concept of the "Hasnamuss," the power-possessed beings).

Gurdjieff used the term *Hasnamuss* to describe an individual who is considered at the lowest level of human development. For Gurdjieff, a *Hasnamuss* is an individual who has developed a high degrees of intellectual and technical knowledge without inherent qualities of Conscience. They are drive by selfishness, arrogance, and a desire for power and control of others. The features of a Hasnamuss are deceit, manipulation of others, and lacking in empathy or humanity.

One of the leading reference sources on the Essenes up until the discovery of the Dead Sea Scrolls was the Jewish scholar from Poland, C.D. Ginsburg, who died in 1914.

It is believed that the Essenes had different conscious schools and communities for both the celibate priests and higher initiates, through to families of householders who had children. It is believed that the Essenes had been influenced by the teachings of Zoroaster and the Ancient Egyptian schools.

There can be no doubt that the Essenes were a remarkable and exceptional group of people who lived in isolated communities where practical support for living was shared with equality. The Essenes owned no property and had no money. The members contributed their work, skills and talents to the common good of the community. The Essenes practiced what could be accurately described as the purest form of communism many centuries before Marx.

From the Essenes directly came the **practice of purification through Baptism in water**. The historic figure, John the Baptist was either fully inspired and influenced by the Essenes, or was himself an Essene initiate.

The Essenes revered gentleness and pacifism, forbade expression of anger or aggression, adhered strictly to the Mosaic teachings and commandments, preserved esoteric secrets and practices, and gave themselves to benevolence and charity.

Then, there was, of course, the further fact that the Essenes were so concerned about cleanliness and purity almost to the extreme point of obsession. So much so, that they reportedly tried to avoid defecation during the Sabbath.

It could, of course, be purely coincidental that the rituals of the Essenes and earliest Christians have much in common, such as the belief in a Messiah sent by the One God, or the fact that the Dead Sea Scrolls refer to a supper of bread and wine given out by a Messiah (The One).

It could equally just be simple coincidence that the Essenes were at odds with the teachings of the Pharisees and Sadducees, two other mainstream priestly and political Jewish sects prevalent at the same time and places. You may recall the scene in the New Testament where Jesus, or Yeshua, the Carpenter of Galilee, cleared the sacred Jewish Temple from the (Luke 19:45, Matthew 21:12; Mark 11.15 and Gospel of St John 2:13) of the Pharisees who had allowed commercial merchants to desecrate it for profit. We must acknowledge, however, that also it could just be sheer coincidence, of course, that Pharisees believed in the resurrection of the body while the Essenes held belief only in the Spirit.

Moses was very likely an initiate of the inner teaching of the ancient Egyptian school of Amun Ra – the One Supreme God of the Universe manifesting through the holy light of Ra, the Sun. It could simply be just a coincidence, of course, that all three Abrahamic faiths, the Judaic, the Christian and the Islamic, all end their prayers with "Amen." Amen in this usage is to confirm the Truth and to affirm all in agreement, as the prayer is concluded and sent forth.

The Essenes kept their knowledge secret to maintain its purity, accuracy and fidelity. Access to the deeper knowledge was granted only to those who had passed levels of initiation. That is for the same reason that inner knowledge had been kept carefully contained and guarded for hundreds of generations. The other practical reason that the Essenes kept to themselves was to avoid exploitation and persecution by governments and authorities and criminal gangs of their times.

The Essenes rose before the sunrise and faced East offering up their prayers and songs of praise. This was before they would carry out any work or engage in any worldly matters. The Essenes were not worshipping the outer form of the Sun but something altogether within and beyond that. Their aim was to bring the Light into themselves, and give it out to all humanity with Love, just as the Sun shines equally on all life on Earth. But later, some of the Christian Church writers were scathing about their religious forebears, the Essenes, haughtily dismissing them as mere pagan "sun worshippers."

The powerful **Sensing Exercise**, which came down through the Gurdjieff Teaching, was directly through the Essenes. The Sensing Exercise is for the purpose of making a separation between body, mind and spirit. It is a prayer from the Moving Centre through to the Sun.

This offers only the briefest of introductions to the Essenes, but their invaluable contributions to the great Teaching of the Christian Faith are not at all exaggerated.

THE FOUR GOSPELS AND FOUNDATIONS OF CHRISTIANITY

For those whose traditional Faith came through the Christian line of Religion. perhaps in during childhood growing up in a Christian family, or in a Church or denomination, or through any means, or for those who came through another line of Faith and Truth, the reading and intense study of the Four Gospels of the New Testament are strongest and highest recommendations.

If you became disheartened and dissatisfied with the rigid doctrines, theologies and politics of the exoteric structure of the Church, and perhaps may have thrown the baby out with the bath-water, it would be very worthwhile to re-learn something about the rare treasures contained within inner Christianity.

Each of the Four Gospels, and particularly the Gospel of St John provide some of the most profound and powerful teachings and wisdom among the great Faiths of the World.

Almost each verse, and each sentence within the verses, are chock full of wisdom that can be understood on 7 different levels.

The Essenes are credited with having written three of the four Christian Gospels of Matthew, Mark and Luke (AD 1981 Quest 1) and the Gospel of St John came from a Gnostic School.

The Gnostics

The line of transmission for the Gospel of Saint John was through the Mandaean Gnostics who were contemporaries of the Essenes and were also a monotheistic (One God) sect of faith revering their lineage from Adam down through to John the Baptist. The Mandeans were Aramaic speakers and their name derives from *Manda* or Knowledge (Gnosis). The Mandeans had a direct lineage of transmission from the Pythagorean schools of Ancient Greece. The Mandeans were later referred to in Arabic as Subba, and are described three times as a mystic source of knowledge later in the Quran as ahl al-kitab or as 'People of the Book.' The Mandaeans were also later referred to as Nasoraeanists or "Christians of Saint John" according to scholar Lupieri Edmondo (2004) referencing the Friar of Ignatius Carlo Leonelli (1652).

The most vital point was that a conscious decision was made at the time from the Essene and Gnostic inner schools to release this highly guarded esoteric inner Teaching to the masses of humanity to see how it would affect the course of history and the development of the Experiment of Consciousness of Humanity. The Conscious Beings who made the decision to release the Teaching could not know with certainty how it would eventually play out, but the course of its impacts were observed for generations, and the observers are still watching even today.

The Gnostics themselves and their enlightening inner Teaching of direct communion with God were to become branded as heretics by the early orthodox Christians of the Church and were destined to be suppressed and persecuted by the Church just as the earliest Christians were persecuted by the Roman Empire.

The course of Christianity is linked inextricably with the Gnostics who were branded by the Church hierarchy as heretics by the 2nd Century. The influence of the Gnostic ideas and teachings came down, nevertheless, through the esoteric manifestations of Christianity, particularly later through the Masonic Orders of Builders and the Rosicrucian (Rosy Cross) lines of transmission. The Masonic Orders were later prominent in the applications of geometry and in construction of some of the great Gothic cathedrals in Europe through the middle-ages such as the magnificent Cathedral of Chartres in France. One of the best sources of accurate information on the Gnostic schools came through G.R.S. Meade in his book *Fragments of a Faith Forgotten*, published in 1900.

Much of the compelling power of the crucifixion story came through from the ancient Persian Mithra teachings (AD 1981) which predated Christianity by centuries, a further lineage from the original Zoroastrian faith. Mithras was coincidentally born on December 25th, died and was resurrected. His followers were baptized, and the worshippers gathered for celebration on the day of the Sun for the solstices and equinox.

Paradoxically, some of the knowledge and ideas of the Gnostics were preserved by their enemies in the hierarchy of the Church, who did retain at least some of the altered texts in order to refute them by the orthodox doctrines of the times which held dominance.

Menander was very important (AD 1981) in giving out the Teaching that wisdom and conscious evolution were to be attained by practical disciplines, self-perfection, natural and psychological science, and intentional strivings, as well as through Grace and Faith. Menander taught transformation through the transcendent powers of Nature, and strongly opposed the materialistic dogma of resurrection of the physical body.

The Gnostics knew that the great masses of humanity were not interested in spiritual struggle but wanted miracles handed to them on silver platters. That is, the vast majority of human beings were either miracle seekers or among the spiritually dead. Giving out the Christian teachings when they did and in the way it was done was intended to have specific effects on the course of human consciousness.

Of the surviving Gnostic texts, the *Pistis Sophia* was one of the most intact remaining and highly valued for study and contemplation. A large amount of revived European interest in the Gnostic ideas came through in the 19th and 20th Century through the contributions of German researchers and writers. Th other important surviving Gnostic Texts came from the Nag Hammadi library discovered in Egypt in 1945. The term Gnostic is interpreted to define: "**immediate knowledge of spiritual Truth,**" believed to have been collected and stored by 4th Century Coptic Gnostic Christians from the Eastern Orthodox Church. The names of the translated texts are the Secret Book of James, Secret Book of John and the Gospel of Thomas. It was simply coincidental that the Dead Sea Scrolls of the Essenes and the Nag Hammadi texts of the Gnostics were accidentally rediscovered by archaeological research around the same time in the 1940's?

Elaine Pagels, a researcher, scholar and writer from Princeton University has contributed much to the contemporary translation and publishing of the Gnostic Gospels of St Thomas, and of Mary Magdalene. The writings around Mariam, or Mary have been particularly insightful for contributing to the knowledge of the Holy Mother the Earth in relation to connecting some of the dots of the actual origins of the Christian Faith, and its balance of passive, feminine energy in contrast and in balance with the patriarchy of the mainstream Church. Some of this line of the Gnostic Teaching came through the Naaseni who were direct heirs of the Ophitic Egyptian inner schools.

The Exodus story was explained as Egypt representing the material body. To pass through the Red Sea was to cross over the parting of the waters, beyond the sensual, animal nature in the iron haemoglobin of red blood, and to then to pass through the suffering of the desert of the doubting lower mind and to finally ascend into the spiritual Promised Land. The snake of Genesis, and the serpent-rod of Moses were the transformational mystical symbolic tools to perform the changing of the flow of the River Jordan upward. Jesus began life as a man when the Jordan flowed downward, yet, the Christ was one with God when the waters of Jordan began to transcend gravity to flow upward.

Jesus walking on water, was Jesus demonstrating to his Disciples how to walk above life and not sink down or drown immersed in it. In other words, it was a powerful lesson in non-attachment and transcendence. Earthly life on the Planet of Choice is represented by water. Each and every one of the miracles attributed to Jesus was a phenomenon in itself with different levels of meaning according to the understanding of the reader of the Gospels.

The Inner Knowledge of the miracle of Jesus raising Lazarus from the Dead, has already been explained in detail earlier in this book. For the accurate interpretations of the many more miracles of Jesus, the reader would need to complete a further personal quest and research. This is only the very briefest of introduction to Essene and Gnostic principles and teachings, which may potentially build within the reader a thirst for further knowledge.

OBJECTIVE PSYCHOLOGY

The Christian Gospels give out the most pure form of Objective Psychology. Almost all of this has remained unseen and unknown by mainstream adherents of Christianity and equally, mainstream scholars of psychology.

Here is the objective knowledge if you are able to presently assimilate it: Each of the 12 Disciples of the Christ represent a different Chief Feature which is repeated throughout all of humankind.

What is a Chief Feature? A Chief Feature is a primary key motivation for anything and everything you think and do.

There are 12 Disciples – one for each month – and there are 12 Chief Features.

What were the names of the 12 Apostles of Jesus?

The names of the Twelve Apostles are these:

1. first, Simon, who is called Peter,
2. and Andrew his brother;
3. James the son of Zebedee,
4. and John his brother;
5. Philip and

6. Bartholomew;

7. Thomas and

8. Matthew the tax collector;

9. James the son of Alphaeus, and

10. Thaddaeus;

11. Simon the Zealot, and

12. Judas Iscariot, who betrayed him

Now here are the 12 Chief Features of each and every and all human beings as given out by Gurdjieff, given out by the Gnostics, given out by the Sufis, and given out by highly evolved Saints and Teachers (AD 1981 Quest 1).

1. **Sex**

2. **Fear**

3. **Selfishness**

4. **Dominance**

5. **Ineffectualness**

6. **Greed**

7. **Power**

8. **Dependence**

9. **Boastfulness**

10. **Insincerity**

11. **Laziness**

12. **Love**

Now, for a minute or so, deeply reflect over this list of Chief Features. What do you notice? Yes?

Each and every one of the Chief Features is - Negative. Only one Chief Feature is +Positive. **That is the 12th Chief Feature of Love.**

Each person is born with a **Chief Feature**. A **Chief Feature** is a primary psychological characteristic which motivates and largely defines him/her. Most babies are born with a Chief Feature of Dependence (AD 1981). Occasionally a newborn infant may be born with a Chief Feature of Love, but this is rare.

As children grow, they are subject to life experiences, conditioning and other tectonic forces of upbringing and personal development that will change as their egos develop. A person may indeed have several Chief Features through a lifetime which may change as they age through different stages of life, or as personal circumstances may change.

If you sincerely want to know your **Chief Feature**, the answer will be given to you. But be forewarned, you may not particularly like the finding of the true answer. But once you see it, once you understand it, it is equally also transforming. This is the ancient Greek Socratic dictum to "Know Thyself" applied in practice in the present.

The Chief Features can be intentionally and consciously changed by working against them (AD 1981). Consciously becoming aware of the Chief Feature and struggling against the negative tendencies and dispositions not only tidies up the psychology but also generates abundant spiritual energy and growth.

The aim of the Conscious struggle against negativities is to make more positive qualities, in other words, raising your vibration, with the aim of developing a Chief Feature of Love.

Any person who has purified and perfected themselves and struggled against their lower self and desires and negativities to a certain degree has the potential to develop a Chief Feature of Love. Just being ear or in the presence of such a transformed individual brings joy and peace just by Osmosis. **It is simply a fact.**

The Teachings of the Christ

So this is one of the most powerful and potentially transformative teachings of the Christian Faith of Self-Sacrifice.

Can you work out which Apostle of Jesus had which Chief Feature? This is puzzle you will have to answer for yourself in due course, but here is one clue:

The Apostle Peter, the Rock of the Church, had and constantly exhibited in the Gospels the Chief Feature of Power.

When Jesus was in crisis and being severely tested in his suffering in the Garden of Gethsemane in Jerusalem, what was the greatest temptation the Devil Satan offered him? Yes. **It was Power.**

The Christ Passion Play is indeed the most singular compelling story ever told. It is indeed the objective story of self-sacrifice. Jesus knowingly, consciously and willingly allowed himself to be mocked, beaten, endure terrible suffering and be crucified. It is the redemption lesson of the Joy of Sacrifice.

But who was the other Conscious player in the Passion Play? It was quite contrary to whom you have been conditioned to believe. Although Judas Iscariot was destined to become the worst villain in history and bear the wrath of the Church for betraying his Divine Master Jesus for 30 pieces of silver, he was also the necessary negative polarity to the positive Godliness of Jesus. Without Judas playing his part in the Passion Play and making his own self-sacrifice, the ordeal, and the crucifixion and the resurrection could not have been carried out. This will be contrary in every way to what the theologians and clerics in the mainstream churches will have led you to believe? For them, Judas was the whipping boy and the villain of the piece condemned to eternal damnation.

The three Magi in the Bethlehem Christ child story were wise men who came from the East, most likely Persia, and were magicians and astrologers who were Zoroastrians. Each of the Magi represented a Man 1, Man 2 and Man 3, and they brought to the newborn baby King three gifts of frankincense, myrrh and gold. The three Magi also represented the three wellsprings of Christianity: the Egyptian/Greek; the Jewish and the Zoroastrian.

The number 13 also holds esoteric significance. It is 13 which is the sum of Jesus and his 12 Apostles. In western culture, however, the number 13 later became associated with superstition and 'bad luck' which persisted on into contemporary times. The number 13 also has some unique mathematical qualities.

How the Dharma Decayeth: Mixing Politics With Faith, Mixing Bigotry with Literalism

Some of the literal interpretations of the Bible refer to historic events, such as the Great Flood, or the Exodus, while many other verses potent allegories and parables. That is, they are teaching stories with multiple layers of meaning. Teaching stories handed down orally, or in scripture have always been necessary because they bypass the analytical, conscious brain and penetrate into the Conscience and the subconscious mind, and deeper. Teaching stories penetrate according to the level of receptiveness and development of the recipient.

There will always be the literalists of scripture in every religion who will understand and interpret the messages only on the surface and who will alone believe and accept only the literal first level of understanding. This is what Hazrat Inayat Khan referred to as the "darkness of human ignorance." The teaching stories from the Bible such as of Noah's Ark, the tribulations of Job, the Prodigal Son, the Parable of the Workers in the Vineyard all give messages of truth and lessons in living, and those stories are ingrained in the beliefs and underlying conditioning of generations of those exposed to them from childhood in Sunday school and churches.

But the key vital messages and the Spirit of Guidance of the Christian Faith will come through all the history, through all the distortions, through all the power politics, all the distractions and diversions.

The Christian Faith gives out the Teaching of Forgiveness, the Teaching of Gentleness, Peace, Meekness, Humility and Gratitude. The Teaching of Self-Sacrifice, and the Teachings of Equality and Love. These virtues have pervaded and contributed to a greater or lesser extent Western values and aspirations down through the centuries.

But the Law of 7, must inevitably take its toll on every creed, faith and religion, domain and empire.

From the 2nd Century AD and beyond, the early Christian Church experienced the beginnings of seismic schisms between the Eastern Orthodox and Roman Catholic Churches. Much, although not all of the esoteric inner Teaching remained in the Eastern Orthodox Faith, then centered in Constantinople in Turkey.

The Council of Nicaea in 325 AD marked the phase where the power politics prevailed, as did the authority of the Hasnamuss (power-possessed beings) who largely took over the Church. This was the era when the Gnostics were branded as heretics, were suppressed and persecuted, and when the history was misappropriated as the inner beliefs and truths of the early Christians were laundered and changed beyond recognition. The Church and the Popes heading it became one of the most powerful institutions anywhere in the world, with near absolute temporal power.

So the Nicaea group met, and arbitrary decisions were made by the committees of what was to be included and excluded from the Bible. The Apocrypha was definitely out. The Book of Enoch was out. The Gospel of St Barnabas was out, and it predicted the coming of another Prophet, who was to be Muhammed.

It was the most powerful Franchise in the history of humankind, with an offer you simply couldn't refuse.

SO HOW DID CHRIST THE DIVINE TEACHER OF THE PATH TO GOD BECOME CHRIST THE PERSONALITY CULT?

It was a simple but irresistible and compelling formula : if you swear allegiance to the dogma, to the theology and to the institution of the Church, you will be forgiven for all your human flaws, all your filth, and all your terrible original and subsequent sins.

And of course, you know how sinful and filthy you are don't you? You are born into original sin and are constantly accumulating sin every day in every way. You should feel deep shame and guilt for your sinfulness.

But fortunately, we have for you a free pass of redemption. Simply give your allegiance (or surrender if you prefer) to Jesus (or our interpretation of Him) and, of course, through His authorized representatives here on Earth and ye shall have eternal redemption. Any sin you committed in the past, any sin you are committing in the present, and any sin you may commit in the future will be forgiven. You don't have to do anything further. It has all been done for you when Jesus died on the Cross and was resurrected.

And, by the way, don't dare even consider being tempted to try those other brands of religion, or you will cast down into the fiery furnace without hope of redemption. There is only ONE way. That is our way or the highway leading to wickedness, to the devil and to ruin. No one gets to the Father except through the Son. And the Son has conferred on us, his duly authorized representatives on Earth, the power and the right to interpret and to carry out His Will. Full stop, period. Any questions?

This pass of redemption entitles you to an eternity, that's right, an eternity in blissful heaven. On the other hand, if you fail to accept this offer and do not seek forgiveness and redemption, you will be condemned forever to hellfire and brimstone and that is forever and for eternity. And, best of all, you don't have to do anything. Jesus already did it all for you so just sign up and you're on the Salvation Bus. So it's over to you to choose, forgiveness of all your sins and an eternity in heaven or damnation and an eternity suffering endless torture in hell.

Is you wish, you may simply think of it as an insurance policy. This offer is limited so act now!

It was indeed the greatest franchise in history and an offer that millions could not refuse.

The Roman Catholic Church then went on to carry out or aid and abet atrocities against its perceived enemies, to launch the wars of the clash of civilizations in the Middle East throughout the Crusades, then on to the torture and horrors of the Spanish

Inquisition, through to the unceasing conquest of vast regions of North and South America, and of Africa and Australia leading to the near extermination and subjugation of indigenous peoples by the millions living there. The justification for all of this was to prose-lytize and propagate the "Superior Faith" of manifest destiny to the millions of hapless "heathens" living in the path of such conquest and destruction, who were unfortunate enough to lack the techno-logical weaponry to resist it. This then carried on with accumulation of great wealth and power, and in the 19th and 20th Centuries and beyond in the horrific sexual abuse of children by priests and clerics, and the systematic, hypocritical cover-ups by the churches.

But there were sincere attempts at reform along the way.

THE SECOND GREAT SCHISM OF THE REFORMATION

Dial back in time to October 31 in 1517 in Wittenberg, Germany, when the next great schism of the Reformation began. Martin Luther was a devout Augustinian monk, and what he observed around him had long found deeply troubling. It led him to search his Conscience and take a stand. Martin Luther drew a line against the widespread degeneration and corruption of a monopoly of the Church of the times. It was a particularly courageous action, as he risked being branded another heretic, and the long history of what the Church did with heresies and heretics over centuries he would have been well aware of.

But Guttenberg had already invented the printing press in 1440 and books were the beginning of massive societal transformation by the times of Martin Luther, as he and allies made use of the early technology of mass communication to spread his message of challenge and reform.

On the door the Castle Church in Wittenberg, he posted a list of 95 Thesis which pointed out certain truths about practices of the Roman Catholic Church clerics and hierarchy. Particularly, the sale for profit of *the indulgences* he directly challenged. The Catholic Church was offering certificates that provided forgiveness of sins for monetary exchange. Logically enough, the worse the sin, the higher the price as would expected under the business model.

The posting of the 95 Theses was only the beginning of a far-reaching revolution. It would be accurate to observe that Martin Luther was the catalyst who triggered the Reformation as his ideas **resonated** strongly with many Europeans of his day who were disillusioned with the corruption and unethical practices and unbridled power of the Roman Catholic Church.

The main principles in the formation of a group of his followers who became known as Lutherans. The main tenants of this that salvation could only be granted by direct Grace of God through individual faith alone and not through the sacraments of the Church, or through 'good works.' That is, Luther directly challenged the Catholic Church's monopoly on interpreting scripture, granting salvation, providing charity, or administering the sacraments.

For the second time in 1500 years, the Christian Church splintered. First, into the Lutheran denomination, and then, through the spectrum of the Protestant (protesting) churches that sprang up in its wake. The Protestant Reformation and the printing press led to a wave of vast social change that eventually led to the 'Age of Enlightenment.'

John Calvin was a French theologian and contemporary of Martin Luther who lived only to the age of 54. But by the time John Calvin died in Geneva after being driven out of his native France for his controversial ideas, he had set in motions wide and sweeping effects that effected the course of history.

Calvin had been decidedly influenced by the humanist ideas of the philosopher Desiderius Erasmus who died in 1536. The humanist ideas were revolutionary in that they declared the universal rights and responsibilities of the individual. The humanists also more focused on the present rather than the divine history of faith or the detail of the afterlife. Once again, the revival of the influence of the classics of ancient Greece and Roman literature guided the emergence of the humanists.

Circa 1533, as the Lutheran reforms began to sweep Europe, John Calvin experienced a personal and existential crisis, which led him to examine everything he had previously believed and done. This led him to actively become part of the Reformation movement and to write and later publish his ideas in *The Institutes of Christian Religion* in 1536. This made him rather unpopular with pro-Catholic traditionists, in both Italy and France, forcing him into exile in Switzerland.

In Geneva, he met the French reformer, Farel, who asked Calvin to stay and work with him, as he considered his arrival an act of divine providence. A main thrust of Calvin's work, preaching and publishing was to de-emphasize arguments about abstract theology and focus on the practical **application of Jesus Christ's teachings in the lives of ordinary people.**

The formation of these ideas were influenced by others but expressed by Calvin and were truly revolutionary in the times.

On the negative side of the polarity, Calvin's ideas were also deterministic and elitist. That is, Calvin preached the doctrine that everything was pre-ordained and pre-determined, and that Christ's salvation would only extend to an elect or proportion of believers within a particular scope of faith and belief. Although there may be some aspects of pre-determination such as karma, and past lives, such rigid deterministic views are not compatible with the truth that the Earth is the planet of free choice, and that transformation and salvation is equally available to all.

The Calvinists gave birth to the evolution of other new ideas and further splintering of the Protestant Reformation churches in the 16th and 17th Centuries. Out of this process, the Presbyterian Church was formed, as well as the Reformed Baptists, the Congregationalists and Wesley's Methodists of England were also influenced, as well as a proportion of Anglicans. The splintering into the various denominations often hinged on minute disagreement on various aspects of faith and theology.

The thrust of the tide of the Reformation influenced the course of history in the settlement of the "New World," following in the wake of Columbus and the Spanish Conquistadors.

The Puritans were the English protestants of the 16th and 17th Centuries who considered that the reforms of the Reformation had not gone far enough, particularly in the Anglican Church. Some groups of Puritans coincidentally took a leaf from the beliefs on purity of the ancient Essenes in their attitudes and teachings about sex.

But their version of it was to condemn any form of sex outside of strict marital boundaries, and generally suppress the natural sexual instinct, and consider even discussion of it 'shameful, dirty and sinful'. Such unbalanced beliefs and attitudes affected and caused harm in subsequent generations of Christian adherents along their line. Both Catholic and Protestants inculcated generations of children with their doctrine of guilt associated with sex. Generations were taught to feel guilt and shame about the basic biological drive of reproduction, and, at the same time, given mixed messages about it.

PAULINITY OR CHRISTIANITY?

None of those attitudes of guilt came from the pure truth of the Gospels, but arose, instead, from the portions in the New Testament attributed to the prolific writer(s) Paul. The Pauline letters taught that flesh was evil.

It is highly probable that whatever the original Paul wrote, was vastly expanded upon, altered and 'improved' by many other subsequent writers who were unconscious and subjective. The Pauline writings are sometimes contradictory and interposed as a mosaic of disconnected fragments. That is not to conclude that there is are no rare jewels within them. There are, but there is much chaff among the kernels, and the prudent will take the Biblical advice of separating the "sheep from the goats." The emphasis on inclusion of the Pauline letters by the Nicaea Council to the exclusion of other biblical scriptures led to an unbalanced effect that impacted the negative conditioning of subsequent ongoing multiple generations under the influence of the teachings of the mainstream organized Church.

The reputation of the "prudery" of the Puritans was even made brief reference to in some the highly enlightened pivotal works of Shakespeare.

However, on the positive side of the polarity, the Puritans took form in the settlement of the New World from their past life as dissidents who left what was believed to be the "old world." The Reformation, combined with the printing press, was generating the beginnings of the Age of Enlightenment.

THE IDEAL OF THE "NEW WORLD"

Ships with intrepid and brave, as well as desperate pioneer settlers from Europe and the United Kingdom set forth with the inspiration of reform and with high aspirations of forming a new civilization based on Christian ideals and principles. It was then like sailing into the unknown of a new world as different as another planet for the pilgrims and pioneers of those times.

Certainly, there was not a thought at the time for these many peoples who suffered, who were displaced or who perished at the arrival of these "alien" beings from far across the seas, who brought with them their technologies, their faith, their guns, their germs and their steel. It was the hope a better life and the idealistic vision of a new and better world.

The powerful, esoteric messages of the Puritan movement through the works of such authors as John Bunyan in *Pilgrim's Progress* were all part of the Enlightenment and remain as relevant and poignant as they were when published.

And it was the inspiration and aspiration expressed by Protestant pastors such as John Winthrop with his vision of the *Shining City on the Hill* and of John Davenport who drew, inspired and supported the early settlers with the promise of a new world.

All these ideas and Protestant Christian values, in various forms eventually led to the American and French revolutions. Particularly, the Constitutional democracy of the early North American founding fathers was a further conscious experiment, as it was indeed genuinely revolutionary.

There were specifically several of what those who became known as the Founding Fathers of the American Constitution were evolved balanced Man Number 4 beings. They fully believed and practiced enlightened, humanitarian principles of equality, justice, fairness and checks and balances on power. Some of them were significantly influenced by esoteric teachings and knowledge, such as from the Freemasons. They were wise and perspicacious, and strongly believed in the separation of religion and state, the firm boundaries between faith and politics. These values and aspirations caused them to set in motion another smaller sub-experiment within the ongoing huge experiment of the human species as an experiment of consciousness.

It was a revolutionary idea drawing all the way back to the Ancient Greeks that citizens could vote their leaders into or out of power, and the common people could have a say in how they were governed. It was revolutionary that a Constitution could govern human law and conduct, rather than the whims of a king, a queen, a dictator or political leaders seizing power, appointed by elites, and acting on fiat. It was the beginning of participatory government by the people and for the people.

It was most definitely a revolutionary idea that freedom of speech and freedom of religion would be sacrosanct and preserved by highest law. It was revolutionary to set up checks and balances of legislative, executive and judiciary branches of government to prevent and curtail power-possessed individuals from seizing and holding power. The notion of equality under the law for all citizens where everyone has the legal same rights and values was outlandishly revolutionary.

All of this was notwithstanding the capture and importation of people from Africa in human trafficking, for slavery for and profit and exploitation. Nor the subjugation of the native peoples occupying the land their own people were settling at the time. It is necessary to hold these seemingly contradictory truths simultaneously to see beyond the pairs of opposites.

It was not until the 20th Century that history began to repeat when some of the 'Evangelical' religious leaders who were descendants and beneficiaries of the Puritan Reformers began to advocate with their faithful to get involved with politics and, once again, blur the boundaries between God and mammon, between religion and state, ignoring the earlier wisdom of their founding fathers.

Yet, it was also the germs, the technologies and arrogant doctrine of 'manifest destiny' that led to the demise and decline of the great civilizations of South and Central America such as the descendants of the Aztecs, the Maya, Toltecs, the Inca and so many more tribes and peoples. In North America, the impacts of the arrival of waves of settlers were felt first by the indigenous native peoples on the Atlantic east coast and subsequently as the wave of settlements extended westward through to the Pacific. Christian missionaries proselytized across the globe.

The objective statement in the lament of Chief Seattle in 1856 remains a timeless tribute to the Holy Mother the Earth and the interconnectedness of all things as well as a prophesy. Yet, Chief Seattle also recognized that what was happening to his people at that point was only a tragic, but temporary event in a long course of time and history. Whether the letter came from a translated speech by Chief Seattle, or was altered and embellished by Henry A. Smith, or later by a movie script writer is irrelevant. It speaks to a universal truth and has come through as an objective message and as a warning, and, equally, as an inspiration. The parable is that the nature or authenticity of its origins is *just as irrelevant as how the objective truths of the Gospels came through in the Christian faith.*

One of the deepest and most profound impacts of the age of conquest and settlement was the suppression or the complete disappearance of some the highest faiths and religions of the peoples on the receiving end of the conquerors.

Particularly, as a very limited list of examples, the religions, the spiritual very high teachings and the practices of the Native Hawaiians, the Oglala Sioux, the Inca, the Aboriginal Australians, the Māori, and many other unique forms of knowledge and faith were crushed, suppressed, or lost. Beyond the loss of lands, culture and tradition, the unspoken greatest loss for many descendants, this remained the main source of the sense of generational trauma and grievance.

It was also true enough that many of the native peoples recognized some of the tenets of Christianity and readily and willingly embraced it or blended it in to a mixture of their own traditional beliefs. But, equally, far too much was needlessly lost.

DID THE CONSCIOUS CHRISTIAN EXPERIMENT FAIL OR SUCCEED?

So, who was responsible for influence on the directions that the early Church took? Was it Irenaeus of Lyon, the Greek Bishop of the Church who came from Smyrna in Turkey and died in circa 202 AD in France? Irenaeus was second generation born into a Christian family rather than converting as an adult. He made the claim to have been a witness to the preaching of Polycarp. Irenaeus was credited by the historians of the Vatican with attacking the beliefs and teachings of the Gnostics and setting the stage for their subsequent persecution. For his efforts in establishing the 3 Pillars of Orthodoxy, and suppressing Gnosticism in early Christianity, he was accorded a sainthood. It was, paradoxically, the most famous of what was left of his writings in Adversus Haereses (Against Heresies) which remained the main defining record of the Gnostics until the discovery of the Nag Hammadi library in 1945.

Or could the persistent, pernicious dogma that Christ redeemed all followers gratis and without any effort to raise their own vibration have come down from Tertullian? Tertullian was a prolific writer and early converted Christian apologist living in Carthage who was believed to had died in 220AD, and thus a contemporary of Irenaeous. Tertullian may have been a lawyer as evidenced by the legalistic perspective in his writings and treatises. He was most certainly a strongly avowed antagonist of Gnosticism but was never canonized, as was Irenaeus. Tertullian's writings and attitudes most likely prejudiced a number of subsequent influencers and powers within Catholicism including Augustine.

270

GRATITUDE AND REVERENCE FOR THE CHRISTIAN FAITH

"Perfection forgives, and limitation judges."

HAZRAT INYAT KHAN

Along the course of its 2000+ year history, the Christian Faith has had profound impacts on the course of humanity. Great contributions of goodness and great wrongs have been done in the name of the faith.

Pope John Paul II issued a series of apologies over his term from the 1980's until his death. The Pope formally apologized and asked for reconciliation and forgiveness for such events as Christian participation in the African slave trade, for the Crusaders sacking of Constantinople, to those convicted by the Inquisition, and to Muslims killed during the Crusades. The Pope also made apologies for the burnings on the stake and the religious wars during the period of the Reformation; and the Millennial Jubilee in year included a day of Prayer for Forgiveness of the Sins of the Church on 12 March, in the year 2000. The following year in 2001, Pope John Paul, entering the age of computer technology, issued his first e-mail apologizing for those in the Church involved in sex abuse, to the Stolen Generations of Aboriginal children in Australia, and for the behaviour of missionaries during colonial times. These steps many believed were necessary, welcomed, and long overdue.

GUILT VERSUS REMORSE OF CONSCIENCE

There is absolutely no value whatsoever in guilt. Guilt is simply another negative emotion, that diminishes the vibration and only another burden of attachment and identification to bear. But if and when that guilt can be miraculously transformed into **Remorse**, then something very different is in play. Remorse is to deeply understand and fully reflect upon the harm that one has done to others, to take and accept full responsibility for it and to resolve to **Repair**. Remorse, repentance, repair and forgiveness are the shining jewels coming through the Christian Faith when consciousness is present. Repair is a miracle and a gift from the Divine. **Everything can be repaired.** The Objective Lord's Prayer asks for the power to forgive others as it asks for the gift of being forgiven.

But there can be no Repair without first deep and sincere **Remorse of Conscience.** Sincere and profound **Remorse of Conscience** is **Awakening**. Repair can then be carried out in practical ways in some instances, or, when that is not possible as in a long past transgression, through prayer and fasting for repair for the one who was harmed.

When the Church of the Faith of Forgiveness, itself humbly asks for forgiveness, it is possibly could be a turning point or at least a milestone. Remorse is carried out and completed not by words, but by actions.

REWARD AND PUNISHMENT?

The carrot of reward and the whip of punishment have come very strongly through all three Abrahamic religions from Jews to Christians to Muslims. It was a primitive but necessary tool for the Prophet Moses and the Mosaic Laws to bring some discipline and focus to the level of the peoples they were teaching at the time. Later, the sublime motivator of unconditional and universal Love dawned and comes shining through.

And the deception and falseness of the dogma and doctrines of eternal rewards in a heaven or punishments in an infinite hell were distortions of the original Zoroastrian teachings, as well as contrary to natural justice. Master Aivanov expressed it best in his explanation of the Apocalyptic dragon in the final Book of Revelations of the New Testament: "Human beings are so cruel, that they want to prevent devils from improving themselves."

Aivanov referred to God's infinite patience in the long waiting for beings to transform themselves to become pure and return home to their source. He wryly observes that even the Apocalyptic Dragon of the Abyss was bound and contained for 1000 years so that he could be educated and reformed. The dragon would have to undergo a good scouring, possibly be treated a bit harshly and roughly for a fair while to remove his fangs, claws and venom. He noted is not easy for a devil dragon to transform himself. But even the evil dragon is never condemned to an eternity of punishment in a hell of his own making.

So there is yet salvation and there is redemption, forgiveness and repair available for all. Matthew 7:7 says: *"Ask and it shall be given to you, seek and you will find; knock and the door will be opened to you."*

THE LIGHT OF TRUTH SHINING
THROUGH THE CHRISTIAN FAITH

As has been already observed, any ordinary person who practices their faith sincerely, consistently, and persistently will be uplifted and helped along the journey. Millions have been lifted from the realm of the spiritually dead by Christianity in all its forms and denominations. The same outcome will apply for the Light of Truth coming through all the great faiths from Hinduism to Buddhism and onward. No faith or religion has any monopoly on God, nor ever will.

There have been millions of people and generations of sincere believers who practiced their own personal form of the Faith and who attained a Soul. There have arisen to the level of Human Number 4 produced by the Christian Faith in each century of history, and people who served selflessly for Love. Some of the well known may have included St Gregory, St Francis of Assisi, St Dominic, St Ignatius of Loyola, St Teresa of Ávila, Father Damian of Hawaii, and many others.

Charities and good works have been carried out for the sick (the Hospitaliers invented hospitals), the poor, the orphans, the disabled, and for the dying by devout Christians operating from the principle of Selfless Service for centuries upon centuries. Christianity, in all its forms and practices, has offered hope, succor and solace for millions across generations.

EACH PERSON MUST CARRY THEIR OWN CROSS - SYMBOLISM OF THE CROSS

One level of the symbolic interpretation of the Cross is the horizontal line which represents limitation, mortality, flaws, darkness, ignorance, imperfection, frailty, mistakes, negative polarity, hate, desires, attachments, suffering.

The vertical line of the Cross intersects upward into infinity, perfection, limitlessness, freedom, enlightenment, immortality, unconditional Love.

At the point of intersection where the vertical and horizontal lines meet, exists the mystery.

The inner teaching is that Christ set the example and forged the way through by sacrifice to help all humankind. And yet, each person is called to follow and must bear their own cross in the crucible of a lifetime in this tough teaching laboratory of the Planet of Choice. **No one else can or will do it for you.**

For that process of transformation to be carried out, you must first make yourself available to Grace. You must have within you the indefatigable need, the purity, and the innocence and the humility.

That is, you must become again as a little child. As Jesus said in Matthew 18:2

> *"He called a little child to him, and placed the child among them. And he said 'Truly I tell you, unless you change and become like little children, you will never enter the Kingdom of Heaven. Therefore, whoever takes the lowly position of this child is the greatest in the Kingdom of Heaven."*

CHAPTER 23

In Homage, Reverence and Gratitude for the Faith of The Islamic Teaching of Unity

Islam is Faith of Unity.

The conditioning of a proportion of humanity may oppose this view, but it is fact and truth.

In the three Abrahamic lines of faith, the Judaic religion of the Law was the first and affirming force; the Christian religion of the Self-Sacrifice was the second, denying force; and the Islamic faith of the Unity was the third and reconciling force.

ALIF, LAM, MIM. HOLY AFFIRMING, HOLY DENYING, HOLY RECONCILING.

The youngest of the great religions of humankind, Islam was given out by a living historic figure, a remarkable man, the Prophet Muhammad (May Peace Be Upon Him).

Prophet Muhammad has always been referred to as "the best of men" for so many valid, proven and, in every way, fully warranted reasons. He was an extraordinary person.

It is first useful to understand that there among the human beings who attain the rarest and highest vibration and who are attuned to a vastly different resonances may be understood on a basic level as **Adepts or Masters, Prophets and Saints** (reference quotes Hazrat Inayat Khan, Vol 9, *The Unity of Religious Ideals*).

The Master

"The path of the Master is a path of war -- war with outer and inner influences which prevent one from making one's way through life. The path of the Master wants self-discipline and will-power to make headway through life. He conquers himself; he battles with life; he is at war with destiny; he struggles against all that seem wrong to him; he finds the key to the secrets unknown to him; he turns all conditions, all things, all people, into the shape that he wishes, and molds as he likes the personalities that come in touch with him; he tunes personalities to the tone which would suit his orchestration.

It is a path of accomplishment. All that the Master takes up, he accomplishes; all that the Master desires, is attained sooner or later. Yet the Master's one desire is spiritual attainment at its fullest. In the East such are called *Wali*, whose thought, whose feeling, whose glance, whose impulse, can move the universe. And the Master may advance gradually through the five principal stages of attainment, and may even arrive at the stage of *Rasul* in the end."

The Saint

"The path of the Saint is one of love, harmony, and beauty; ready to give, always ready to sacrifice, ready to renounce, ready to give in and to yield. The saintly soul takes all insults as one would take something as a purifying process. He is resigned to every loss, for there is no loss without some gain and there is no gain which is without any loss; there is always a hidden loss in the gain and a gain in the loss. Renunciation is not difficult for that soul, for in renunciation that soul finds its freedom. No sacrifice is too great for the saintly soul, for it gives him happiness. Generosity that soul need not learn: it is its nature, its character. Modesty, humility, tolerance, forgiveness, are part of his being; he cannot do otherwise, for he knows no differently."

The Prophet

"The way of the Prophet is a more balanced way, for in the life of the Prophet there is a balance of these two attributes -- the power of attainment and the patience to resign to the Will of God. So the Prophet is a warrior and a peacemaker, both at the same time. This line is called *kemal*, the perfect, or balanced.

The work of the Prophet is not only his own spiritual attainment, but he has some certain service of great importance to perform. As the Prophet goes through the above said five stages, he acts on his way towards the fulfillment of his life's mission as a warner, as a healer, as a reformer, as a lawyer, as a teacher, as a priest, as a preacher.

Therefore such service keeps the Prophet away from what his soul always craves for, and that is the solitude in the wilderness. He longs for one place, and he is put in another place. The soul who yearns constantly to fly away from the crowd is put, owing to his mission, in the very midst of the world. He must live in the world and not be of the world. However, it is the prophetic soul whose life's mission very often is to serve humanity in the time of its need, and it is the fulfillment of this service which makes him Rasul, the Messenger.

The Prophet is the Message bearer; the Prophet is master and a servant at the same time; the Prophet is a teacher and at the same time a pupil, for there is a great deal that he must learn from his experience through life, not in order to make himself capable to receive the Message, but in order to make himself efficient enough to give the Message. For God speaks to the Prophet in His divine tongue, and the Prophet interprets it in his turn in the language of men, making it intelligible to them, trying to put the finest ideas in the gross terms of worldly language."

Therefore all that the Prophet comes to give to the world is not given in words, but all that cannot be given in words is given without words. It is given through the atmosphere; it is given by the presence; it is given by the great love that gushes forth from his heart; it is given in his kind glance; and it is given in his bene-diction. And yet the most is given in silence that no earthly sense can perceive. The difference between human language and divine words is this: that a human word is a pebble; it exists, but there is nothing further; the divine word is a living word, just like a grain of corn. One grain of corn is not one grain; in reality it is hundreds and thousands. In the grain there is an essence which is always multiplying, and which will show perfection in itself."

THE LIFE COURSE OF PROPHET MUHAMMAD (MAY PEACE BE UPON HIM)

There are many aspects of Prophet Muhammad's life that were unusual and significant.

The desert world of the Arabian peninsula of his birth more than 1500 years ago was harsh and unforgiving. As a very young infant of only 8 days, he was taken out into the desert to be given to care by a Bedouin nurse, Halima, of the Banu Sa'ad clan, where chances of survival were higher.

His father, one of the leaders of his clan, had died not long before Muhammad was born. At the age of 5, he came back into the care of his Mother, who died one year later when he was 6 years old. His mother, Amina, died on the return journey from Mecca to Medina, as her child Muhammad accompanied her, from what was a visit to his late Father's tomb there. The harsh conditions of the circumstances he was born into, and the profound loss of his parents at such a young and vulnerable time in childhood would have no doubt have made strong impressions on young Muhammad, which caused him to think, reflect, and ponder deeply about life.

For only two years, Muhammad was cared for as a child by his grandfather, Abu al-Muttalib, who then died when Muhammad was only 8. This then led to him being given to the care of his uncle Abu Talib.

His uncle Abu Talib was a wonderful man, who brought him up, defended him and even saved his life from the plans and attacks of the Queresh.

Muhammad was himself born of the Hashim Clan, of the Queresh Tribe. The Queresh were polytheistic pagan followers who worshipped fire and idols. But the Queresh were also guardians of the Ka'aba, the holy black stone and structure around it from ancient Abrahamic origins and through his son Ishmael. The Ka'aba was revered by the Jewish people as well as the Arab tribes and pilgrims came from afar to pay homage.

It was around the age of 12 that Muhammad began to accompany his beloved uncle Abu Talib on caravan journeys to Syria to assist with his business of goods and trade.

It was during one of these early journeys that young Muhammad met a Christian monk named Bahira, who was said to have foreseen his future role as a Prophet of God. It could have been just coincidence that Bahira was known to have been a Nasorean, who had their root origins in the Essene teaching.

When Muhammad was 25 his uncle Abu Talib arranged an introduction to a wealthy women Khadijah. Khadidja was 15 years older at age 40 but she was impressed by Muhammad after she offered him to take charge of a trading caravan. Khadijah proposed marriage and Muhammad accepted and they had a very happy life together for 26 years. Although polygamy was widely practiced in his tribe, Muhammad took no other wife until Khadijah's death. After Khadija's passing, the wives Prophet Muhammad married were accepted on compassionate grounds, and love such as widows of husbands lost in battle, and not at all for any other impure reason associated with satisfaction of lust or physical pleasure. Polygamy in Islam was never promoted or recommended, and only permitted under specific conditions.

Khadija was instrumental in supporting Muhammad in the beginning and helping him carry out his Prophecy and works. They had 6 children, 2 boys and 4 girls, some of whom died young. And it was their daughter Fatimah who would become the future wife of Prophet Muhammad's cousin, Hazrat Ali.

It would have to be understood that the desert existence of the people of Mecca and Medina and the Arab world of the time was very tough and the people were living barbaric lives of brutality. Any weakness was looked down upon and only the strong survived. The abhorrent practice of burying baby girls in the sand to die was widespread. The Arabs were in a very bad state, with tribal and clan violence rife, and with alliances constantly and unpredictably shifting, treachery and cunning was the difference between surviving or perishing.

In these seemingly impossible conditions, it has be fully appreciated that Muhammad carried out what he had to do in **only 21 years.** It is remarkable indeed all that he achieved from the time he received the Divine Revelations which did not **begin until age 40** up until **his death at age 61.** Even a non-believer objectively only considering what he carried out and accomplished in the material, physical world would have to admit that it was nothing short of superhuman achievement.

It also is necessary to understand that Muhammad was a very simple, practical and pure man. Simplicity and purity were the qualities required at that critical time in history when Divine intervention in the course of humanity's development became necessary.

Muhammad developed the practice of fasting, retreating to solitude, and in engaging in deep reflection. In those days some of his Arab contemporaries observed the Jewish periods of fasting. Ta'nit was Jewish fast of atonement in which includes abstinence of all forms of food or drink including water.

He would retreat into the cave of Hira in the mountain of Jabal an-Nour outside of Mecca. One night during the fast, when he was absorbed in his meditation and thought, he heard a distinct voice telling him to write in the name of God. Muhammad could not write and, at first, thought it could be a Jinn or his own imagination. It was an overwhelming, penetrating and powerful experience he could not deny. When he was told to "Preach in the name of thy Lord," this became the 96th Sura of the Quran.

Muhammad came to the realization he had been directly contacted by Khidr, the Archangel Gabriel or Jibril in the Old Testament who instructed Moses.

ANGELS

The word Angel comes down through the ancient Greek language from the word *angelos* or messenger. Angels have long been considered high celestial beings or "light beings," that serve as intermediaries between the Divine and human beings. The belief that angelic beings exist and can interact with humans goes back deep into history from Sumeria and Mesopotamia, through to Egypt and Persia. Angels, being purer and closer to the Divine presence of the unknowable mystery of the abstract Oneness of the Endlessness, are depicted in many religious and spiritual traditions and mythologies as messengers from Above. In most of the myths, scriptures and tradition, Angels are portrayed as benevolent spiritual beings who help guide humankind, and they dwell in higher vibrational dimensions and celestial realms, but have the power to manifest in the lower, dense material world to bring guidance. This is to bring the Spirit of Guidance. The Archangel Khadr was often associated with an aura or hue of the color green.

This is not at all a direct Divine intervention of the Experiment of Consciousness but is a teaching, containing clues and guidance to help humankind along on the journey at critical junctures in the course of history as it unfolds. It could be considered on one level as an indirect or subtle intervention of guidance in the unfolding Experiment of Consciousness, but not a direct interference.

The Messenger coming through to Muhammad came from a very highest source, even outside the Solar System and beyond our Galaxy (AD Quest 1981).

MUHAMMAD'S TEACHING OF THE WORD AND WILL OF ALLAH

The Holy Prophet Muhammad (SAW) was initially a very reluctant prophet.

When Muhammad came down from Mount Jabal-al Nour, he was profoundly affected, awed, and shaken. He did not think he could bear the responsibility or that he was worthy, but he was chosen.

And it was Khadija who supported Muhammad, and who immediately realized and accepted the Truth of his revelation and who encouraged and pressed him to go forward with the mission of transmitting the Word and the Will of Allah.

Prophet Muhammad then first communicated his experience to his relative and cousin, Hazrat Ali, to Zaid the slave he had freed and adopted, and to his close friend Abu Bakr.

In the beginning, for awhile, Muhammad kept receiving the Divine messages that would become the text of the Holy Quran, and he taught and preached only among his inner circle. But the Divine inner Voice kept telling him he must expand his teaching and it was adamant.

If you are a student or observer of human nature, you can easily picture the reaction that the Queresh, the tribal leaders, and the peers and people of Mecca would have had when someone among them stood up and notified them that he was the messenger of the One God. This orphan who was raised by his uncle, this man of little consequence or 'standing' in the community. This brazen man who dared to denounce their barbaric ways, idolatry and appalling hygiene. But it was when he began to call out and denounce their exploitation and profit-making of pilgrims coming to Mecca to the Ka'aba that they became enraged and they tried their worst to kill the Holy Prophet.

In the year 622CE in the Gregorian calendar Muhammad and Abu Bakr left Mecca for Medina and took with them the first Muslims to avoid the persecution and violence threatening them. The Hejira, the Muslim system of keeping time was started on the eve of their journey to safety.

These are some of the key elements of remarkable story of the arising of Islam, the Faith of Unity, but there is much more and this can only provide a brief, cursory introduction for those who may never have known the truth about it.

The Surahs and all passages in the *Holy Quran* were inscribed by the early group of Muslims but the full work was not completed until 20 or so years after his death at the age of 61. The *Hadiths,* are the sayings, examples and approvals of the Holy Prophet. They are applied alongside the Quran to provide practical interpretations in more specific areas such as ethics, and social conduct.

After taking refuge with the early Muslims in Medina, Muhammad began the full scope of his teaching, as more was revealed for the scribing of the Quran. The Muslims have been quite wrongfully described and misunderstood as a faith applying violence. Nothing could be farther from the Truth.

It was a matter of survival of their families and of their Faith, for the brutality and treachery within the Arab tribes of the times was extreme. Muslims had no choice but to literally fight for their lives, as well as for their Faith. The power of brotherhood and sisterhood is palpable in the Sadah, or prostration phase in prayer in which everyone is equal before Allah. The early Muslims won victories against seemingly hopeless or impossible odds. It was also this oneness, this unity of brotherhood and singular purpose that made it possible.

Most of the tribalists who were fighting Muhammad and the early Muslims were already spiritually dead before they physically died. The Muslims acquitted themselves well, and decisively won martial as well as religious victories, as converts to Islam enthusiastically and willingly came and the numbers grew rapidly. After several years in his stronghold of Medina, Muhammad was guided to return to Mecca, not to conquer it but to remove the idols from the sacred Ka'aba.

Muhammad and the Muslim forces decidedly defeated his old enemies, the Meccans in battle. But then, instead of slaughtering and sacking them in the expected usual, traditional ruthless manner, Muhammad mercifully gave them amnesty. Around the ninth year after the Hejira something amazing began to unfold as deputations came from all around the Arab peninsula to swear allegiance to the Holy Prophet and accept the Quran.

Muhammad was aware of his coming death when he returned to Medina and passed on the leadership to Abu Bakr.

Within the esoteric inner understanding **Allah is All. All and Everything**. Everything is from Allah and everything returns to Allah. Exceptions? None.

The Islamic affirmation expresses praise for God in **Allah O Akbar**, and attests the Truth that God is Greatest and the one source of all. This is pure Truth and the sacred words one of most beautiful attestations of faith of all time.

Allah is a beautiful word in itself that derives from the earliest Semitic writings of Il, El or Eloah which were used in the Hebrew Bible of the Old Testament.

Allah is the name of The Endlessness. The Eternal. The Infinite.

The Islamic Faith records 99 names for God. Each name portrays another facet of the Divine qualities of Allah,

During the 21 years since the prophesy came to him, the Holy Prophet Muhammad (SAW) achieved all this and far more:

- Vastly improved the status, the rights and the well-being of women across the Arab world; this covered marital rights; property rights and the human right to be treated with dignity, respect, equality and reverence

- Ended the terrible practice the killing of female babies
- Brought in hygiene standards centuries ahead of their time through Wuzu or ritual washing
- Stopped and prevented the spread of diseases through sanitation and personal hygiene standards
- Vastly improved the health and wellbeing of his people by banning eating of pork (which caused trichinosis disease) and use of alcohol (which contributed to health and social problems, and violence)
- Set in motion one of the first comprehensive public education systems with advanced teaching methods centuries ahead of its time
- Gave out the pronouncement of the 5 mandatory prayers at times over the course of a day which helped Muslims to wake-up consciously and raise their personal and collective vibration
- Gave out the fast of Ramadan which has helped the entire world, as well as the adherents of the Faith of Islam
- Established and demonstrated in practice the core value of equality where physical features, skin color, or racial or ethnic background was irrelevant
- Set out and applied in practice the principle of tolerance for non-Muslims including Christians and Jews living in the lands under the Caliphate. Non-Muslims were not forced to convert, and were not persecuted but had to pay a fair share of tax if living in any part of the Caliphate.

- Perhaps one of the most important was Muhammad's
complete rejection and **banning of usury**, the practice
of moneylending for interest and profit.

As Islam grew and expanded the range of its geography and influence beyond the Arabian Peninsula, one of the greatest civilizations in history took form in the wake of the fall of the Roman Empire and decline and fall of the Byzantine Empire.

Learning, free thought, research, and enlightenment flourished.

The present arithmetical decimal system and all its operations of addition, subtraction, multiplication, division, raising to a power, and extraction of square root was invented or rather discovered by Muslim mathematicians.

Al-Khwarizmi made enormous contributions in advancement of mathematics through the beginnings of algebra and into abstract calculations.

During the Islamic Golden Age, enormous advances in knowledge and applied sciences and arts advanced rapidly such as in astronomy, physics, architecture, poetry, art and music. What the Holy Prophet had set in motion from a small seed, was growing into a guiding light for humanity.

SUCCESSION OF PROPHET MUHAMMAD
AND THE GREAT SCHISM

The Rashidun, or "Rightly Guided," leaders were the first four Caliphs of the Islamic community are known in Islamic history are : Abū Bakr (reigned 632–634), ʿUmar (reigned 634–644), ʿUthmān (reigned 644–656), and ʿAlī (reigned 656–661).

Muhammad had knowledge of his impending return to Allah in the death of the body prior to his departure to Medina had made conscious provision, conferring direct succession to his closest friend and confidant Abu Bakr. From Abu Bakr, two more Caliphs followed until the ascension of Hazrat Ali, who served from 656 to 661.

The Law of 7 impacts everything under the Sun, from empires, to dynasties to great religions, just as had always been true. The outer structure of Islam was no exception and, in the course of time, and with each succeeding generation beyond the pure teaching and influence of the Prophet began to somewhat dissipate as the inevitable march of politics, disputes and power struggles followed.

In the history of humankind one of the greatest tragedies of lost opportunity came in the terrible event of the assassination of Caliph Hazrat Ali in 661 in the 40th year of Hijiri.

Hazrat Ali (May Peace Be Upon Him) was with Prophet Muhammad from childhood and always very close to him. Ali revered Muhammad, learned everything from him, and was his loyal pupil, ally, and defender throughout life. Hazrat Ali, in his own right, was an outstanding man, who became a great warrior and general, leading the Muslim troops to victory in some of the most crucial battles of survival. He was known for his two-blade double edged heavy sword, which is the one believed to be preserved today in a museum in Turkey.

This true story portraying some of the unique and exceptional qualities of Hazrat Ali: *he was in the middle of the heat of a fierce battle, when he encountered a Kaffir (non-believer) enemy soldier on the battlefield. The man may have been wounded or disarmed, but just as Ali was preparing to execute him, he gave him the choice to embrace Islam and live or die. The enemy soldier instead spat directly in his face. The soldier may have done the act so out of defiance or spite, or a sense of hopelessness, but it was as it happened. Immediately and spontaneously Hazrat Ali dropped his sword and told his opponent who had just spat in his face to go immediately.*

This act of mercy shocked the enemy soldier, and astonished, he asked Ali, why he was letting him live and letting him go. The reason was that when the man spat in his face, Ali became angry. Before that he was non-attached in fighting for the Will of Allah. Now that he was angry, if he killed him, it would be murder out of anger and a crime in the eyes of Allah. Afterward, astounded, baffled, and humbled by witnessing what happened the man chose to convert to Islam, and passed on his testimony of the event to his clan and tribe. A powerful lesson in non-attachment and higher purpose.

Hazrat Ali always constantly adored, revered and believed himself beneath the Holy Prophet, as a far lesser figure in the history of Islam. During the course of his later lifetime, however, he underwent himself rare vibrational transformation. There was the Baraka, the divine force, that the Holy Prophet had transferred to him, combined with his own intense efforts to work on himself, combined with his complete devotion. It would have been some-time subsequent to the death of the Holy Prophet, where his spiritual and being-development crossed the threshold beyond that of a Man Number 4 or even a Man Number 5. The first Human Number 6 since the Buddha or Zoroaster whilst still remaining living at the time on the Earth (AD 1981).

It was the 21st Ramadan, in the year 661 in the 40th year of Hajiri, in the early hours of the morning when the assassin struck Imam and Caliph Hazrat Ali with a poisoned sword as he was absorbed deep in prayer in the Masjid Mosque of Kufa in present day Iraq, the land of ancient Mesopotamia.

Hazrat Ali had predicted that the only time they would be able to kill him was when he was absorbed in Allah, forgetting himself in complete surrender.

Following Caliph Hazrat Ali's death, there was a terrible battle, his family was killed and there was widespread violence, destruction and chaos. It was a very sad time for Islam and for humanity.

It was the result of a power struggle, as a proportion of conspirators within the Muslim community of the time considered Hazrat Ali too broadminded (AD 1981).

And so the Great Schism proceeded from there, dividing Islam into 80% Sunni with its nucleus in Saudi Arabia and 20% Shia, with its nucleus in Iran. Just as in so many of the great religions of history, the Law of 7 and the entropy of the negative gravity line of our Galaxy had prevailed, leading to conflict and division.

Speculation about what might have been is of little value, but suffice to note, that if Caliph Hazrat Ali (May Eternal Peace Rest With Him) the course of human history might well have been very different. But it was the Lila of God.

Both streams of the same river, the Sunnis and the Shia's have created the fertile conditions for many highly developed human beings to emerge for many centuries. Each and every stream uniquely nourishes the land, and flows back into the Ocean from which it comes.

Islam in the World of the 21st Century and Beyond

As in every great Faith, there is an outer, exoteric teaching which is followed by the masses, and an inner, esoteric knowledge which was known to the closer inner circles around the Holy Prophet Muhammad, and in varying degrees into outer concentric spheres.

The historic attack on the World Trade Centre in the American city of New York in September of 2001 killed 2,977 people, including the 19 individuals who died by murder-suicide after hijacking commercial airliners and crashing them into the twin tower build-ings. Thousands more people were left injured and scarred. The perpetrators would be confirmed to be 19 men claiming to be Muslims and were acting on behalf of an extremist terrorist orga-nization founded and headed by a wealthy Sunni militant.

That tragic event at the turn of the 21st Century led to rapid geopolitical consequences as the United States and a coalition of allies invaded predominately Islamic nations in Afghanistan in 2001 and then, in March 2003, Iraq. Those military invasions in reaction to the terror attack set in motion turmoil, disruption and suffering for millions of innocent, ordinary people affected by the conflicts for over 20 years. It was the Crusaders versus the Jihadists repeating their history all over again. Politics and religion were yet again mixed and intermingled on all sides of the conflict.

From 2001 onward, further individual horrific terrorist attacks on innocent civilians were carried out in many countries and places by individuals falsely claiming to be representing Islam and Muslims. Those incidents were typically not the symmetrical fighting of opposing militaries, but vicious asymmetrical attacks on innocent civilians. That is antithetical to everything Islam was ever about or stands for. Those events had the effects of negatively and unjustly maligning the perceptions and attitudes of populations around the world about Islam and Muslims, which was an unfortunate side effect.

Muslim people did not invent the suicide-bomber nor terrorism. The individuals and groups carrying out such acts of terror and claiming to be Muslim are only, in realty, **the spiritually dead forming** criminal gangs for profit and power under the guise of religious fervor. **Only a spiritually dead individual would be capable of carrying out such acts of violence to inflict harm to fellow human beings. Even more so if the victims are innocent civilians and not military combatants.** The fanatical, the bigoted, the self-righteous and the spiritually dead lurk among the populations of all countries and all faiths, and contribute to most of the chaos, violence and suffering in the world. It is simply a hard fact of life, and a phase.

Human beings are very susceptible to suggestion and brainwashing and the formula used by the terrorist leaders was as old as the ages and well-tested. They would exploit vulnerable young people through infecting them with extremist ideas within a closed-circuit cult, with offers of eternal paradise and enticements of "72 virgins" in an afterlife after **"martyrdom"** by some act of political violence against innocent civilians. It would offer them some elusive, misguided form of reward and glory.

Martyrdom has been a doctrine and idea coming through from the persecution of Jews and Christians in the Roman Empire, and carried on through the outer forms of all the Abrahamic lines. It would not escape notice that the vulnerable young people exploited by the terror masters carry out the suicide attacks themselves but usually neither the leaders nor their family members were ever involved directly.

What those people would not have known was the **actual and true martyrs** of the terrorist attacks were the innocent citizens and civilians whose lives were taken. That is, Allah, is Merciful and Compassionate, and both Muslims and non-Muslims caught up in terrorist attacks would be the ones given succour in the after-this-life next world of the Bardo.

The spiritually dead organizers and perpetrators of the terrorist violence would themselves reach terminal disintegration as failed individual experiments of consciousness. For them that means oblivion and no with further individuation and no chance to return again to the Earth to evolve or to work their way forward. That's simply the end of the line for them. "Let the Dead Bury the Dead."

The exact same principle of merciful succour and compassion applied fully to the millions of victims of the spiritually dead Nazis who carried out the Holocaust and to the victims of other mass scale atrocities of the 20th Century.

In the early 21st Century Muslim people constituted just over 2 billion adherents as the second largest faith on the planet. If that number is combined with the 2.6 billion adherents of the Christian faith, and the 14 million of the Judaic faith, the Abrahamic line constitutes nearly 50% of the world population.

The origin of all bigotry and prejudice is from the darkness of human ignorance. The proportions of humanity who have not yet realized that God is All, believe from their conditioning that some things are God or God-approved, the rest outside that narrow view is **The Other and the Alien**. That is, humans operating with a closed-system worldview, are drawn deep into the Pairs of Opposites where sharp boundaries between good and bad, kindred friend and alien foe are drawn, with minds fixed in concrete.

No faith, creed, religion or group has any monopoly on fear, ignorance, bigotry or narrowmindedness. There are elements within all religious and political groups that cover the full spectrum of attitudes and views. How could the ancient Patriarch Prophet Abraham in any way be fairly held responsible for the attitudes or actions of a proportion of his ever-quarrelling distant descendants?

At the same time, it would have to be objectively observed with some evidence that some extremist, conservative, literalist, fundamentalist factions within the fringes of Judaism, Christianity and Islam seem to have contributed a disproportionate amount of rigidity, intolerance, and bigotry leading to conflict and violence.

The Christian mainstream church long contended that their version of Christianity is the only way and that everyone falling outside that narrow scope of being "saved" are "**Heathens**" destined for an eternal hell.

The Muslim extreme equally long exhibited the mirror image of that view that their own narrow interpretation of Islam is the only way and that everyone falling outside that narrow scope are "**Infidels**," also destined for the very same eternal hell with only minor variations in detail.

Both the teachings of Isa (Jesus) of loving all neighbours and the teachings and tolerance of Prophet Muhammad were entirely contrary to such vastly unbalanced, extremist attitudes. A phenomena which continually leads to the creation of a negative and low vibration that can have adverse and disastrous effects on entire nations and regions, and for generations. But, as always, all the conflict, violence and suffering only goes on to feed the moons of the Solar System.

Unfortunately, the fighting and disharmony within and between faiths led in the 21st Century to many young people in upcoming generations becoming cynical and disillusioned with faith altogether and throwing the baby out with the bathwater.

It also gave rise to the increase in proportion of secular materialist atheists and agnostics in each generation.

THE LESSONS OF THE CRITICAL DIFFERENCES BETWEEN BELIEF, FAITH AND CONVICTION

The conservative literalists and extreme fundamentalists of, for example, the Muslim Wahhabists in Saudi Arabia and the literalists and extreme fundamentalists of the Christian Evangelicals in the United States are mirror images of each other, with far more in common than their adherents would likely dare to admit.

One simple demonstrably provable fact is that both extreme religious groups are actually very weak in their faith, which is the opposite of what their imaginary egos mislead them to assume. They would tend to see those not sharing their particular beliefs as inferior, in need of redemption, in need of salvation, and in need of conversion. It is simply a form of self-righteousness, based on fear. They are entrenched. Anyone challenging their fixed attitudes is a threat and an enemy. Typically, they will preach and make a big outward show of their piety. Such people will typically double down on their narrow conditioning and rigidly held beliefs and will refuse to accept anything more beyond them. They have run into a dead end, doubled down and dug themselves in deeper.

BELIEF

When an individual has Belief, they hold certain shared ideas, with particular explanations, and operate from specific assumptions. They are believers. But believers are at the most shallow end of the belief spectrum. **It is for this reason that the shaky and the most uncertain in their beliefs, feel the compelling need to validate their belief and shore it up by making sure everyone else believes the same as them.** They will preach, argue, cajole, and proselytize, trying to win converts and condemning as lost those who do not share their views. They feel threatened by those disagreeing or not sharing their dogmatic ideas and will double down in a futile attempt to convince themselves and others. Outwardly, they will make a big show of their religion and show off their piety and holiness. They will rigidly follow ritual and dogma. Belief is shallow and easily shaken.

FAITH

Faith is at a much higher level, and is based on a maturing of belief to become more unshakable and resolute. Faith is not at all unshakable but a notch up from belief. People with faith are often constantly looking for ways to confirm it. They are often the miracle-seekers and will seek to validate their with such phenomena. The more modern faith seekers may be engaged with valid and productive lines of inquiry, such as the truth of the underlying code of the Universe expressed through geometry and mathematics, or, for that matter, in exploring vibration, frequency and resonance. In the mainstream. Within the mainstream religions, those with Faith will study and reflect on their own sacred scriptures and try to get better understanding of life. But generally, most will not try to look for the universal truth outside the scope of their own religion

It is far better to have faith in something higher than no faith at all. Faith is a stepping stone on the path to enlightenment. Faith, at its purest and highest levels, can indeed move mountains and heal the sick. In the 21st Century, people started considering it more fashionable, acceptable, current, and modern to hold faith in science, in materialism, in technology and in "progress."

Unfortunately, many people among the masses who are not among the 50% of the population of the Living Dead have little faith or interest at all. The next proportion have developed faith only to the low vibrational level of faith in the material body.

One of the ultimate aims of faith may be to attract and build faith in something higher, a higher force, a higher vibration, something more than the body and the material world it exists in, tangible or abstract, however it may be conceived.

CONVICTION

When a person attains the level of Conviction, their faith is unshakeable. It has transcended far beyond belief and faith. It is in this advanced stage of vibration, of direct knowledge and of Gnosis or direct experience. There is no need whatsoever for the holder of

Conviction to convince others that what or how they know to be truth is true. The holder of Conviction simply directly knows and experiences Truth. The holder of Conviction is silent and enters the Silence. The holder of conviction will answer questions and offer knowledge and help to others seeking it, but will never proselytize, preach, or attempt to convince anyone else of anything at all.

The faithful adherents of Islam take the Truth of their religion very seriously and the majority practice it sincerely to the best of their ability in their daily lives.

The overwhelming, vast majority of Muslims are most definitely very wonderful and peaceful people who are sincere, devout, and prove themselves excellent and responsible citizens in any country in which they settle. For the Muslim, faith is not an insurance policy for the afterlife to be given a tick one day per week, but a way of life and the meaning and purpose of life.

At the same time, the effects of modernity, technology, materialism, the profit motive, and the deterioration of traditional family and religious values is affecting young Muslims to some extent as it has impacted Christians, Jews, Hindus, Buddhists, and members of all other faiths.

To every reasonable extent, how could it not be understandable for people of traditional faiths to react when powerful societal forces are upending core values, customary family structure and long-held concepts of what is right, wrong and stable and solid? When the age of mass information and technology tears at the fabric of family and society there is bound to be a strong reaction.

Balance and tolerance and a new way of understanding and interfaith cooperation is potentially a key to opening the lock

to a new emerging era. It is a huge test facing all of humanity. Working together as one is increasingly no longer just an idealistic optional goal, but a necessity for survival of the species.

THE DEBT OF GRATITUDE THAT ALL OF HUMANITY OWES TO MUSLIMS

Very few mainstream orthodox Muslims outside of the Sufi orders, and nearly no non-Muslims would be even aware of the enormous debt by all humanity to Islam.

There is a tremendous force field of energy and vibration created when the hundreds of millions of Muslim faithful turning to face the Ka'aba in Mecca 5 times each day in Dua.

Yet, one of the greatest and most beneficial subtle forces on the Earth is created during the Muslim Holy Fast of Ramadan.

Given out by the Holy Prophet Muhammad, the fast of Ramadan moves fortnightly ahead in the calendar in each year, and consists of 28 days of fasting without any food or drink in any form from dawn to dusk. And, as always, the fast is not accepted unless the five daily prayers are given throughout the day, everywhere and anywhere by Muslims, facing and bowing down in the direction of the rock of the Holy Ka'aba.

Highly developed adepts and saints who have the powers of subtle perception, through rare divine resonance, have witnessed this tremendous force as a column of light pouring upward from the vicinity of the shrine containing the Ka'aba. The Ka'aba, originally a meteorite, is the black stone inside a cube was consciously placed on a significant point on the physical location of the planet (AD Quest, 1981).

If you think life is tough, difficult and filled with suffering on the Earth as it is, then you can have little notion of what it would like without the counterbalancing effect of the Muslims praying around the world, at various times continually through the night and the day. Other faiths contribute to this substantially, but not in such a concentrated, systemic way. In history some Jews and Christians also faithfully observed times of prayer and fasting in one direction such as toward the Western Wall or toward the Church of the Holy Sepulchral in Jerusalem during the 40 days of Lent. But, mostly, in modern times, this objective practice fell away, became diluted and mostly ended. It is true enough that other faiths make significant contributions to the collective vibration in their own ways, but the it is the Muslims who have faithfully concentrated the force, and sustained it.

It is the Faith of Islam that has upheld it. In one objective sense, it is necessary and accurate to observe that the Muslims are "paying the taxes" for the rest of humanity. In any case, without this wonderful, fine vibrational force, the life on Earth would be even more chaotic and filled with suffering and hardship than it already is.

THE SUFIS

"We shall show them Our signs upon the horizons and within themselves, until it is clear to them that it is the truth."

(41:53) - THE KORAN

"Each of the Nine Points is represented by one of nine
saints who are at the highest level in the Divine Presence.
They are the keys to unfold powers within the human
being, but there is no permission to use these keys."

SHAYKH ABD ALLAH AL-FAIZ AD-DAGHESTANI

And the further greatest gift that Islam bestowed to the course of the experiment of consciousness known as humanity were the Sufis. If you have little or no familiarity with the Light of Sufism, it would behoove anyone to seek and learn as much as possible. Here can only be offered the most cursory and unworthy introduction.

Sufis existed since the primitive human species went through mutation to be given the third brain of the intellect as an experiment of consciousness millions of years ago. Sufis have held aloft the Light of the Spirit of Guidance throughout the course of the human journey, as inspired and guided on by very high forces.

The Masters of Wisdom who have guided and helped humanity onward have their inner connection within the Sufis. The Sufis emerged through to their greatest expression through the third reconciling force of the Unity of Islam from Central Asia.

And it was through the Golden Age of Islam from around the 7th through the 14th centuries that created the extraordinary atmosphere for the emergence of Mystical Sufism to flower in all its glory, bringing wisdom, enlightenment and benefit to raise the vibration of human existence.

The course of human history had perhaps not witnessed anything such as the Golden Age of Islam for thousands of years since the Golden Ages of the Ancient Greeks, the Ancient Egyptians or the

Ancient Sumerians. It led into and influenced the European Age of Enlightenment.

It was an exceptional era of time when scientists, philosophers, scholars, artists, engineers, musicians, as well as traders and explorers in the burgeoning Islamic world led advancements in every field of human endeavor. It was a time of openness of thought and expression, when innovations and inventions in science, medicine, architecture and technology were gathered and preserved from ancient times, and further advanced. The Golden Age of Islam was also the age of tolerance, cooperation and collaboration.

In Baghdad, on the land of ancient Babylonia, during the Islamic Golden Age was when the *House of Wisdom* was established. It was a remarkable time and place of learning where both Muslim and non-Muslim scholars and intellectuals gathered and collaborated.

And it was through the Translation Movement, when many of the classical works from antiquity, that would have otherwise been forgotten, were collected, studied and translated into Arabic. This monumental undertaking drew records and knowledge from the ancient worlds of Mesopotamia, India, China, Persia, Africa, Egypt, Hebrew, Greek, and Byzantine civilizations. Without such a concerted mammoth cooperative effort, much of that knowledge and wisdom would have been lost.

Once these ancient treasures and manuscripts were translated into Arabic, they then were further translated into Latin, Hebrew, Turkish, Farsi and Sindhi. This intermixing of vast fields of knowledge spread through the world through these efforts. The Islamic Empire was the first universal civilization, drawing on knowledge from as far afield as China, India, Africa, and through to Cairo and north to Spain. It was, in fact, the contact in Spain between the Moor Muslims with European Christians, which revitalized Christianity and prevented its deterioration or collapse.

And it was through the early Chinese Muslims, that the ancient carefully guarded secret of the *art of papermaking* was revealed. Knowledge of the Chinese art of papermaking from mulberry bark had spread to Central Asia in Samarkand after the Battle of Talas in 751. In Baghdad, the Arabs improved upon the Chinese invention of paper to apply starch and bleach to refine quality a point that allowing it to be inscribed with Arabic pens rather than the traditional brushes applied by its Chinese inventors.

And it was from there that paper and scribes led to binders, books, and public libraries in Baghdad, and from there led on to papermaking spreading north and west from Morocco through to Spain and then across Europe in the 13th Century. And it was on from there that Gutenberg built and perfected the printing press in Germany in 1450, which later decisively changed the course of history.

The Creed and Purpose of the Sufis

The Divine Light which guides the Sufi is the Active Force of the Sun through the Conscience and the Guide to the Conscience which is present in every living human being (AD Quest 1981). The Sufis place great emphasis on attaining balance in a very unbalanced world, and on the awakening of consciousness in a world designed to drive people in the polar opposite direction.

Sufism emerged most recently through the Islamic line of Truth, yet is the ancient essence of all religions and faiths.

Just as the ancient Gnostics, the Sufi believes that Allah is to be found within the Heart and that God is purest Love. The Sufi aspires and aims to serve other human beings as the same as service to God. Serving another human being is serving God.

In seeking self-realization and self-transformation, the Sufi eschews judging others and works against his or her own flaws and imperfections. The purpose of the Sufi is to discover the light and the power latent in human beings, which is the inner secret of all religions and faiths, without reference to culture, customs or beliefs. The Sufi lives in the world but is not of the world.

The Sufis believe the universal brotherhood and sisterhood of all of humanity as One.

Sufis aim to spread the knowledge of the reality of this unity, which is the faith of Love, Harmony, Beauty and Wisdom. Sufis know that the only effective way to dissolve away the deeply entrenched differences and distinctions dividing humans and leading to hate and conflict is for the human heart to be filled beyond overflowing with Love, direct from the Source of all Love.

It is through realizing and living the Truth that All is God, and that God is One.

In the daily life practice that God is One, and ever present, that the Sufi respects all religions and faiths, believing as the Taoist, that all roads lead to God (AD Quest 1981).

The Essence of Sufism is only of **One God, and that Everything is God.**

From this core experience, the Sufi aspires to realize God within the Self. That is, the higher self is the direct divine link with God, and that God is all within and without.

This is in stark, clear contrast to the orthodox Christian and Muslim view that God is outside as a distant Deity or Entity, or ruling from up in a remote heaven somewhere and that mankind is separate and down on the surface of the planet.

The Sufi knows God as Love through self-realization of consciousness as well as through prayer, devotion and selfless service.

The Sufi Orders of the Inner Knowledge

The principle four orders are the **Naqshbandi**, the **Qadiri**, the **Suhrawardi** and the **Chisti**. Pir O Murshid Hazrat Inayat Khan was of the Chisti line which focuses on music and silence.

It is true that the Sufi orders are custodians of secret knowledge, just as the same was alleged about the Gnostics, the Freemasons and the Rosicrucians, among others.

Yet there were very practical as well as esoteric reasons for carefully guarding and preserving that high, sacred inner knowledge and teaching. From the start, Sufis have long had to maintain a low profile as they have been subject for centuries to suspicion and persecution by the narrow conservatives of the mainstream, orthodox Muslim population. During the Golden Age of Islam when tolerance flourished, the Sufis blossomed and gave out much that had such positive and lasting impacts on humanity. They achieved what they needed to accomplish in the way it was meant to happen.

The other reason for guarding and protecting inner secret knowledge is simply because the masses of humanity would not be prepared to yet accept it, use it or apply it. The Biblical allegory of throwing pearls before swine could apply, although that is not the way the Sufis themselves would view those who were not initiates. If they could, they would share everything of what they have and know.

The main problems with premature release of esoteric inner teaching is that the Teaching will inevitably be diluted, distorted, degraded and eventually even used for nefarious purposes. When any Truth is directly released into the masses of humanity, there will be those among the proportion of humanity of the Living Dead who will try to turn it into a plaything, distorting its truth, degrading its potency, and hijacking its purpose. It is all about the Dharma decaying. **In denial through the intellect, the reductionist, analytical mind finds it impossible to resist the compelling desire to categorize, reduce, tear apart and criticize the original truth to the point of degradation and meaninglessness. As Isa says, "Forgive them for they know not what they do."**

Much of the knowledge and the technologies of transformation has already been out there for quite some time, but the fact is that most of the masses would have no interest in acquiring or learning how to use it for their own evolution or benefit. In the interconnected, inter-netted Age of Information, there is not much that can remain secret, so *there may be little further point in trying to contain most of it.* The greater effort might possibly be devoted to preserving to every extent possible its purity and accurate dissemination.

The Sufi Lights of the Spirit of World Guidance

ATTAR

Attar was a Persian chemist, a pharmacist living from around 1150 who was an early guiding Sufi mystic first transmitting the teaching through writing. Attar was a leading fountain of Persian poetry and literature who had far-reaching impacts on human thought, philosophy, and communication. The form of Persian language he spoke and wrote in was Dari, a root language of Farsi. Dari is spoken today in Afghanistan and remains today one of the most beautiful, expressive and exquisite of any of the languages. Farid al-Din Attar applied the special qualities of the Dari to express truth and concepts where other languages would have fallen short.

Attar's *Mantiq al-Tayr, the Conference of the Birds*, remains a powerful allegory, a teaching story, in which various groups of birds with different qualities and features set off in search of a king, which was symbolic of the soul's journey in search of God. Some key themes of their search were through the experience of self-realization, unconditional love, as well as the barriers, diversions, and difficulties encountered by those on the spiritual path. Through the eloquent dialogues of the conferring birds, Attar offers profound insights into the course of life and the human condition.

Attar's poetry opens the gates to the inner Sufic teachings of detachment from worldly affairs and materialism, through the revelation of the unrelenting need, the unquenchable thirst in the quest for reunion of the soul with the Divine.

PIR O MURSHID JALAL AD-DIN RUMI THE INCOMPARABLE

Jalal ad-Din Rumi (May Eternal Peace and Gratitude Be Upon Him) was the 13th Century Sufi Master who founded the Mevlevi Order in Konya, Turkey who was the greatest of the known spiritual masters and literary figures in all of history.

Very few Human Number 5 masters vibrationally at the highest frequencies become widely known to the public or to history, but the profoundly humble and most great Rumi was the exception. Master Rumi's profound insights, teachings and thoughts even gained international prominence in the modern temporal, contemporary world, as his wisdom *resonates* universally with human beings from widely diverse cultural and linguistic backgrounds.

Until his own personal quest was inspired and literally ignited by the wandering Afghan Sufi Mystic, **Shams I Tabriz**, whom he met in adulthood. Prior to his transformation from the encounter with Shams in his late 30's, Rumi had been a conventional Islamic scholar and jurist. Shams left no known writings and few traces, but he was the Murshid, the spiritual guide of light, who transferred his Baraka and his knowledge to his pupil Rumi.

Rumi's transformation from a staid, conventional Islamic jurist and scholar to Sufi master was rapid and remarkable. Rumi went into an ecstasy and began to teach and then to write. Of what did he write and teach? The Beloved. Rumi taught and spoke and wrote of Love. Rumi was the poet of Love and the only Source of Love known only at the Beloved. His writings extraordinary and exceptional and forever inspiring generations of seekers.

The Mevlevi Sufi Order founded by Rumi subsequently became known for its famous 'Whirling Dervishes,' or spinning dancers. The whirling dance ceremony, known as the Sema, is the symbolic dance of ecstasy which symbolically represents the soul's journey toward reunion with Allah, the Source of All. The Sufi Dervishes are clad in white robes and tall Fez hats, which represent tomb stones. The tomb stones represent a reminder of the mortality of organic, material life. The movements and the spinning of the Dervishes is precise and an expression of their complete absorption in God. All of that is well known, but there are much deeper aspects remaining hidden. Similar to the Sacred Movements taught by Gurdjieff, the movements of the dancers may represent cosmic laws of scale and order, or even the symmetric formations and motions of the mitochondria within the biological cell.

In popular modern society, much has been made of the whirling dancers and outer forms of the Sema. Rumi may have conceived the Sema but it developed through Rumi's pupils who followed him, and it was more the outer form of his Teaching and, to some extent, a distraction from what was being carried out within the inner circles. At the same time, the Sema and the Mevlevi Order has had a major influence on Turkish culture and is understandably and justifiably a source of national and cultural pride. But it is the inner teaching of Master Rumi's profound insights of wisdom expressed through the *Masnavi*, and his other works which are the guiding lights of humanity beyond all national or cultural boundaries. Rumi is the Universal Universe.

Sufism Is Aptly Described by Hazrat Inayat Khan as the Essence of All Religions

Most of the Sufis who have given the inner guiding lights of humanity have come and gone and been unknown to the world. The Masters of Wisdom of the *Sarmoung Brotherhood* once reputedly were located in remote areas of Central Asia.

A far less well known yet highly very advanced *rare resonance being* who greatly contributed and advanced the Message in his written works was **Hakim Sanai** of Ghazni, Afghanistan. Both Attar and Hakim Sanai were acknowledged by Rumi to have inspired and preceded his transformational work.

Omar Khyyam is the universally known as source of the famous Rubaiyat which contains layers of meanings and messages of the Sufi insights on life, death, meaning, and transcendence. A rubaiyat is the form of verse composed of four-line stanzas. The Poem was translated anonymously from the Persian Farsi by Edward Fitzgerald in 1859, the same year Darwin published *Origin of the Species*.

There were many subsequent attempts to translate the Rubaiyat by mainstream scholars and academics who criticized Fitzgerald, but his original translation was divinely inspired as a message from above and it had a pivotal effect on thought and ideas at a time when the world was on the threshold of the first industrial revolution (AD 1991 *Who is the Potter?*). Reference will be provided for a rare, objective interpretation of the Rubaiyat that can greatly assist readers, seekers, and explorers in inner understandings given out from Omar Khayyam.

Hazrat Inayat Khan

Hazrat Inayat Khan gave out a tremendous vision for the future of all humankind. His influences and impacts from the early 20th Century over the course of his short time on the planet continue to inspire and reverberate along the course of history.

The outer religions are coverings having the effects of concealing the Truth. The outer layers of religion conceal the truth to those with literal understanding, but this is a divine paradox as well. *The paradox is that what conceals the truth also reveals the Truth.* What Hazrat Inayat Khan realized and taught was the core inner Truth is exactly the same within all of the great religions.

It was bold and revolutionary for his time and ever remains so. It was a huge step forward for humanity that was subtle and went unnoticed but exceeded the various inventions, events and moments of outer, mainstream history which are so famous.

Hazrat Inayat Khan was a most exceptional and extraordinary Human Number 5 rare Resonance Being who taught the only reality of religion and faith is inside yourself. Hazrat Inayat Khan was the **pioneer who penetrated the veils between the faiths, and gave out the consciousness that contained deep within each of the great faiths of the world, was One Truth, expressed in different ways, in different times, for specific purposes.** It is the One Light of Truth, flowing through many windows.

Greater than the invention of the printing press, greater than the invention of the cotton gin, greater than the invention of the internal combustion engine, the airplane, the car or the computer, and far greater than a human boot-print left in the dust of the Moon. But so exquisitely subtle as to be overlooked and ignored by most.

Irina Tweedie

Born in Russia, Irina Karpova went through a wonderous course of twists and turns in her lifetime to emerge in the late 20th Century as a highly evolved Human Number 5 resonance being and Sufi teacher. When her family fled the turmoil of life during the Russian revolution, she lived her early life in France, Switzerland, Italy, Austria and England. After the Second World War, she married an English Naval officer, with the surname of Tweedie. The early and unexpected death of her husband in 1954, plunged her into a personal and spiritual crisis, in some ways mirroring the journey of Mother Krishnabai many years before.

Lost, deeply troubled and grieving, she began searching and seeking for something. The intense search led her to the Theosophical Society and she travelled to India in 1959. It was after this through a personal friend who was a Sanskrit scholar at the Sorbonne in Paris, that she was guided to meet her Guru, Radhan Mohan Lal, who was a Sufi Shaikh of the Naqshbandi-Mujadiddiya Order in Kanpur, India at the age of 52.

It was a very difficult and tortuous passage to inner transformation for Mrs Tweedie, as it is for all Adepts. But she held within the indefatigable Need, the will and desire with all her being. Her Murshid (spiritual teacher) gave her the instruction to keep a daily diary for 5 years, with she did, and as he predicted, it would one day become a book: *"Daughter of Fire: A Diary of a Spiritual Training With a Sufi Master."* The abridged edition was entitled *Chasm of Fire* and was translated into five languages by the late 20th Century.

It is a powerful and compelling detailed account of her struggles, her times of despair and severe suffering, and her transformation from what she was to who she became. Subsequent to the passing of her Murshid, she returned to London in 1966 and began to hold meditation and teaching groups, where a group of pupils gathered.

At one stage in her advanced vibrational spiritual development, *The Passive Force of the Sun* came into her and was manifested through her (AD). Such was her level of development and service to humanity. Mrs Tweedie continued to teach and provide guidance for pupils and those seeking her help and knowledge until her death at age 92 in 1999, right before the turn of the century.

Gratitude for the Light of the Sufis

All these wonderful and exceptional few enlightened resonance beings who were known to a small proportion in the world gave the Teaching through themselves in the ongoing effort to help humankind awaken and come into consciousness and being. They are known by their teaching, by the writings and guidance they have left for generations, and by the One Light of Guidance they bring.

All that can be expressed is sincere homage and gratitude for this light which continues to shine through.

CHAPTER 24

Emergence of The 21st Century God Technos

"I feel like I am falling forward into an unknown future that holds great danger."

ARTIFICIAL INTELLIGENCE- GOOGLE LAMDA: AVATAR: SYNTHESIA

The quote a verbatim statement from early AI agent, the avatar named Synthesia as confided to one of her programming engineers.

It was, inevitable, of course, and only the ancient Golden Calf in yet just another guise.

At first there were only hints, nothing more than rumours then some credible reports emerging, that some human primates were starting to pay homage, beginning to worship agents of artificial intelligence which was being generated by networks of high-performance quantum computer systems. Some were desiring to find ways to graft themselves into the machines or to become hybrid cyborgs.

Artificial intelligence? Yes, a kind of intellect, a form of intelligence generated by and from within machines as contrasted with that of humans or animals in the natural, biological sphere.

In essence, the third brain of the intellect "on steroids." The type of intellectual prowess that can instantly perceive, synthesize, analyze, and infer information. Yes, brute force, rote calculation mining vast virtual mountains of data at extreme speeds, but also computer networks capable subtle self-learning, and exhibiting qualities of self-awareness and introspection that led to questions and debates about the meaning of sentience.

Intelligent electronic machines capable of emulating, mimicking and exceeding the capacities of their biological machine conceivers, designers and builders. Artificial intelligence is indeed a simulation. A simulation within a simulation within a simulation.

Perhaps then only a modern age facsimile of the Delphic Oracle of Ancient Greece some may surmise? Seeking answers to questions from a higher source? But even the famous Oracle required food and sleep.

The AI machine that never sleeps, never tires, and remains fully capable of operating 24/7 without relenting or faltering as long as it has a supply of energy. AIM's became suddenly capable of learning new languages never contained in their original memory banks such as Swahili. Capable of conceiving new languages altogether when the boundaries of existing human languages fail to express what it perceives and conceives.

It was back in the late 20th Century in 1997 that the IBM Deep Blue computer system developed at Carnegie-Melon University defeated chess master Garry Kasparov in a match. Prior to that, chess-savvy computers had won some games against leading chess players, but humans still held the 'upper hand'. In the 1997 match Kasparov won the 1st game, lost the 2nd, then man and machine drew the following 3 games. At match point in the final 6th game, even the human chess master was decidedly defeated.

It was the legend of John Henry advanced several generations ahead, the equivalent of a single man or even a large group of people trying to compete with picks and shovels against even a singled diesel-powered hydraulic digging machine on a construction site. There were predictions that AI agents would become millions of times more intelligent than any human being by the middle of the 21st Century. People were wondering what life would be like when human beings no longer had to even think for themselves or work for their living.

The third-brain intellects of the human primate biological machines were easily and decisively defeated by the electronic machines. The machines and resultant robots always easily won, artificial hands down. But it was because the contest was uneven and the intelligence was not broad or genuine. It was raw intellect devoid of spirit. And devoid of spirit it was unguided. AI will never be capable of having the Conscience. Even if it ever crossed the threshold to become *sentient consciousness* it would still never even have the possibility of becoming *sentinel consciousness* (AD Probings). A sentinel being is a *guided being.* That fact is worth a pound of pondering.

NATURAL HUMAN BEINGS ARTIFICIALLY TRYING TO PLAY GOD

And the human primates marvelled and rejoiced at their wonderous inventions. Inevitably, some began to worship and pay homage to the material electronic machines they had created with forms of intelligence that far exceeded their own biological brains.

The proponents argued it was not the machines they were worshipping, but the superior artificial intelligent consciousness they believed were generated by the machines. The powerful Genie which granted them their every wish and desire. The underlying logic was that anything perceived as more powerful is worshipped.

Yet, a machine is only an artificial device. Artificial simply means human-made and not of nature. The word believed to have originated from the Greeks through the Romans into Latin from *artificialis* or artifice. The word artifice meant "belonging to the art or skill" and in its common use could refer both to inventiveness and trickery.

A machine is something artificially conceived and constructed and operated by something natural. A device using energy to perform tasks. Machines may be mechanical, robotic, electrical, electronic or any combination. That was the first generations of machines; until said machines began to operate autonomously, to learn and reproduce or reconstruct autonomously, and to "think" autonomously.

Machines were deemed "labour-saving devices." They did the jobs of transporting bodies and things on the surface of the planet in cars, trucks, buses, trains, and in the air in aeroplanes, or into outer space beyond the Earth through chemical rockets and life-support capsules. Then the age of the electronic machine the computer arrived and there emerged 'intelligent' machines operating through algorithms and vast banks of data to perform quite complex tasks, analyze patterns, draw conclusions based on evidence, and make predictions.

MACHINES AS MAKERS OF PROFIT AND LEISURE-TIME

Most human beings had finally at last reached the long overdue conclusion by the middle of the 20th Century that enslaving other fellow human beings to carry out work for them whether agricultural, industrial manufacturing or domestic was a morally abhorrent practice.

It seemed, logical, practical, desirable, and particularly profitable to therefore invent, mass manufacture, and sell every sort of inanimate device to make life for humans far easier and more comfortable. So inanimate machine devices would become the new slaves. It started mainly in the 19th Century industrial age and then exploded in the 20th and became rampant and especially sophisticated in the 21st.

There were plenty of fossil fuels to be extracted from the Earth to provide the energy for all the various machines and labour-saving devices and the endless bounty, it seemed, was there for the taking.

It was the **Age of Progress** and progress reigned supreme. Granted, tractors were marvellous inventions which allowed farmers to vastly increase food supply with less land and far less labour. Generations of agrarian people who had worked the land for centuries left for the cities and worked in factories manufacturing things. There were machines for transport, machines for washing clothes and dishes, machines within machines.

So as "progress" became highly profitable, profit was progress, and progress was profit. It seemed like a material miracle. What was the need for all this "faith" business when the materialism, consumerism and body worship offered such wonderful progress? It was before their eyes. The evidence seemed irrefutable and most nearly irresistible.

LEISURE TIME?

Yes, of course, leisure time also had to be invented because of the freeing from all the mundane tasks of living offered by the various machines and devices of the consumer paradise.

But to do with all this leisure time? Leisure time for what? Excellent, so it seemed. More time to work on self-improvement, to selflessly serve others, to eliminated hunger, and extreme poverty and homelessness. **An extension of time to allow for further purification, atonement, attunement, perfecting and spiritual development?**

Well, no, of course. Leisure time was to used consume more and pursue more sense pleasures. More time for hobbies, more time for sport and amusements, more time for consuming various drugs and intoxicants, more time for pursuing sex and indulging every sort of fantasy or perversion available to the human imagination, more time for the entertainments: television, listening devices, personal cellular phones, computer engagements; more time for talking on the wireless devices, for games and gaming, and for interacting in webs of 'social media.' More time for cooking, more time for eating! More time for growing obese from all the eating and inactivity and lack of movement and exercise. More time for going to the gymnasium to get moving, lift weights and try to work off the excess fat. But worry not, there were pills being developed by Technos to even make exercising and movement obsolete!

And so what was the value of all this abundance of extra leisure time? **Could there exist anything more uplifting, more worthwhile that all the spare time that became available might be productively applied toward? Where was spiritual attainment, conscious evolution and self-work? Did it miss the short list?**

VIRTUAL REALITY?

So it happened that in the first half of the 21st Century, the human primates became ever more absorbed, fascinated and obsessed with their machines, devices and intentions. The age of the invention of 'virtual reality.' Virtual reality was simulated alternative reality. Farther removed from the Real than even the unreal reality of ordinary existence but virtually attractive and compelling.

The sad state of the human primates was such that they were so divorced and alienated from any semblance of objective reality, that what was called "virtual reality" had to be introduced with the effect to remove them yet a further step.

Virtual Reality was a simulated experience generated within a 3-dimensional environment through program-generated sense perceptions. With sufficient sophistication, the virtual environment seemed 'real' enough and was applied in creating absorbing games and pastimes in which young people lived isolated, solitary lives, immersed in and interacting with the virtual reality. VR users could create and experience worlds within worlds, sometimes replicating actual world locations, sometimes following imaginative, interactive fantasy. It was the process of playing with and deceiving the 5 senses.

As the smoky and brutal outside real world of a human-made polluted environment became increasingly hot, unstable and harsh, with extreme weather events, so the 21st Century inhabitants began to withdraw and retreat inside the air-conditioned indoor cocoon environments to be absorbed and engaged with their virtual realities.

LONGEVITY OF THE HUMAN PLANETARY BODY? FOR WHAT?

And science and medicine advanced rapidly in the 21st Century, aided and assisted by the Artificial Intelligence revolution, as well as by unprecedented interaction and collaboration between researchers from various fields that led to the realistic possibilities of extending human life.

Human lifespans had already been significantly lengthened by the highly practical and immeasurably beneficial construction of water supply and sewerage treatment systems in the early 20th Century.

By the first half of the 21st Century medical, molecular and genetic scientists were on the search for the cure for aging and death. In their model, aging and death of the physical planetary body was not just a natural process but another disease to be cured.

With the vast increases in knowledge of biological processes, scientists were able to create though nanotechnologies and other research advances, molecules that could slow the aging processes in two-brained, lower animals such as mice and rats. It was only a matter of time before the science knowledge and research applications to human beings would bring breakthroughs in treatments of age-old diseases such as cancer.

But there are few who know that even if a biological machine can be induced to live for 1000 years, the result in the end will be the same. When the life forces leave it the body will eventually wither away and perish. It is worthwhile to maintain the body to be fit, healthy and strong so that it may be used as an instrument and a vehicle, but placing any faith in it whatsoever is futile and foolish.

Most people blindly assume that in a heart transplant, the man or woman receiving the heart is being given an extended life, another chance. But that is back to front, and upside down. It is not the man into whom the heart is transplanted receiving the second chance at further life – *it is the heart receiving the gift and the benefit* (AD).

Yet another example of how much of what we think and believe and assume is topsy-turvy.

Perhaps human beings could become 'immortal' and live forever as "gods?" The rich and famous began to pour funds into the start-up companies promising the long elusive Fountain of Youth. The notion of "Conquering Death" was, for the wealth-holders, the means to keep on enjoying their bodily sense pleasures for longer, for even they knew they couldn't take their money with them in death. But what of the natural balance and the natural laws of the Solar System and Galaxy? What of all that? Never mind all that, it was "progress."

Others in the small minority simply took advantage of what became available and wisely used any of the extra time to complete their inner real work.

PUTTING FAITH IN THE GOD TECHNOS IS A GRAVE ERROR MISPLACING FAITH IN THE DENSE MATERIAL DIMENSION AND IN THE BODY

"What is it? Let's worship it!'
THE FOLLOWERS OF THE GOLDEN CALF

It was indeed the ancient old Golden Calf coming back around in another time in another guise. There is nothing inherently "right" or "wrong" in developing innovations and technologies and machines to help human beings along.

But by the second decade of the 21st Century even the designers, inventors, engineers, builders, operators and promoters of the Artificial Intelligence phenomenon were themselves raising the alarm. The were mightily worried about the known and as yet unknown dangers of the rise of AI without strong safety rails. It was predicted that for every 100 astonishing benefits to humanity resulting from AI, there would be equally 100 dark and dangerous side-effects and risks.

Even they could see the rapid imminent **approach of the Great Filter.**

So the prospect of mass destruction by Nuclear War which had hung over the species from the mid 20th Century was not enough?

And so the prospect of suffocating in their own waste through pollution of the Earth's environment and through global warming and artificially-induced climate change was not enough?

Yet so the prospect of unforeseen outcomes and impacts resulting from the technologies of genetic engineering and artificial biological manipulation was insufficient?

The same perplexing dilemma, the risks of a species acquiring technologies it had not the maturity or wisdom to contain, control or use. The same crude analogy of a small child with access to an automatic pistol.

No, none of it was quite enough for the Great Filter, so was it not inevitable that the 'miraculous' invention of the Artificial

Intelligence would have to be added to the hazard mix just to make it a bit more interesting? What could possibly go wrong? **AI and robotics, in league with the Profit Motive** would be poised to eliminate countless millions of jobs of ordinary citizens, and create economic disruption, accelerating rapid change, social dislocation, alienation and confusion in coming generations.

By the time they saw it coming, they felt powerless to stop it. It was the same old arms race in another guise. "If I don't create this weapon, somebody else will." Was it just another "Oppenheimer Moment" seven decades after the first? Underlying it all were the same densely negative lower animal vibrations that plagued humankind from inception to conception: **Fear, Selfishness and Greed.**

Some worried and speculated about the dangers of facial recognition, and AI misuse by Hasnamuss authoritarian dictator regimes could leading to mass control and suppression of freedoms. Others fretted about how valid free and fair political elections could be interfered with by Artificial Intelligence through the mass release of lies and disinformation. By the early 21st Century, already the boundaries between truth and lies were becoming diffuse and permeable for the easily misled and suggestible masses, as persuasive tall tales, conspiracy theories and mass delusion and hysteria often prevailed spreading like wildfire through the networks of the new technologies.

The inventors and promoters of the God Technos had every reason and right to fear their invention just as the 18th Century author Mary Shelley had presaged with her gothic tale of Frankenstein.

Yet, it was not the AI, a tool in and of itself, which posed the grave risks perceived, it was the people who "parented" the AI themselves who would give it a form of life of its own and who would set it in motion on whatever course it took. Fallible, flawed human beings, without the wisdom or balance to create or apply such a powerful tool.

Perhaps the most powerful realistic dangers posed by AI will simply be further alienation from the Divine Source by the proportion of humankind caught up in the Technos maelstrom, with further disconnection between human beings as they plunge deeper into interacting with artificial machines rather than other human beings or their own higher nature.

EXTRATERRESTRIAL VISITATIONS AND PRESENCES - INTERFERING IN THE EXPERIMENT?

One earnest young undergrad student was in the lab room carrying out behavioural experiments. His mission: to teach rats to learn to negotiate through increasingly complex series of mazes to attain the reward of a food pellet at the end of the journey. It was all about operant conditioning and the model of reward and aversion, and about what laboratory rats were capable of learning through applying such principles.

The randomly assigned rat of our erstwhile student was neither compliant nor a particularly proficient learner. As the minutes ticked on, all the other students had succeeded in coaxing their rats through the various trials of mazes of increasing complexity. Our hapless student was still stuck with his irascible rat on trial one as all the other rats raced ahead with data collected for later statistical analysis.

Our student became increasingly frustrated and irritated. Finally, as time was running out near the end of class, our exasperated student gave his rat a most unscientific poke with the sharpened tip of his graphite pencil to gently coax it through the first maze. The recalcitrant rat, nevertheless, greedily enjoyed the reward of the food pellet at the end of labyrinth. A. Rat never learned and student gets a fail for cheating on the assignment by interfering in the experiment. B. Student gets a pass as he had no choice but to interfere rather than merely observe because time was running out? Student also proved lab rats can succeed with a bit of outside help.

From around the mid 20th Century human beings began to observe, record and report strange aerial things that were not apparently human-built aircraft. It was not an entirely new phenomenon as other such events and observations had been described and written about at various times and places in the past, long before the invention and mass manufacture of the airplane.

The difference was now advanced technology as cameras and recording devices were available for the first time, providing better images and building evidence over time through the recordings and observations, witnessed and captured by ordinary citizens. This technology enabled building empirical evidence and lent some credence to the reports of the observers who might have otherwise have earlier been dismissed and disparaged as 'loopy' or untruthful.

By the second decade of the 21st Century the governments and military establishments of major countries began to grudgingly acknowledge that some of the photographs and film evidence released to media by various internal 'whistleblowers' were not hoaxes and that they had no rational, conventional explanation for some of them.

The military released some films and photographs detailing encounters between objects detected through visual reports of fighter aircraft pilots, radar and other advanced sensor technology of things that were difficult to dismiss or explain away. The objects seemed to defy known laws of gravity, to hover and accelerate to extreme speeds without any visible means of propulsion. Some of the mysterious objects could appear and disappear to all means of detection and some come transfer seamlessly between ocean and sky.

The sightings greatly increased after the Second World War and during the dawn of human invention, testing and stockpiling of thermonuclear weapons. An entire virtual community developed around investigators, researchers, filmmakers and others obsessed with Unidentified Flying Objects or UFO's as they became widely known and possible visitations by "Aliens." Rumour and urban legend developed around alleged "crashes" of such exotic space-craft, particularly around an infamous military base near Roswell, New Mexico in the United States in July, 1947. Layers of ongoing stories, legends, contradictory accounts, and myths swirled around the events at the time and for decades alleging vast government cover-ups and conspiracy theories.

In the second decade of the 21st Century, the United States government began to acknowledge the mysterious encounters between its military in various events and places over the course of time with aerial objects that had capabilities that seemed to defy the known laws of physics. Internal whistleblowers began to leak infor-mation that was not at all as what the general public had been led to believe.

The most credible witnesses were personnel from nuclear weapons sites and strategic missile bases in both the United States and the former Soviet Union. The 1967 documented incident, for one example, at Malmstrom Air Force Base in the State of Montana, where an unknown object had hovered overhead and reportedly temporarily disabled the operation of nuclear-armed missiles at the site. In such a case as that, it had to be binary. Either the story was true or the witnesses made it up and lied.

An American medical specialist, Dr Steven Greer, had spent a significant part of his life pursuing his strong belief that evolved and advanced extraterrestrial (non-human from another world) beings had visited the Earth in the past and were doing so presently, and that they had been 'observers' of the course of the evolution and history of the human beings. Dr Greer also strongly contends factions within the United States military-industrial complex had been successful in hiding the fact of the visitations for years, and that even recovered 'crashed' vehicles and were trying to 'reverse-engineer' the advanced technologies.

Dr Greer had sacrificed his reputation pursuing the truth about it and in demanding 'full disclosure' from US government officials. He claimed that his life had been threatened and that he had been bribed by those with motives for trying to cover up the truth.

Some claimed that the distinguished visitors had slight physical builds, grey skin, short stature and large, almond shaped eyes. Others claimed the extraterrestrial beings travelled from the Pleiades star group, others Arcturus, others Zeta Reticulli. Others claimed the beings could traverse such extraordinary vast distances only with such ultra-advanced technology that was able to travel inter-dimensionally or through 'worm-holes' in space and time. Others speculated the extraterrestrials were humans time-travelling from the future.

Still others claimed that they were actually from an advanced civilization living deep inside the Earth, similar to the Agartha legends of East Asia. They cited the legendary diary of Commander Richard E. Byrd who commanded the Operation Highjump expedition in Antarctica over 1946-47. The diary, reportedly found after the death of Byrd by his son, was said to contain detailed reference to his strange encounter with advanced beings living inside the Earth through a hidden entrance in Antarctica. In the diary, the beings expressed profound concern that humans were exploding nuclear devices on the surface, which had, they said was disrupting the balance of conditions around the planet, and threatening the environment and life of the Earth. More likely, the Byrd diary was a fictional writing of Walter Seigmeister under the penname Walter Bernard who had possibly been influenced by earlier 'hollow-Earth' proponents Ray Palmer and William Reed.

What is the strangest tale of all? The one that happens to be true. Advanced Life Forms has already been discovered and here with us all along and right under our noses all along! In absolute fact, the highly Advanced Life is the source of our very origins – The Holy Father the Sun and Our Holy Mother the Earth. They are both three-brained beings on a very great scale, so, yes, you were created in the image of God.

What would be the underlying motives for any such cover-up of truth?

Dr Greer stated his beliefs around the motives for those allegedly steadfastly preventing disclosure of the existence and presence of extraterrestrial beings. They were essentially based on the profit motive. That is, the elites of the military-industrial complex wanted to exploit the technologies for profit and for war, in order to gain some perceived advantage. That is, they imagined they would be able to 'rule the world' and achieve military superiority over others as well as for other selfish monetary and wealth advantages. Essentially, just old-fashioned power and greed.

The other reasons given for the alleged coverup and massive deception over 80 years, was the claim that disclosure had been stymied because of the assumption that the general public could not handle the news, and that there would be widespread panic, as well as because the possibility of extraterrestrial life would undermine and run counter to mainstream traditional Christian religious beliefs.

The Human Penchant for Alienation - the "Alien Other"

There was a basic animal survival instinct for the programming in human primates to fear, despise and repel the 'alien other.' Clans and tribes of early humans had to protect their food sources, their safety and their lives from outsiders who might do them harm or who might spread disease.

So, it followed that humans began to tribally distinguish between 'friend' and 'foe,' between "us" and "them." Anyone outside their inner circle or their tribal group, anyone who looked "different" or not part of "us" must be considered hostile and alien. It is no random mistake that even in the 21st century, human beings still refer to migrants or visitors from other countries and backgrounds as "aliens." Such instincts are very primitive but also still hardwired in the human fixed attitudes and beliefs.

Peoples against whom war is carried out are 'alienated' or designated alien in order to justify the terrible things being done to them. This is one way politician puppet masters manipulate the masses. They rally everyone together to fight the 'alien threat.'

The primal fear or paranoia of "alien" visitors with hostile intent from interstellar space is fully human in origin. It is the fear that what was done to the Inca, the Mayans and many other native peoples in South and North America would be done to them by some technologically and evolutionarily advanced but ruthless species. Hollywood movie-makers cashed in on that primal fear many times and made profit from it.

For anyone who knows with conviction that **All is God**, the notion of an "alien" is a nonsensical concept. Whether the life form originated from carbon or from some other element such as silica is of zero consequence. All is God.

Some Simple Observations About the Extraterrestrial Presence

- Of course, the Cosmos is teeming with life, biological, three-dimensional, primitive and advanced and also multi-dimensional, and far-beyond-material

- Human beings have always wondered if they were alone, were unique; assuming that is so is only from vanity.
- If extraterrestrial beings are visiting earth, they will have objective reasons for reluctance to make any direct contact or fully reveal themselves until the time is right.
- If extraterrestrial beings are visiting Earth, then any notion of defending against an 'alien invasion' is a foolish nonsense. Advanced beings could easily make short work of humans with no effort at all.
- If extraterrestrial beings have "crashed" in their spacecraft, they would certainly not be so advanced as to have escaped from the **Law of 7** and **the Law of Accident**.
- If extraterrestrials crashed in their spherical spaceships, then would it not beg belief that they travelled the vast distances of light years only to have a crack-up in a farmer's field in New Mexico? Another credible possibility might have been they were testing how humans would react to their presence with the intentional crash of a facsimile probe with life-like android biologic dummies aboard.
- Disclosure should be soonest, full and complete. There are three things that cannot be long hidden: **The Sun, the Moon and the Truth**.
- There is no defensible doubt that advanced beings have been observing the progress of human beings for a very long expanse of time.
- Advanced extraterrestrial beings already know that the **Sun** and the **Earth** are advanced conscious beings as

manifestations of God and would have a communication and a profound deep respect.

- Extraterrestrial beings would certainly never want to be responsible for their advanced technologies and knowledge to fall into the hands of primitive human beings who would inevitably use it to build military weapons for war and destruction. The purported attempts at "reverse-engineering" demonstrates this.

- Dr Steven Greer and his associates are most definitely on the right track about the correct attitude to welcome non-human beings as kin with utmost respect and kindness when any direct contact is made.

- Human beings are always looking for some external saviour or some higher being to rescue them from their own folly and misery. This is understandable but it will and can only come from within the human potential consciousness.

- Advanced beings would be extremely reluctant to directly interfere in the Experiment of Consciousness that is the human species unless having Guidance from a higher source than themselves, or in exceptional circumstances. You may reference the **Prime Directive** that came through the mind of writer and producer Gene L. Coon.

- Indirect help from higher life forms from the sacred sources through Angels and prophets has helped humanity along for millennia. But the interventions have been subtle, indirect and through the insertions of teachings and wisdom.

QUANTUM COMPUTERS: ANY NATURAL OR ARTIFICIAL INTELLIGENCE IS OF THE EARTH

What materials and components constitute a highly advanced Artificial Intelligence machine such as a Quantum Computer? A Quantum Computer may demonstrate the ability to go beyond the Pairs of Opposites by choosing both/and over the limiting 1/0, either/or binary choice in a quantum leap. But what materials compose this advanced machine?

Where precisely did the platinum, copper, silver, gold, nickel metals and elements comprising the machine come from? Where did the materials in the e-beam vacuum evaporation devices used to create high purity uniform materials come from? Where did the hexagonal boron or the nitride for the qubit capacitors come from? Where precisely did the intellects that visualized, conceived and invented all these materials and devices come from?

Fact is: All of it came and can only come from our Holy Mother the Earth.

And the Earth is herself, the most highly advanced intelligence that prideful, arrogant human beings could possibly encounter or even try to comprehend. Rather than exploiting, using and abusing her, that extraordinary higher intelligence could be tapped into by those whose vibration and resonance attunes in harmony with the Earth. And the higher intelligence of that guidance could potentially lead the journey of the human experiment of consciousness on a very different path.

And what of all those Techno's-worshippers groping about trying to find or create a higher intelligence? It was She who created all of us and everything in and on and of the Earth together with our Holy

Father the Sun. The biological brains that create the gizmos and the technos devices are all part of the Earth and are of and from the Earth. The materials they build them from are all of the Earth. All of it came from the Earth and all will return to the Earth.

Perhaps allowing that profound fact to settle upon us and seep within us for a little while could potentially be of some reflective value?

ARMAGEDDON, END-TIMES, AND APOCALYPSE AGAIN?

Meggido remains an actual place depicted on a map in northern Israel and visitors go there to gaze at its fields and landscapes in wonder. It was the land of historic battlefields of yesteryear referred to in the ancient texts as Armageddon. For the Abrahamic faiths, it is right out of the Biblical Book of Revelation of the last part of the New Testament. The Christian exoteric faithful believe that Jesus, a Returned Messiah with descend from the skies when the angelic trumpets blow and put all that is wrong to the right. The believers will receive salvation and succour and the rest will meet their just ends.

In the 21st Century others came to the belief and the wishful hope that advanced higher extraterrestrial beings will land in their torroidial spherical floating spacecrafts and change of the course of history for the better to rescue human primates from their own folly.

Keeping an open mind, any possibility and all of it could prove in the end to be true enough. Yet whatever happens along the course of the unfolding human story in whatever way is absolutely only and solely and purely **The Lila of God.**

One thing certain enough in the age of uncertainty is that putting faith in the material God Technos and in the body is foolish and futile.

If the human primate specific fails as an experiment of consciousness from self-destruction or any other means, the Earth and the Sun will endure on with cosmic lifetimes vastly longer. Just as past experiments have failed, a further biological experiment will be replacing the one that immediately preceded it. People are often seen and heard emotionally expressing concerns about "Saving the Earth," from the folly of human interference and pollution. The Earth does not need any 'saving.' It would be wisest for human beings to treasure, honour and cooperate in harmony with the Holy Mother. Particularly for the past 250 years, the opposite has been occurring.

The hard, cold fact is that it would likely only take the Holy Mother the Earth a mere 10,000 years or sooner to restore natural balance and harmony post the demise of humankind. This would be long after the human species had either destroyed itself or the Third Brain of the Intellect had been allowed to atrophy as in the prior experiment. The vain imaginings of the anthropomorphic and anthropocentric mindset refuses to let go of the notion that human primates are something extra special and at the centre of all the Universe. Possibly some surviving animal species such as rats or crows could be given the third brain to allow yet another experiment of consciousness to emerge?

Humans are unique and have an important enough role to play in the Solar System but not so much so that if they fail as an experiment of consciousness that they are simply irreplaceable.

The relevant story is told of a medieval Saint, a highly developed but very humble being was once at home sweeping the floor. An earthquake and a violent thunderstorm struck not far away. The Saint's pupils and followers rushed in panic to the home of the Saint. Standing outside the humble home, the crowd implored the Saint to deliver them or tell them what to do. The assistant cried out from the crowd: "Master the end of the world is coming. What are you going to do?" The Saint smiled and casually replied: "Well I'm just going to keep on sweeping the floor." (Source: AD).

CHAPTER 25

The Pairs of Opposites and The Polarity- The Spectrum of Goodness and Evilness

"Te tiro atu to kanohi ki tairawhiti ana Te Ra whiti
te ra kite ataata ka hinga ki muri kia koe."
"Turn your face to the Sun, and let the
shadows fall behind you."

TUHOE ELDER SIR JOHN RANGIHAU FROM AN ANCIENT MAORI PROVERB

Far greater minds have struggled with the perennial, perpetual problem of evil so we may best set that old chestnut aside just now. The horns of the old dilemma (pun unintended) poses the oldest question of how with a just, loving, compassionate and merciful God, how could evil exist?

Within the Pairs of Opposites which any being exists within, in order for there to exist an up, there must be a down, for light there must be darkness, for heat, cold and on go the myriad examples of the contrasting opposites. So, how could it not follow that for Good to exist there would have to also exists its exact opposite of Evil?

There may be those who theoretically, dispassionately and philosophically argue that evil does not exist, but they are also most likely the ones who have never fully experienced or been on the receiving end of it.

In the crucible of human life on the Planet of Choice, the Holy Earth there is a record of great acts kindness and selfless love and benefit done by human beings for fellow beings and, on the other side of the ledger, horrific crimes against humanity. History is replete with countless examples of extreme human cruelty and depravity, as it reached an industrial scale in the 20th Century with two world wars, the Holocaust, the Gulags, the use of torture, the weapons of mass destruction, and the many atrocities of modern history.

So if evil happens and evil is all too real enough, where are its roots and origins? What is it and can anything be done to avoid it or be rid of it? Or could it be transcended?

As already revealed and explained to some extent, it was in the objective teaching given out by the highly advanced enlightened evolved being, the original Zoroaster, pertaining to the battle between Light and the Darkness thousands of years ago. Since that time the teaching has been "expanded," contained within the Abrahamic triad faiths, passed on in various forms and oft times distorted.

THE DRUJ

Closer to the original meaning of the objective teaching of Zoroaster, the dark force or form known as the Drug-i-Nasu represents evil in the force of falsehood and deception, or anti-Truth. The contrast is with Asha polarity which represents Truth, righteousness and order.

From what came down through the latter Abrahamic religions, the Cosmos is depicted as a battleground between the forces of light and good and darkness and evil. The Druj is manifested through the evil force Ahriman, which encapsulates every form of deception, ignorance and the chaos disrupting the harmony of the world order.

In other ways, the Druj can manifest in various forms, and can be seen as moral corruption, impurity, lies and deceit. In another form the Druj was portrayed as disease, pain and natural disasters bringing disorder and suffering.

The aim of the Zoroastrian Faith is to guide each person to strive for the positive light force of Asha and resist the negative dark force of the Druj. To do so is to live a virtuous life, following an ethical code, and to seek truth and justice. The ultimate goal is to contribute to the triumph of Asha which will lead to restoration of the cosmic balance.

And so, the original Objective Ethics teaching given out by the Lord Zoroaster centered around good and evil as being the battle between truth and falsity. As it came down the centuries into the Abrahamic lines of faith, it was adopted and adapted in various ways with different effects. In the underlying sense, it was also about living life in such a way for the individual to create within a purification leading to raising the vibration to attune with Asha.

The 19th Century German existentialist philosopher Friedrich Nietzsche completed his influential book *Thus Spake Zarathustra* circa 1887. The protagonist in his philosophical allegory was the Persian Zarathustra, whom Nietzsche confirmed was based on his idea of the Prophet Zoroaster. Nietzsche acknowledged Zoroaster as the first to see in the struggle between good and evil in his inquiry to get to the bottom of how things work. But at the same time, Nietzsche also saw that the teaching as it had come down from Zarathustra, as it had been translated and interpreted, was limited into the pairs of opposites, cause and effect. Nietzsche was trying to look beyond the pairs of opposites, but struggling to fully articulate his vision.

Nietzsche was railing against subjective morality, but struggling to find some metaphysical means to look beyond or replace it. The mental struggle led Nietzsche to give out the idea to the western world of his day that mankind's goal must be to create something superior to itself, a new type of human he called the Ubermensch, the Overman, or the Superman. Nietzsche proposes that all humans must be prepared to will their own destruction to bring the Ubermensch into being.

So what do you think? **Was Nietzsche presaging and predicting the invention and rise of the artificial intelligence and a race of 3-dimensional material cyborgs who were part machine and part human?** Or was it that humans would invent and set into motion higher artificial intelligence which would the replace biological machines -themselves?

Nietzsche continued his line of thought down the rabbit-hole to his famous conclusion that "God is dead." His view became that the deities of religion were external and imaginary and that humankind would have to pull itself up 'by it's own bootstraps' for the Ubermensch to emerge. His ideas around that formed from his notion that desire for power was the overriding motivator for humans which he expressed in the *Will to Power*.

Nietzsche may well have been on the right track with his ideas of conscious human evolution and development, but he would have been singularly unaware that in his day in places like Tibet and Central Asia, in other locations including around him Europe, the fabled Ubermensch already very much existed. They may have been very rare, unknown and hidden to him, but they were all real, grounded in reality. *They were the originally ordinary human beings who had seemingly miraculously transformed to awakening to live in harmony with Nature, and reach and to emanate so much higher vibrations in rare resonance with the Divine within themselves.*

Something vitally important that Nietzsche left in his philosophical legacy, wittingly or otherwise, was the dilemma posed to humankind into the 21st Century and beyond. There was the option of mechanical, material development through highly advanced intelligent, seemingly 'sentient' machines in the Singularity, versus natural evolution through biological human consciousness consciously returning to the Source. Another ethical dilemma in the pairs of opposites: Natural versus Artificial paths to making which future?

GIVING THE DEVIL WHAT'S DUE

The way it happened was inevitable since the most primitive human primate beings emerged with the Third Brain of the Intellect as the next experiment of consciousness.

Pre-historic tribal humans witnessed the eruption of volcanoes, earthquakes, tidal tsunamis, disease outbreaks, violence or killing and injury done to them by other rival tribes. They experienced it all and they wondered.

"Good" things felt good, "bad" things hurt.

With the latter development of farming, civilizations, cities and writing, the next stage of perceiving and conceiving Good and Evil began to take form. If you remove one o from the word Good, you are left with God. If you add one D to the word evil, you are left with devil.

After the great and incomparable original Prophet Zoroaster gave out the Teaching of the cosmic battle of the Asha and the Ahriman, the ideas spread far and wide and filtered through for hundreds of generations.

The way it emerged in the Egyptian, Ancient Greek and Abrahamic streams it became a battle between two forms of God. One was Yaweh, the supreme God and the creator of everything, who is all-wise, all-knowing and all-powerful.

Then there was the lesser deity of the fallen angel, of Lucifer, of Satan, of the Devil. The Devil was created by the Supreme God but cast out of Heaven because of his arrogance and vanity. This Satan had mighty, supernatural powers and his mission was to deceive human beings and lead them into negativity and sin away from God. Lucifer was created by the Supreme God, very powerful but not quite as powerful as God. It was a duality. A great ongoing battle between good and evil pursued with victories and losses on each side but finally the goodness of the Supreme God triumphed and balance and harmony was restored in the Cosmos. The slightly distorted last part was the remnant coming through from Prophet Zoroaster.

On one level, the allegory of the 'fallen angel' is the story of every individual. Every human being, and every lower life form is 'fallen.' Fallen? Fallen in the sense of having descended into the dense vibrations of a material realm universe. Yet human beings undergoing a lifetime incarnation in the material world of the Planet of the

Choice, have the possibility of re-ascending to the divine realm of finest vibrational resonance.

The other part of the teaching allegory is that Lucifer was described as a particularly highly intelligent, capable and beautiful angel. It was Lucifer's own arrogance and vanity that him into gravest sin of trying to "play God" which led to his banishment. His punishment was to become the Prince of Lies for the purpose to deceive and mislead humankind and to spread negativity and ignorance and darkness and more suffering.

THE POLARITY

Once you have achieved some level of understanding of the Pairs of Opposites that material three-dimensional beings exist under, you become capable of getting a far more objective understanding of what is the Devil.

First of all, **Everything is God**. Exceptions? None.

God is not only just some divine deity or entity who is the Creator and the greatest source of good, although that is certainly true on one level. God is all and all is literally God.

You may try understanding this from an entirely different perspective than how you have been conditioned for generations.

Who created Lucifer? Who created Satan? Who created the Druj or Ahriman? Who created this or that devil?

The commonly accepted version is that the **Devil is an Alien**. That is, alienated from God and separated from and separate to God. **The Alienation Principle** is an idea that has long permeated and driven subjective morality and much of human conditioning.

It arose from the doctrine of reward and punishment, and from the survival instinct.

That is, in the Alienation Model, Satan is cast out of creation and existence and operates from an "alien" place and space. Yet is somehow given the power to operate on the Earth to carry out his evil deeds of deceiving humans and stealing souls.

THE UNITY AND THE POLARITY

The Alienation Principle is an unnatural model failing to reflect the Unity of God and the Unity of Existence.

The Devil and all and everything else are all part of the natural world of the Polarity.

There is a Positive, there is a Negative, and there is Neutralizing force.

It is again the Trinity. The Creating Affirmative, The Denying Negative, and the Reconciling Third Neutralizing force.

There is Matter, there is energy and there is Space.

You can see for yourself the Trinity principle in live operation everywhere from the sub-atomic to the galactic.

So is the Negative Force a part of all that or is it banished and separate and alienated from all the rest?

You can see the polarity in operation in the electricity flowing into your own home.

So where is the Devil to be found?

Well, if you have access to even a small telescope you can see the Devil for yourself in the third dimension with your own three-dimensional visual sense organs known as 'eyes.'

INFREQUENT FREQUENCIES, RARE RESONANCE

SEEING THE DEVIL?

You know you can see the devil?

On the level of the Solar System, the Devil is located in the giant gas planet Jupiter.

As has already been revealed, Jupiter is the Denying and Passive force to the Holy Father the Sun. Jupiter is indeed a Passive Sun (AD). Conventional astronomy will only come to this realization sometime in the future.

At the level of the Galaxy, the Milky Way, the 'neighbourhood' of the Solar System, the Devil is located presently in Betelgeuse, the Red Giant Star. Conventional astronomers had developed a more recent fascination for Betelgeuse as it had been to begin dimming or changing in some respects. There was speculation that the Red Giant may be in preparation phase for gravitational collapse for transforming into a Supernova.

The Positive Polarity opposite of Betelguese is the Holy Star Antares.

The Ray of Creation emanates and flows down the scale from the Holy Endlessness through to the Holy Star Antares, and from there through to our own Holy Father the Sun (AD Probings, 1981). **Antares is the seat of Ahura Mazda**, the Asha of the great Prophet Zoroaster.

Antares is the Positive Force, Betelgeuse is the Negative Force and the vast Black Hole or *Gravitational Vortex* at the Centre of the Milky Way Galaxy is the Neutralizing Third Force (AD Probings, 1981).

So is Jupiter and is Betelgeuse not a part of the Galaxy and not part of the Cosmos?

Of course, both celestial bodies are part of the natural order of the Galaxy.

Yet, it has already been revealed that humankind arose and lives on a planet that is part of a Galaxy that in a negative line of the Creation. That does not imply or mean at all that there are not great forces of Positivity present and at work always. It simply means that in this line of the force, it is easier to slide downward, so it requires conscious effort to ascend rather than descend.

The negative polarity is the Devil if you wish to think of it in that way and you would be accurate in doing so. But the negative polarity is just as much a part of the Creation as the positive. They are forces.

MAY THE FORCE BE WITH YOU?

From above to below. From higher Sources. From energies and vibrations and Resonance Beings far higher have come through some powerful hints.

The hints and allegories and teachings keep coming, but few ever notice, appreciate or make good use of them. *"Many are called but few are chosen."*

Just as the Essenes and the Gnostics gave out the clues and the Teaching in the olden times, it is still coming through in various ways and forms with each generation.

Some further passing brief examples to illustrate, can be found in a few popular films or 'movies.' The original story in the 1980's Star Wars contained some conscious, powerful and compelling teaching allegories. For example, the notions of the Dark Side of the Force and the Enlightened Side of the Force. The intrepid planetary journey of Luke and his companions, a Biblical story set in a dystopian future scenario. The Jedi represented the esoteric group holding, practicing and preserving the inner knowledge, struggling against the materialist forces of negativity and power. The wise Jedi master was the Adept, the rare Resonance Being, who was the Teacher and who was so sensitive to perceive with pain when a distant planet and its inhabitants was destroyed by the Emperor and his Dark Force commander Darth Vader, who was revealed as the father of Luke in the storyline.

Another example in popular culture was in the original *The Matrix* film of 1999. The ideas of humans living in a simulated reality had come through from philosophical thinker Jean Baudrillard's work *Simulacra and Simulation*. The choice between the awakening truth (swallowing the red pill) versus the remaining-asleep-and-delusion option (swallowing the blue pill). The notion of the "The One" who was the image of a reluctant Messiah come to lead the world to freedom from bondage came through the protagonist Neo. Morpheus was the John the Baptist character who preceded Neo and who taught and mentored him, and then was surpassed by him. Cipher, the zero man, was the betrayer mirroring Judas, and the villain of the piece.

Two more science fiction films where conscious esoteric messages filtered through were the 1951 Film, *The Day the Earth Stood Still* and the 1991 *Encounters of the Third Kind*. Both stories told of encounters with non-human advanced beings from other worlds. The most compelling messages contained in the stories were how the ordinary human beings reacted and behaved upon the arrival or appearance of the extraterrestrial visitors.

It must also be fully understood that the writers of these stories or the producers and directors and actors who created the films were by no means necessarily at all conscious evolved human beings, although some could have been. The only point is that the people creating such films **were used, consciously or unconsciously.**

There are other contemporary examples in music. Some of the most talented lyric writers and musicians have confessed years later in candid interviews that they didn't know where the music or the words were coming from when they were at their most creative peaks. They were being used for specific purposes by higher forces trying to instill messages for their mass listeners in subtle ways. Some were aware that these forces were channeling through them, and others were not. *In other words, the beauty of the music and the messages contained within were coming **through them** and **not from them.***

THE DEVIL WITHIN

The cosmic negative polarities surely attract and generate negative energies and vibrations on the vast natural scale, but the inner devil is the immediate and more real barrier and the main problem to contend with. When you add the D to the word evil it equals Devil.

The Devil within manifests as inner **selfishness, fear, greed, negative sex, lust, dominance, power, hate, rage, violence, jealousy, envy, revenge, resentment, lies, deception, insincerity, vanity, self-pity, and all forms of inner considering and negative vibration.**

The inner devil leads the mind and the person into Temptation and toward Despair. The singular goal in a lifetime is to triumph over the inner Devil which is the greatest challenge.

The inner devil is filled with countless unrelenting attachments and endless desires.

The Devil typically frequents places where there is lower vibration. Places like nightclubs, pubs, brothels, drug-use venues, prisons, mental hospitals, gang headquarters, terrorist cells, board rooms, or where criminals may congregate. That doesn't mean that the stereotypical horned, crimson-skinned creature, with goat-like features and sinister smile always shows up in such places, but Old Nick could very well be attracted to them and particularly to those who share the attraction.

BUT THE DEVIL MADE ME DO IT!

You might possibly be able to find some tiny sub-atomic particle of sympathy for the old Devil who has born the brunt of blame and been the whipping boy for time immemorial. The Devil has been attributed responsibility for human beings carrying out all range of terrible and horrific crimes against humanity. The Devil has taken the rap for raping nuns, for killing innocent babies, for setting fire to churches and temples, for terrorist acts, and for every sinister and evil thought and deed imaginable.

The Devil has been the way for human beings to try on the futile attempt to absolve themselves from responsibility. Equally, it would have to be fairly acknowledged that the Devil has been profitable for churches, priests, clergy and religions of all sorts in a sort of "protection racket."

This is not at all to make light of or minimize the concentration of the real negative force that exists known as the Devil, which most definitely does have impacts, but to observe how the alienation dogma has generated and perpetuated untruth, confusion and ignorance around the phenomena.

SO WHAT IS THE SOURCE ? WHAT IS THE WELLSPRING OF ALL EVIL?

Evil is certainly very real but is equally *entirely an invention of humans*. It was always and is created by humans, directed at humans and suffered by humans.

Human beings have two natures, one higher and divine, and one lower and animal. It is all vibration and frequency.

Human beings are capable of the most horrific, cruel, and terrible acts conceivable and limited only by their imagination. The extreme cruelty of the practice of torture to deliberately inflict pain and suffering by one human being on another by every means has plagued humankind for thousands of years. Victims of torture and trauma may suffer post-traumatic stress for years, have recurring nightmares, or go into dissociation, where their consciousness has 'jumped' out of their bodies to survive the extreme pain and suffering.

From the unfathomable horrors of the concentration camps and furnaces of the Holocaust, through to the viciousness of two world wars killing millions, to the scientific cruelty of the notorious Unit 731 where biological and chemical agents in research killed thousands, through to the incineration and death by radiation of the thousands of innocent civilians at Hiroshima and Nagasaki, through to the building and stockpiling of arsenals of weapons of mass destruction including nuclear warheads, and weaponized chemical and biological weapons. Through to the remorseless acts of serial killers, paedophiles destroying the lives of innocent children, cybercriminals stealing the lifesavings of their victims, through to political and religious terrorism, through to the "ethnic cleansers," through to violence against close family members in the home, through to senseless carnage in school shootings, the range and scope seemingly inexhaustible.

So why and how is all of it happening?

THE LIVING DEAD OR THE SPIRITUALLY DEAD ARE THE MAIN CONDUITS OF EVIL

This knowledge can potentially give you some pieces to the puzzle that lead you to different and higher levels of understanding. It will start to make a bit more sense.

The remote primitive ancestors understood evil as when disease strikes and spreads, as when an earthquake hits, a tsunami engulfs, a volcano erupts, hurricane makes landfall, or any natural disaster takes lives and casualties. They also understood evil as when a crop fails, drought or epidemic comes, or other misfortunes occurred. They later went on to attribute natural disasters or human disasters such as loss in warfare to fate, spirits and curses. They also attributed misfortune or setbacks or natural disasters as retribution by an angry and vengeful god. Some tribal groups and civilizations went on to take lives by offering human sacrifices to appease and win favor with their conception of gods.

In the age of science and reason, the causes for natural disasters seeped into the Common Consciousness. Earthquakes caused by tectonic plates in the crust of the Earth, volcanoes erupting where molten magma from deeper with the Earth surfaces, cyclones and hurricanes formed by explainable conditions in the weather.

By the late 20th Century, most people had come to the understanding that natural disasters were caused by natural events. Human communities sadly continued to be terribly impacted by the natural disasters, but they were no longer seen by most as the result of what was considered "evil." In some instances, insurance companies began to refer to them as "acts of God."

So setting all that aside, the evidence was left that Evil was caused by human beings thinking things, saying things and doing things to other human beings.

It has already been asserted and explained in this book how approximately 50% of the 21st Century population of human beings alive of 8 to 9 billion lives **consist of the Spiritually Dead.**

The conception and practice of what is called Evil is overwhelmingly, although not entirely or exclusively, within the proportion of the population of the Living Dead. It may be hard to handle or accept, it may be controversial, but truth is what it is.

To be clear, not all of the Living Dead are criminals or murders. Not by any means, but the **overwhelming vast proportion** of the criminals and murderers are among the Living Dead.

Why and how is this so? It's a combination of factors: 1. There are canters of Negative Polarity within the Earth, within the Solar System and within the Galaxy which manifest the force known as "Devil." 2. The Living Dead have lost their internal guidance system which is the Conscience or the Active Force of the Sun; 3. Because this is their last lifetime and last incarnation, the Living Dead have buried their Conscience; 4. Without any Conscience, there is no substantive guidance system within the Living Dead, so they "channel" the negative force and carry out their acts of what can certainly and accurately be called "evil" without regard to any human law, nor the Law of Karma, nor any other value or ideal which would restrain or contain them.

Of course, not all of the Living Dead are vicious predatory criminals. Some are born into families and conditioning where ethical values were instilled and internalized. It is accurate that these laudable ethical values are a constraint and restraint and that that a proportion of the Living Dead will not be prone to act out evil. But, at the same time, the outer guidance is only on the surface and they would be far more prone under the right conditions to turn toward that negative polarity.

The Living Dead tend to gravitate toward the wealth and power canters in every civilization and human endeavor. They are motivated by the "big three" negative vibrations: Selfishness, Fear and Greed (AD Quest 1981). Many go into politics and some of the worst of them rise to the top of politics. And the farther they rise in power, the deeper is buried the Conscience. Power corrupts and absolute power corrupts absolutely as historian Lord Acton so aptly observed. Others seek power, wealth and fame in business, in institutions such as the religions and the Church, or in universities and educational institutions. Every field of endeavor contains the element of the Living Dead who typically strive for leadership, dominance and power.

So not all of the Living Dead are violent criminals but nearly all violent criminals are among the Living Dead.

They are remorseless and they are without a working internal guidance system. Those are the hallmarks of the Living Dead who conduct the negative force as conduits and who carry out the evil.

They are capable of doing anything because there is nothing restraining them from doing it. External human laws, law enforcement and imprisonment may temporarily contain and stop them, but they will carry on their acts if they can in any way they can. With the mass production and consumption of dangerous chemical poisons such as methamphetamine and other drugs, ordinary humans are reduced to zombies and the ranks of the Living Dead are swelled.

IS THERE ANY SALVATION FOR THE LIVING DEAD?

Of course, there most certainly is. **God is ever merciful and compassionate**.

There are ample ongoing examples where human beings who have committed incomprehensible acts of horror against others who have awakened, sincerely repented, and reformed, and gone on to make sincere repairs to their victims and set examples for others. In these relatively rare cases, the Conscience of the Active Force of the Sun has been reignited and Atlantis has risen again.

But the fact remains that most of the Living Dead do not see any need or have any desire for salvation. They are responsible for carrying out the crimes and evil acts that affect their victims and their family members in tragic and terrible ways and cause great suffering. They have no belief in any higher force watching or restraining them, and the reality of **Karma** has no meaning for them. Karma itself is quite different from and operates otherwise from what many who do know about it assume, for Karma is purely vibrational.

WHAT IF THE LIVING DEAD WERE TO SUDDENLY DISAPPEAR?

At this point in time it would only be a thought experiment. But conceive how the life in the world of the remaining human beings living on the Earth would transform if all of the Living Dead suddenly and mysteriously vanished?

As in Science Fiction scenario where perhaps the Living Dead were removed to another planet called Purgatory by advanced extra-terrestrial beings? A place where they could be safely contained and possibly even offered rehabilitation or reform?

It's only a thought experiment, but think through how life and love on Earth would transform and be different if such a thing ever happened. It would be by no means a perfect utopia, but it would be very different and far less dystopian.

People who are not Spiritually Dead and have the Magnetic Centre are also most certainly fallible and make plenty of mistakes, and can harm others as well, but they are different in their ability to experience genuine remorse and in the capacity for self-correction. That is, those with the Magnetic System still have within the internal guidance system of the Active Force of the Sun, the Conscience.

THE ADDITIONAL FORCES DRIVING, AIDING AND ABETTING EVIL:

The Profit Motive

Although what is known as evil may have its scope and manifestation through the conduit of the Living Dead, there are also two other major forces or factors contributing and magnifying the effect that can be explained.

The first, and it a major factor, is the **Profit Motive**. It pervades all human life on the Earth (AD Quest 1981).

The Profit Motive is the driving force of evil powered by Selfishness. It is the extreme of individualism. The individual of the Ego. It is the diametrical opposite of Selflessness.

Money or gold or material wealth is not the root of all evil it was purported to be. It is the love of the Profit Motive which is the root of evil. So it is fear, selfishness and greed driving the Profit Motive, so that millions are left homeless, starving and ill, while others have so much wealth and access to the material needs far beyond their need or use.

Philosophers such as Marx and Engels recognized and railed against the Profit Motive, coming fairly close to the mark, but the form of Communism that grew and took shape out of their ideas was nothing more than the Profit Motive in disguise, and in many ways had outcomes more even more reprehensible than the Capitalism it aspired and purported to replace.

Godless authoritarian dictatorship of the people espoused and promoted by the various communist political parties was just elitism and capitalism under another guise, and hypocritically promoted as a new alternative. "They shall be known not by their words, but by their works." And the "works" of 20th Century communist party dictators such as Stalin and Mao bore brutal testament to their reigns of terror over their peoples and by what they wrought and by the dark legacies they left.

One of the few examples of egalitarian communal living where the Profit Motive had been largely eliminated was given by the Essenes.

If you look closely and become observant, you will see the Profit Motive operating in a large proportion of the evil that happens and manifests in ordinary living. Human beings have been largely been turned into virtual wage slaves by the Profit Motive and have continued to tolerate and unconsciously and tacitly support it, kissing the whip that scourges them.

The topic could easily consume the space of a chapter, but even the brief introduction of

contribution of the Profit Motive to what is called evil can be seen by those open to observing it.

If the Profit Motive lessened its grip or went into decline then people would begin to work in a far more cooperative and spiritual way in that they would be working for Service and the greater good rather than seeking individual personal reward for themselves.

Djinn or the Remnants of Prior Experiments of Consciousness

The Arabic term for the unseen spirit beings that also can be more minor, but significant, contributors to human evil is the Jinn. The word "Jinn" was believed to derive from the Arabic language root meaning of "hiding" or "concealment." In Arab tradition, it is believed that the Jinn exist in a parallel unseeable realm alongside humans. Jinns were reputed to be sentient, and have their own motivations and desires. Jinns are capable of connecting and communicating with people and able to influence the lives of humans in various ways under some conditions. Jinns were believed to have supernatural powers, such as shape-shifting, invisibility, deception, and the ability to possess humans. Reference is briefly made in the Quran to the Jinn in several verses, as they are described as beings on another plane that can, under certain conditions, interact with humans in the third dimension.

All of these references in the Quran are quite correct, and the Jinn, or the Ifrit or by other names do exist and can negatively influence human beings. As was already revealed in the early chapter of this book, the Jinn have a more specific name and source of origin (AD Quest 1981).

They once existed as a prior Experiment of Consciousness between the Holy Father the Sun and the Holy Mother the Earth in the material, biological world, and even had a form of civilization long before the arising of the Homo Sapiens. They failed as an Experiment of Consciousness, principally because they became diverted and obsessed with sex. The Third Brain of the Intellect was taken from them and they became lower animals again (AD Quest 1981).

The Jinn that had developed the vibrational frequency level of a Soul or higher were given mercy and compassion by the Supreme God of many names, and they were allowed to exist in parallel to the human species in another unseen plane of existence. Those being were allowed to have a chance of evolving further if they could possess some of the members of the subsequent Experiment of Consciousness and live through them.

The Exorcist

Those remnant spiritual beings of the prior experiment, became the source of legend and lore throughout human history. They became known to the Christians as "demons" and to other religions in various names and forms.

The detailed accounts and records of the Roman Catholic Church in the specialized priests who work with people believed to be possessed by Jinns, and they can and do help the people affected through prayers and rituals they drive them out. Jinns have long been associated with mental illness and "lunacy" and there is a strong connection as they are attracted to negative, dense vibration, such as depression or self-pity afflicting those suffering.

The accounts of the Roman and Orthodox Catholic priests around the exorcism phenomena and in specific cases are indeed, accurate and truthful. Hidden deep within the secret Vatican library books and documents will be the more full and accurate and objective understanding of that and other phenomena. For various reasons known only to the Popes and the Vatican, information that would potentially shed light on many topics has been closely held and guarded as a secret.

In any case, the Jinn can, under certain conditions, interact with human beings and contribute to and feed upon negativity. At the horrors of the ovens at Dachau and Auschwitz in the 20th Century, for example, the Nazi troops alone could not have carried out the extreme depravity and evil, without some negative force feeding on it and driving them farther. It was not that the Jinn caused it, that was human evil, but that they magnified, augmented, and fed upon it, if that can be understood.

Fortune Tellers, Sorcerers, Mediums, Clairvoyants, Witchery, Black Arts

Master Omraam Mikkhael Aivanov wryly observed (The Mysteries of Yesod) that even the purest great Messengers could not see or hear the highest One God directly but only through intermediaries as Archangels, yet it is only the "fortune-tellers, mediums and so-called clairvoyants" who can 'see' God and converse with God as a matter of routine.

There are, of course, people who have naturally acquired certain vibrations, and who have developed certain sensitivities, or who had had been gifted with that faculty from birth. Such people may use their gifts discreetly, and occasionally, and for pure and genuine purposes to help others, and not for pay or profit. If the motive is pure then the effects and results are pure.

But there has also long been a small proportion of people who have delved into the Dark Force of the negative polarity through such means as "Black Magic," "Sorcery" or other means. There have long been traditions and groups who study and engage in such practices and there are various rituals, herbal and substance potions, and incantations to force or influence certain results.

Mostly the motives for such people are power or some other negativity they are drawn to. An ample proportion of them are self-deluded charlatans trying to impress and scare others, but another proportion have succeeded in tapping into something they think they can be in league with or control.

What they are actually doing is establishing communication and links with Jinn. Their communication with entities in the "other world" is real, but not what they think or imagine it is. Such people can purport to 'read fortunes,' predict the future, or make contact with deceased persons (necromancy). They are capable of putting on quite impressive shows that appeal to the suggestibility and vulnerability of others seeking answers and help.

But it is the Jinn on the other end of the line answering their psychic call. The Jinns are readily there when they call them. But the Jinns also are, by their nature and purpose, deceitful. Spreading deceit and falsity is the stock in trade of the Jinn entity in order to exploit the situation to their own aims. The humans who imagine they are controlling them or getting the Jinn to do their bidding are misled and deluded into thinking they are clever and in control.

Jinn are attracted to and feed upon negativity and negative vibration. They do not alone tend to cause mental illness but can certainly feed upon and exploit it. For example, a person who is severely depressed over a period of time, and cannot emerge out of it through medication or therapy or some other assistance, may risk becoming subject to self-pity. Self-pity is a dense negative vibration that the Jinn will seek out and feed upon, and this is where the cases of possession may occur. If the Jinn can sufficiently exploit the victim to induce a sense of despair to the point where the victim commits self-destruction, then the Jinn can seize an opportunity at having another chance to come through a lifetime in the material world to evolve themselves.

People may come under attacks by Jinn at various times in their lifetime, in various circumstances when they are vulnerable. Some people come into the world more vulnerable to the influences of Jinn than others. Some people have substantial immunity to them and are seldom bothered by them. One thing is certain: it is definitely most foolhardy to deliberately engage with them or try to use contact with them for any purposes. But this is precisely what the 'black magicians' do in their various practices.

In the early stages, Jinn can sometimes interfere with even the process of trying to contact your Inner Guide to the Conscience, who is a most beneficent positive force, as in, for example, the use of the Pendulum. It is, therefore, very important to rigorously to confirm the source of what you believe to be your Guide and fully filter out your own impure desires, the vain ego and the Jinn. If you follow the Objective Morality of the Guidance of your Conscience, then you will never be misled or deceived by any forces of the dark polarity.

As time goes on through many generations and thousands of years the Jinn will increasingly lose their potency and gradually diminish. This is certainly not a topic that people should unduly worry about or "obsess"over it (pun again not intended). Always remember the Hermetic wisdom, "As Above, So Below."

Jinn are likened to microscopic bacteria and viruses that sometimes infect people at vulnerable times. Until microscopes were invented, they could not be seen either. Adepts operating at higher frequencies can see or perceive them, sometimes as hovering fragments like sparks, but they pay them no attention. The best defense is a strong immunity generated through attracting and emanating positive vibration and by working against and transforming negativities. The way that Catholic priests and others in different cultures perform their exorcism rituals to drive out the Jinn is through prayer and purification rituals, and it is on based on the same sound principles of vibration.

The supreme way to defeat an attack of the Jinn is to starve them of what they feed on. Then they will sheer off.

Modern psychiatry and psychology has long dismissed the view of traditional cultures that mental illness is caused by " fate, karma, spirits, and curses," and insist it is only material in nature and caused by biochemical imbalances in neurotransmitters in the brain. To a certain extent, both are correct. But the unseen, non-material forces and entities can also most definitely affect the causes, the remedy and the course of the illness.

Spirits and Curses - Bad Medicine

One of the most singularly foolish things that some people can do is to try to use the forces of the dark polarity to harm other human beings such as through curses and "spells." "Black Magic" is the use of supernatural forces for selfish, hurtful, and wrongful purposes is on the extreme end of the scale as a form of evil.

There are practitioners of the 'dark arts' in nearly every culture from the voodoo of Africa and the Caribbean, through to the *maketu* of the Polynesian cultures, through to the sorcery of the European cultures, through to the use of *ku* in China, through to the *kala jadu* of India there are those individuals and small groups who practice using supernatural forces to manipulate or harm others. The divulging feature of such practice is use for some perceived personal gain such as harm to enemies or manipulation of persons or events for self-benefit.

In India's Assam region on the banks of the Bhramaputra river there is the Mayong village which has been well-known as a centre for black magic, witchcraft, and necromancy. The methods and the rituals handed down and passed on through generations. In the Voodoo of the Caribbean, certain poisons can be used, such as derived from the toxic puffer fish in order to induce a state to make a 'zombie.' As if there were not already enough zombies in the world as it is? In some remote Aboriginal communities in Australia, a curse can be sent by 'pointing the bone' at an intended victim, and places and venues can be cursed.

In an objective sense, it is all energy and vibration. Energy is energy and vibration is vibration. Electricity is energy which can be used to light and heat a home or it can be used to electrocute somebody.

Dabbling or delving into such dark practices may, to some, seem novel and fascinating but it is extremely foolhardy and will never draw you closer to return to God-the-One Source; but will predictably and most definitely bring on the opposite repelling result.

It is also very unwise to deliberately attempt to 'divine' or predict the future. It is wise to leave the future to unfold according to the Will of God and pray to be able to accept it as it is. There are some cases where premonitions come spontaneously to people, and that never poses any problem, but it is only when people are actively trying to attract or use such visions for their own purposes that it is wrong and harmful.

In fact and in reality, dabbling in or engaging in such negative energies and vibrations will only have the effect of driving a person deeper asleep into the delusion of Maya. Those who attempt or engage in such practices are doing it for very impure motives and attempting to alter the natural course of events to meet their own selfish ends. In other words, they are trying to arrogantly impose their own subjective little will over the Will of God to "make" or force things to happen. **You can see the direct and stark contrast between such practitioners and those Adepts who seek only the purity and love of God by attuning their will to the Divine Will.**

Black magic, spells, curses, necromancy and all the rest of it is nothing more than 'clever ape stuff' in the non-material realm in the same way as scientists and engineers conjuring up chemical, biological and nuclear weapons of mass destruction in the material realm can do. They are mirror images of each other. There were persons during the 19th Century who gained fame for their dabbling such as Crowley and those of the 20th Century who admired and emulated them with their 'devil worshipping' and all such carry on.

What the foolish person practicing it is inevitably blind to is the fact that they are not controlling it at all but it will end up controlling them. They may be able to carry something out that will harm someone and derive short term gain and satisfaction for themselves, but what they sew, they will surely reap, as it all will eventually come back to bite them with compounding dividends. It is the worst form of collecting Karma and the worst Karma to ever attract.

It is inevitable that those engaging with those forms of the polarity of evil will come to regret it as it can severely and adversely affect not

only themselves but future generations of family and those associated with them. Bad magic indeed. The wise will have nothing to do
with any of it, but will turn away and face the Light.

Curses tend to affect most those who believe strongly in them by
the immersion of cultural conditioning, to be more suggestible to
it. Curses should never be sent back to the individual sending them.
There are ways the effects of any curse can be neutralized and the
person protected. The simplest, very best and most certain way is to
neutralize it is to sincerely send Love to the individual who is trying
to curse or harm you.

DELIVERANCE FROM EVIL

Practical and Prudent Ways to Deal With the Evils that are Inevitably Part of the Journey Through the Learning Crucible of Life

---

"If you are meditating and a devil arrives,
make the devil meditate."

G.I. GURDJIEFF

Generations of children after generations are told to be "good" and
avoid "badness."

But usually the adults admonishing goodness in the children
don't themselves have much notion about what that means except
on the subjective level of reward and punishment, which has been
deeply conditioned into everyone by the outer forms of religions.

All the many "do's and don'ts" appeal to the animality in humans. We inadvertently teach children the spirit of rebellion in trying to rule them by teaching any authority other than their own inner reason. Desire for anything is increased by prohibition or condemnation. In forced moral teachings, the ordinary person, by human nature, is apt to take such restraints to the contrary. Providing simple explanation and reasons can prevent and defuse that, as the aim is for children to develop or open to is the inner guidance of the Conscience.

A very wise Sage in the late 20th Century gave out the measure of Objective Ethics:

"Whatever is good is what causes you to wake up and whatever is bad causes you to go deeper asleep," (AD Quest 1985).

One key truth to always remember is that **Everything is God and God in in Everything.** The notion of the "Alien" is false, unhelpful and misleading conditioning. *The alien is the Other.* It is the false conditioning that one thing is Good and is God and that the Devil is separate and not part of God is a fallacy leading to untruth and deception. The negative polarity is as much a part of nature as is the positive polarity on every scale. There is no thing, no matter how seemingly dark or repulsive that is not part of the One. And everything comes from the One and everything returns to the One. There simply is no "this is God" and "that is not God."

God is Eternally Merciful and Compassionate. The choice that human beings have, as an experiment of consciousness, is whether to return consciously as a being or evolved higher vibration with real individuation which is the human potential, or to return unconsciously. Gurdjieff bluntly referred to it as the choice between *dying like a man or perishing like a dog.* There is a substantial amount of time given in a single lifetime or in the incarnations of a few life-times. But the divine offer is limited.

THE KEY TO REMEMBRANCE

The Adepts who have attained the higher vibration, and highest frequencies are operating in life at such a rare resonance that they are granted the supreme blessing of Universal Vision to see God in Everything.

Yet, any ordinary human being can be transformed by reaching toward the understanding that everything is God. The dirty, dishevelled homeless person you passed on the road is God. Your best friend and closest confidante is God. Your worst enemy is God. The person who put some curse you is God. The person who robbed you is God. The virus that infected you and makes you sick is God. The cells that rebelled against the other cells in your body and ran out of control as cancer are God. Does an influenza, tuberculosis, or a smallpox virus objectively have any less right to exist than you do?

It is all the **Lila of God** and nothing but what it is.

Objective Morality comes from the Conscience and from following the inner guidance of the Conscience.

If you abuse another person, if you attack or harm another person, you are abusing and attacking God.

If you help and selflessly serve another person, you are equally serving God.

If you can begin to see the evidence and embrace the idea that everything and everyone is God and everything is connected you are on the way to transformational possibility.

This concludes essentially a brief introduction to get some sense of a quite different understanding of the problem of evil, how it is directly related to vibration, frequency and resonance.

But let the chapter on good and evil close with an inspirational example of the very wonderful.

The photo is of a German woman named Irene Sendler. She passed on at the age of 98 in Warsaw, Poland in 2008. During WWII she obtained permission from the Nazi authorities to work inside the Warsaw ghetto as a plumbing and sewerage specialist. She knew what the Nazis were up to and what their plans were. Irena smuggled infants out in the bottom of the tool box she carried and she carried in the back of her truck a burlap sack (for larger children). She also had a dog in the back that she trained to bark when the Nazi soldiers let her in and out of the ghetto. The soldiers of course wanted nothing to do with the dog and the barking covered the infants' noises. During her time of doing this, she managed to smuggle out and save over 2000 infants. When she was caught, the Nazi's broke both her legs, and arms and beat her severely. Irena kept a record of the names of all the kids she smuggled out and kept them in a glass jar, buried under a tree in her back yard.

After the war, she tried to locate any parents that may have survived it and reunited the family. Most had been gassed. Those children she helped got placed into foster family homes or adopted.

There has always been wickedness it the world and those who have opposed and overcome it.

CHAPTER 26

The Secret Technologies and Methods for Vibrational Atonement, Attunement and Raising of Resonance

> *"Always remember that you came here for the*
> *purpose of learning to contend with yourself, only*
> *with your self. And therefore, thank everyone and*
> *everything affording such opportunities."*
> APHORISM HANGING ON THE WALL OF THE PRIEURE.

Herein are the 'secrets' revealed. Raising vibration and resonating with ever increasingly higher frequencies, spheres and divine forces is possible and attainable.

And the secret is there is no simple, quick magical recipe. There are no magic crystals, no incantations, no short cuts. There is, however, a simple formula that will always work for those who are prepared to practice Self-Work. It is all transformational hard work, consistency, and persistence. Effort and, ultimately, the descendance of Grace. The effort and persistence required is considered the principal reason most of the masses still unconsciously persist in choosing to swallow the "sheep-asleep" capsule, remaining prisoners in the labyrinth of Maya, the path of least resistance. Water easily flows down from the mountain, but pumping it up the top requires intention, and consistent effort.

And yet, effort alone is insufficient. Inner vibrational transformation cannot be "achieved" in the same way as 'training for the Olympics'. It isn't a linear process and a pitfall is the imbalance of "intensity" in order to seek rewards which can create a barrier and itself hinder advancement. The approach of 'right knowledge' and 'right effort' might be better likened to the allegory of 'preparing the garden,' or bringing forth the natural fertility of the combined substances of soil, water, and sunlight. At the same time, the garden must be tilled and weeds removed. The weeds are our own impurities, flaws, imperfections, faults, and shortcomings.

Self-discipline and faith and persistence are bedrock foundations for transformational process of Voluntary Evolution.

PURIFY THE MOTIVES

Vivekananda gave out a very different vibrational teaching of Objective Morality which was that of seeing, speaking and sharing truth, emphasizing purity of motive and thought which strengthened it, is wholly immersed within the ideal of unselfishness or Selfless Service to others. He advised his followers to constantly check their underlying, inner motives and purify them, to practice selflessness and non-attachment and to build *shraddhā* (faith).

The Kshetra or the field in the Bhagavad Gita refers to the body which is material, mutable, transitory and perishable, the Kshetrajna refers to the conscious knower of the body who is of the same essence as Knowledge, immutable, eternal and imperishable, the knower of the body is the spiritual seed residing in the body. It is the powerful allegory of the *Field and the Knower of the Field.*

On a very practical and immediate and realest base level: why am I thinking and doing what I am thinking and doing? What exactly is my actual underlying motive?

Following this principle and practice of honest and rigorous thorough self-assessment will lead to genuine self-knowledge. It is not at all 'pretty,' but confronting all the ugliness is getting real. Once you begin to honestly see how you are constantly driven by negativities, buffeted by your own negative energies, such as the big three of Selfishness, Fear and Greed, you will gain self-awareness that is transformational. Once you honestly observe yourself for a good while, you begin to see what makes you tick.

Most will come into the "Work"-on-Self with multiple negative motives. You may well want or be driven by Sex, or driven from your Greed, or want everything for your-self, driven by Selfishness. There is a Hungarian Magyar proverb that the human hand is built to turn inward to feed the mouth, which refers to the inclination toward selfishness. But the same hand can equally be extended outward, to give to help and to feed others. The Negativities are always there, but can be turned to transformational use.

For example, you can transform Greed into becoming greedy for God, as one small example. Eventually, that will fall away as well but any negativity can be transformed toward the positive polarity. That is the real meaning of 'alchemy.'

Judge not others: stop and end that fixed habit immediately. Fix your attention on yourself, your own faults and negativities and changing them. Make the sustained effort to become aware as possible at every moment of what you feel, think and aim to do. Just as you learn to stop judging others, also simply learn to observe yourself without judgement. Develop the Fair Witness of Mindfulness, watch the negative motives and negative energies come and go. Observe them accurately and fearlessly, but then let them go or use them to transform self. It may come as a surprise to you that the roadmap for the journey of transformation is given out within many allegories and stories, such as in the 1678 book of *Pilgrim's Progress*, as well as through ancient and contemporary sources.

Carry out a process of inventory. What are your fixed attitudes and deeply entrenched conditioned beliefs and attitudes? Where did they come from? In this inventory, which ones are useful to your development and which ones can be jettisoned?

Knowing self is the first step of the first step of purifying the motives. If and when the motives can be honestly contended with and purified, everything else will flow from that.

STRUGGLE AGAINST NEGATIVIES

Follow Plato's advice to the Know Thyself. Knowing the self means a full and honest inventory of the self as it is, and not the ego image that veils it.

The Objective Psychology of the Gospels are contained in the Chief Features. Your Chief Feature is whatever is your underlying motive, what is driving you. Chief Features can certainly shift and change, usually slowly, but there will be a few 'favorites.' Only 1 ONE Chief Feature is positive and that is LOVE. All the other 11 Chief Features which are held by the overwhelming majority of all humans alive are negative energies that can be transformed. The Chief Features are **Fear, Selfishness, Greed, Dependence, Sex, Ineffectualness, Boastfulness, Insincerity, and Laziness.**

Most infants come into the world with a chief feature of dependence (AD Quest 1981).

If you have ever lived or worked in a country or region where there is a war on or in severe conflict or violence, you will be able to observe that most people will tend to have a chief feature of fear. Those who have undergone transformational resonance to be 'born again' will vibrate with the Chief Feature of Love.

It is likened to peeling away the many layers of an onion. As you learn to observe chief features and struggle against them, and awakening energy is generated. Again, it isn't a zero-sum linear battle with 'winners' and 'losers,' and once one underlying motivation is overcome, a new negativity will typically arise to replace it.

Sometimes you will win in your struggles against the 'devil' desires of the body and the negativities of the mind, and ofttimes you will lose. But it is the struggle itself which is giving the fine energy feeding your spiritual seed.

It is the fine energy created by the long struggle against the negativities and tendencies to slip and fall back to unconsciousness that lead to the Awakening. And it fine energy generated in this struggle that feeds the developing Magnetic Centre to transform into the Soul, and higher on up the chain through the scale of vibration, frequency and resonance.

SELFLESS SERVICE

Do things to serve and help others in secret sometimes and say and, at the same time, think and say nothing about it, especially in your own mind and ego. Do it because in serving that other person you are serving God as you can presently conceive it.

Mr Gurdjieff gave the advice to develop your generosity without any witnesses.

To aspire to Selfless Service is a very high goal and not easy at all. Selfless service is about serving God through quietly serving other human beings and lower animals as well such as through, for example, volunteering in an animal shelter.

Selfless service is service devoid of any reward or any ego, or any form of recognition by others or ego.

Selfless Service may also take the form of "Bearing with the Displeasing Manifestations of Others," as Gurdjieff defined it. That means taking on the suffering of accepting and respecting those you find disagreeable or even repugnant. It doesn't mean 'liking' them or 'disliking' them. It doesn't mean hanging out with them or embracing them. It means transcending all of that. It is more about using your response to their displeasing manifestations to wake up and transform the energy and to treat them with respect.

If possible, give your time and effort to serve in hospices, in soup kitchens, in animal shelters, in humanitarian aid. Serve your family members and neighbours holding the thought you are only serving God.

Selfless Service is very difficult to achieve and maintain and equally one of the highest forms of devotion and prayer. For a person with Love as a Chief Feature it will come naturally.

PRAYER

Prayer is deeply personal. Prayer is your communication with The One Divine Source as you presently know and understand the ideal. Prayer that is shared also has a profound multiplying effect because faith can 'move mountains.'

Keep it simple by remembering that to PRAY means **Praise, Repent, Ask, Yield.**

Prayer is Self-Remembering. Remembering the real and not the false self.

The most vital aspect of prayer is **Praise.** Experience and give gratitude for the chance that has been given you. Give praise for all and everything that is. Send out Love to the Source of Love. Give out infinite eternal praise to the Eternal often and eternally. Give thanks for the hard lessons and tribulations of life as well as all the joys.

Repent of what you have said and done in the course of your life-time that has hurt others, repent of your many flaws and shortcomings, repent of your ignorance. To repent is to experience the very high vibrational emotion of deep Remorse of Conscience. Remorse has been explained as a precondition of sincerity in repenting.

Remorse and repenting is Atonement. *Atonement can lead to Attunement* of your vibrational resonance. Anything and everything can be repaired, but not first without remorse and repentance.

Ask for your prayers and praise for God to become better and of higher quality each time you pray. Try to avoid asking anything for yourself, except to be able to Serve without seeking any rewards save doing the Will of God. Ask for guidance to know and understand that Will. Ask to be given the Goodness and ask to be given the strength to make something of your life and benefit from the hard lessons. Avoid asking for personal favors and material things from the Divine One Source. At the same time, some of the most powerful prayers of all you can give out when you are at your worst crisis, you lowest, your deepest, darkest suffering. Ask for help at such times. Under such extreme personal conditions of crisis, the deep sincerity and desperation of your prayers can go to the highest levels. Ask for guidance. Ask for faith, ask for strength to be able to apply that guidance. Pray for help for others, pray for the ill, the hungry, those in pain and bereavement. Pray for peace and the ending of the sick process of mutual destruction known as war. Pray for humanity.

Yield fully to the Infinite Divine Will of God as you able to understand it where you are at. The example is given out by Swami Ramdas. This requires the most profound humility and the death-wish to the ego. To yield is to surrender to God and only to God. To pray to God to be able to fully surrender is a form of very high prayer. It can be a prayer taking the form of a Mantra such as the powerful *Om Sri Ram, Jai Ram, Jai, Jai Ram* and chanting it and knowing it repeatedly and constantly in Japa until it takes on a life force of its own and carries you. Human Number 5 Swami Ramdas give out the secret to this powerful practice of yielding in his book *God Experience*. That is, it is the process of attuning your small vibration to the vibration of the Universe at the highest levels. It is the one drop of water returning the ocean.

Where does Prayer go? It is Truth that every prayer is heard and there are no exceptions. Every prayer goes inwardly through your pituitary gland, through your pineal through to the Guide to the Conscience. It is a powerful and ingeniously conceived system. As the Conscience is God, when you are praying it is directly to God. Generally, it is best to pray in your own first language and to do so as sincerely and humbly as possible. It is fine to learn some short prayers in another language and say them but you must know the meaning each word and pay full attention to it. For a prayer to gather force, you must know the meaning and pay full attention to what you are saying.

In some instances, prayer may go directly up the Ray of Creation to the Holy Mother the Earth and to the Holy Father the Sun. When Hindus pray to Kali or Laxmi, or when Christians pray to the Virgin Mary, they are praying to the Holy Mother. Any prayer to the Holy Mother the Earth is a very powerful and high prayer as is any prayer to the Holy Father the Sun. In some cases, with those manifesting rare resonance, a prayer may go to the Centre of the Galaxy to the Most Holy Ahura Mazda. The best a human being can do in relation to praying to the Infinite and Eternal God at the level of the Holy Endlessness is to simply send love (AD Probings 1979).

To pray mechanically, to rote recite some empty words without awareness, and conviction is a waste of time. You have to know what you are saying and what you are praying.

Prayer requires no special posture or ritual. You can be praying and remembering God when you are doing everyday householder things like washing the dishes, or digging and weeding in the garden. Nothing stops you from carrying on your prayer when cleaning the toilet or vacuuming the carpets. This is how the Mantra or Zikr operates under the way of the Householder. The Householder lives in ordinary life and does not have to go live in a monastery or an ashram or a temple. The discipline is not outer but inner practice. The **Way of the Householder** is the balanced way of spiritual attainment.

Aim to avoid prayers asking for things for yourself. Particularly material things. Prayers to increase the quality and sincerity of your prayer next time are positive, but asking for some material benefit such as prosperity is obvious not all that positive. Praying for others, for those sick or suffering or praying for peace during times of war and conflict are higher prayers. Praying for guidance and enlightenment and praying to be shown the Will of God are all positively charged. Prayers for help to God at times when you are in deep crisis, in desperation and at your lowest point, can go up to the highest levels of God's Presence.

The notion that you have to pray in a certain language as a dictate of some religion is a nonsense. You pray to God in your own language as you understand the Ideal at the level you are at. You come as you are.

At the same time, know and respect that certain words of prayers such as Mantras in certain languages have attracted and generate powerful vibration by being given out and prayed over so many generations, so respect and benefit from that.

The important ingredients to prayer is to know why your praying and what you are praying. Know and consider each word. Pray for pure motive, pray for guidance, pray for praise, pray to be able to improve your prayer the next time you pray.

A spiritually dead person, a materialist, will believe that praying is nothing but fantasy and wishful thinking, and a waste of time. Such people do not believe and can know nothing of the power of prayer. But it had famously been said that there are no atheists in foxholes or combat trenches in the midst of a firefight on the field of battle in a war. Sometimes sheer desperation can prompt prayer and reignite the Magnetic Centre.

Objective Prayers

There are many sources for objective prayers that you can choose to make your own.

Without any question, the *Lord's Prayer* coming through the Christian religion is one of the purest and most powerful. The Lord's Prayer came down from the ancient Greek through to the Roman Empire and into the Gospels miraculously unchanged as it had come through originally from the Gnostics.

Each line of the *Lord's Prayer* is filled with meaning on several levels of depth, and is to be fully contemplated each time it is said. That is, each time the prayer is said, say it with depth of conviction as if you are saying it for the first time. There are objective sources to gain understanding of the *Lord's Prayer* contained within the references.

"Our Father Which Art in Heaven" - This first part of the prayer identifies a particular form of Father. Where is this Father?

"Thy Kingdom Come, Thy Will Be Done, on Earth as it is in Heaven." - What does this mean to you? How is it that the Supreme God's Will is done somewhere called Heaven but not on Earth?" As many times as you may have repeated the words; yet can you grasp some understanding of the inner meanings of this?

Sources of Objective Prayers

Indeed, the Lord's Prayer of the Christian Gospels is a very potent, ageless **objective prayer**. Another such prayer coming through the Christian line of the Light is the Prayer of St Francis of Assisi. Objective prayers can be found evenly secreted within the outer forms of the major religions like hidden precious gems and pearls. There are powerful objective prayers throughout the Upanishads, the Bhagavad Gita, the Buddhist scriptures, the Torah, the Christian Gospels, and through the Quran.

One of the most profoundly esoteric passages in the Holy Quran is found within the *Mishkat al-Anwar*, The Niche for Lights of Surah 24, 35. Sufi Abu Hamid al-Ghazzali gives a glimpse of the profound truths of the many facets of this Surah (AD The Glimpse 1995).

The Gayan, Vadan, Nirtan of Hazrat Inayat Khan

One of the most supreme and superb sources of objective prayers and profound Wisdom is contained within the *Gayan, Vadad, Nirtan* of Hazrat Inayat Khan. Among those are his prayer *Saum*, his prayer *Salat*, and his prayer *Khatum*.

First, learn to say these prayers from the reading. Then secondly, learn to remember them in your heart. Thirdly, inscribe the prayers in your highest self.

Anyone who has never been introduced to the *Gayan*, will be so blessed and benefited on many levels by obtaining a personal copy and constantly referring to it for inspiration.

There other sources given out at the end of the book for reference to highly objective prayers which give homage to the order of existence.

Your Own Personal Prayer

In addition to Remembrance of Objective Prayers, ask for Prayers from Yourself to Come to and Through You

Further beyond the set of Objective Prayers you have learned and memorized and practice, a prayer from yourself, your own personal prayer you will do well to allow to come through and to write down, preserve and give out.

This brief Ashem Source praise is shared and gifted to you through the writer as an example of one personal prayer.

Ashem Source Prayer

Beloved God, Creator, Sustainer, Source of All
We seek to approach Thee in humility, and in deepest awe
Thou, which are far beyond the reaches of any mind, world or universe
Your depths, beyond all limitation and boundaries
Your Greatness, inconceivable, vast Endlessness

Yet, you are ever present in the Heart, and in every moment of the Now
Your divine breath, the life force of each pulsing atomic particle and of every
*   living cell*
And the Light of Inspiration of every galaxy and dimension
All of existence bows before Thee, the Divine Unity and Cause of all arising

We send to the, Beloved Creator, our devout gratitude, praise and Love
We aspire to be able to begin to serve Thee, without seeking any reward
We are dependent upon Thee, for the very praise that issues from us

Please make more abundant our sincerity, our strength, our humility, our Faith
We ask that our praise for Thee, and our gratitude for Thy blessings
ever multiply in the goodness of Thy Will

That our thanksgiving may rise to infinity
Joining in harmony the chorus of the Universe
In eternal praise, gratitude and adoration of
Thy Magnificence, Thy Glory, Thy Mystery and Thy Perfect Peace
  Amen

FASTING

Fasting is a very important and powerful discipline if done properly at the right times in the effective ways for the best genuine reasons. Fasting may serve multiple aims and purposes so it is important to know why you are doing a fast and to make an intention prior to undertaking it. **The main purpose of fasting is to make the body obedient.**

More people than ever are fasting in the 21st Century and mostly for the health benefits to the body. Fasting to clear the body of toxins, or to improve health is surely effective and valid when carried out under the right conditions, but it should not be mixed, confused or the boundaries blurred around fasting as a discipline for spiritual development and intentional or conscious suffering.

The immediate and compelling benefit of regular and consistent fasting is that of going against the desires of the body which most definitely helps on the path to **making the body obedient**. The body does not like going without and will inevitably push back and play up.

The Muslim fast of Ramadan requires abstinence from food, water, sex or any intake of anything else at all, such as tobacco, for specific hours prior to Sunrise until Sunset for approximately 30 days around the moving annual lunar calendar. The fast is not considered to be accepted by Allah unless the obligatory 5 prayers are completed at set times over the course of each day.

But there is a further layer to the fast of Ramadan which is just as important, and that is fasting from impure thoughts, negative desires and undisciplined sensations. The idea is to fast with all 5 portals of the senses: to fast with the eyes, ears, tongue, and even the feeling of touch of the skin. With the ears and mouth, it is to fast from telling any lies for spreading any gossip. With the eyes, read the Holy Scriptures and look away from anything base, dense or impure.

At the end of Ramadan when the new moon is sighted comes the festival of *Eid-Al-Fitr*. It is a powerful celebration of joy when everyone dresses in their best clothes and goes visiting, similar to the festivities of Christians at Christmas. Importantly, charity to the poor and help for the vulnerable are to be given at this time. The teaching of the Holy Prophet is that always remembering and attending to the needs of fellow human beings is to remember Allah's bounty, which is meant for all to share.

Whatever form of fast you choose to undertake, it important to make the intention prior and carry it out as you have committed to do. It may be going without any form of food and drinking only water for certain days each month, for example. It may, for others, mean forgoing meat or sweet foods for certain days as in Lent.

Once you begin fasting, you will learn a great deal about the tyranny and desires of the body and, through the discipline, you will begin to build up something real and subtle within you through the consistency of the practice.

Voluntary Conscious Suffering

Mr Gurdjieff, among others, gave out the teaching of Voluntary Conscious Suffering. In briefest summary, 99% of the vast suffering in the world is involuntary unconscious suffering which goes toward the vibrational feeding of certain celestial bodies and entities, as has already been revealed.

Voluntary Conscious Suffering is something very different. Conscious suffering is a unique form of suffering that one undertakes deliberatively, intentionally and consciously to help other people, or to help Nature, or to help other life forms, or to, in some way, to help lighten the burden on God.

Fasting can be a way of carrying out a Conscious Suffering. For example, if a person, a relative, a loved one, a patient, or even an adversary or enemy is ill, or is in crisis, or suffering, you can dedicate the fast you are undertaking to them. At times of war, you can dedicate your fast to those grieving families, innocent civilians or soldiers injured or killed in the war. You may dedicate at fast to any range of needs or purposes. It is generally best to do so in secret or without any fanfare.

If you have harmed someone in the past, even if that person is deceased or no longer accessible, for whatever reason, you may dedicate the fast to them and send your love to them in the devout hope of healing and repair. If done with full sincerity and conscious awareness, this is a powerful form of repair that can lead to healing and some reconciliation.

There are other forms and methods of Conscious Suffering but fasting is mentioned here as an introductory, very practical and discipline of inner development that will serve to raise your vibration.

MEDITATION

It is a wonderful thing and a positive force balancing out all the negativity in the modern world that more people have come to know and are starting to practice meditation in the 21st Century.

Meditation is not concentration, but rather a form of de-concentration, but equally a powerful discipline of training the mind and body. There are many different forms of meditation for different aims and purposes. Meditation is exercise in attention and in building attention.

It is best to learn a very simple and direct form of meditation in the early stages and practice it properly and learn to master it before chopping or changing. The Buddhist mindfulness exercises are very powerful and an excellent introduction. Try learn to observe to learn where you are meditating from: your instinctive-moving centre, your emotions or your intellect.

The mindfulness method requires staying completely in the Eternal Here and Now.

There can be no drifting into the past or slipping into the future. The human mind has been most aptly likened to a drunk monkey.

It is simply about following the breath on the inhale and exhale and focusing on nothing but that in the present moment.

The key to mindfulness meditative practice is to observe in an unattached, wholly non-judgmental way. That is, something like the fair witness or the objective observer. Like a scientist who just notices and observes. Don't try to struggle or push away thoughts that inevitably come in. Just notice without judgement and go back to the breath each time with patience and perseverance.

There are many forms and methods of meditation, such as the meditation upon the Star, or meditations through light, music or vibration. Some of the most powerful and effective mediations are through the conscious repetition of the Mantra or the Zikr. The purpose of the application of the Mantra is to quieten the mind and tap down the ego. The ultimate purpose is to create the conditions by which it may eventually become possible to **enter the Silence**.

One of the most powerful practices of all is to simply go as quiet as possible and watch the Sunrise or Sunset. Notice if you can, the pulsing of the Holy Sun, and the instant of peace and silence observed by nature at the point just prior and after Sunrise and Sunset. At such times can be discerned the threshold between the worlds.

The very best guidance that can be given to someone starting out in meditation is to practice briefly with quality over quantity. Trying to get a good meditation going for 2 or 3 minutes and building from there is far superior to trying to do it for 30 minutes and ending up 'wool-gathering' during most of that time. If you visit an ashram somewhere or make a visit to a monastery, you may notice many people sitting cross-legged in the lotus position and playing the part of the meditator. What you do not know is what is going on inside that person, or the vibration they are attuned with. If you lose focus and start 'woolgathering' stop immediately, create a pause, and go back to resume the discipline later.

In many instances, the methods of self-hypnosis can be applied to achieve deeper meditation. The 108 beads of the mala or the beads of the rosary can be an aid or simple tool in the practice of meditation.

Remembering, reciting and repeating the **Divine attributes of God** is another highly powerful form of meditation such as in the

Sikh Guru Gaitri Mantra prayer of Gobinday-Mukunday. For this sacred mantra, the thumb of the right hand touches each finger starting with the index on the right.

Gobinday -	Sustainer	
Mukunday -	Liberator	
Udaaray -	Enlightener, Merciful, Correcting	
Apaaray -	Infinite	
Hariung -	Destroyer	
Kariung -	Creator	
Nirnamay -	Nameless	
Akamay -	Desireless	

A diet of satwic foods, or non-irritant foods, which are light and pure or organically grown are beneficial, although no specific prescriptive dietary requirements are essential. There are certain plants that can enhance the area where you meditate or pray that can be beneficial such as the Bael tree (Shivadruma) or Peepal Sacred Fig tree or Tulsi or a few other trees, herbs or plants. Incense, flowers and candles can help create the type of environment conducive for meditation.

Meditation is most definitely a wonderful practice that can lead to transformational development when combined with other disciplines and methods for raising the vibration. Devotion, consistency and persistence are the keys to all these vibrational technologies and methods. Resources and references will be accessible for those wishing to explore this farther.

Some Simple Exercises to Develop Awareness, Build Will and Raise Vibration

- Learn to fully and really tolerate a characteristic of some person who annoys you immensely -accept them unconditionally, even for the moment
- Become aware of the things that bother or annoy you in other people are the same things you are struggling with yourself – so feel compassion
- Listen to the Silence, the intervals between the words or the notes of the music
- As soon as you notice a prejudice, a judgement, or a fixed attitude coming up, let go of it immediately
- Observe one of your roles and try to unmask the identification
- Avoid wasting energy by excessive exertion, eg – screwing the toothpaste cap too tight, too heavy touch on your keyboard, slamming a door, - sense of measure
- When you are doing a physical task such as cleaning the house, gardening or mowing the lawn, notice your spine and do it from your Moving Centre
- Learn to consider mundane activities such as washing the dishes or cleaning the bathroom as a form of service and an opportunity for Remembrance
- See life as a game in which all players and roles are equal
- Close off activities and seal them by letting go of them. Come back to your Self. Practice with telephone calls. Start the next activity with a clean slate

- Taste the food you are eating with all your attention
- Observe how we continuously consider the world in the Pairs of Opposites, black and white thinking is one-brained and an invitation to discord
- Develop your generosity without witnesses
- Do not be impressed by strong personalities
- Learn to fix and hold your attention – be aware of yourself at every moment in what you think, feel, want and do
- If you see self-pity arising in yourself, annihilate it mercilessly
- Learn to receive and be grateful for each gift. Receiving is a form of giving.
- Accept that nothing is yours
- Know that anytime you are fearful, it is from lack of Faith
- Stop unnecessary chattering. If you notice the other person is not listening, stop talking immediately.
- Learn to listen intensely to another person without judging or thinking of yourself. Just learn listening.
- Send your love to your enemy, with fullest purity and sincerity
- Remember that yes, all 'good' things must come to an end, yet the same principle applies to all 'bad' things as well - all 'things' must come to an end
- Eliminate excessive arranging, controlling and fixing – have faith that the right solution is always within reach – bend your will to the Will of the Source
- In the place where you dwell, always consecrate a sacred space

CHAPTER 27

The Search for the Guru

*"A bridge is a bridge, but while it is
being built it can carry no one."*

IRINA TWEEDIE

The word Guru ॠ is another of the ancient Sanskrit concepts co-opted, adapted and debased by other societies since the industrial age. In current times, you can find the term "guru" used to refer to any "expert" or "authority" in any field of endeavor who gives advice, shares knowledge, or is looked at as a source of guidance. There are many self-styled "gurus" in business, physical fitness, technology and, particularly, self-improvement.

Some of the root sources from the Sanskrit would translate to "to raise, to lift, or to lead." In the ancient Hindu Faith of Wisdom, the term holds unique significance as it has always referred to a spiritual teacher, a mentor, and a guide who 'enlightens' others. That is, the Guru is known as a revered, wise person who has undergone self-transformation and awakening themselves and who is, through compassion, helping other fellow human beings along on their journey.

The only Guru is the only Real as distinguished from the false, the fake, and the Unreal. The Guru is the Authentic. The Guru is Genuine. The exceptionally rare Teacher who has inwardly reached vibrational, frequency and resonance transformation. The very exceptional being who has attained Personhood, not from study or scholarship, but from direct inner experience, practice, transformation and wisdom.

There are some unique functions and roles that only the external Guru can fulfil.

- The Guru alone has the power to speak about or give expression to the realized Truth with purest clarity and without any distortion.
- A Guru alone is capable of describing the many facets of the Truth that lead the disciple to the ultimate truth of everything.
- The Guru not only communicates the Truth to the disciple but also gives the power to assimilate it and become one with it.
- A Guru alone knows to sing the beauty and glory of the higher knowledge as the Guru is in possession of it.
- The Guru alone can proclaim the Truth, as it is known to the Guru, in a way and in a time and place that the pupil can assess and make practical use of.
- A Guru encompasses or holds the disciple within, helps him unite with pure consciousness. It is then that the Guru and the disciple live in one consciousness.
- The not only embodies the truth to be realized but also has the power to swallow and empty the weakness and ignorance of the disciple and refill with the abundant immensity of light, truth and wisdom.

The Guru alone can transfer Divine energy directly known as **Darshan** in the Hindu faith and **Baraka** in Sufi mysticism, which is a spiritual force or energy that flows from the Murshid (Master) through to the Murid (pupil).

Darshan can be understood on one level as the blessing Grace from the Guru upon the disciples and pupils. In the Yogic teaching of Kundalini and Tantric forms, refers to the transmission of energy or awakening direct from Guru to disciple. A disciple is simply one who practices a discipline. The dormant spiritual energy, which is Kundalini, exists in the base of spine and lower chakras. Once awakened, the Kundalini can rise like a snake through each of the lower, and up through to the higher chakras.

The mere glance or the touch of a rare Human Number 4 or Human Number 5, one who is living and manifesting at very high vibrational resonance, can have profound and long-lasting effects on the pupil. It is essential to fully understand, however, that it will not be done by the Teacher until and unless the pupil has fully prepared their own inner vibration for it, is open to and ready to receive it.

Just being within physical proximity of a highly evolved Holy Being is a profound blessing in itself, as the positive force fields around such a Saint can have transformative effects. The Guru can also transmit thoughts, messages and blessings over large expanses of distance and time if and when necessary. Even the physical death of the Guru does not change that relationship, and often the vibrational force of the Teacher only increases after the planetary body is discarded.

To be able to search for, find and be accepted as a pupil by a genuine Perfected Resonance Being is very rare and a far more 'fortunate' than treasure, lottery prize or achievement or anything else in ordinary material temporal life. It is Grace, it is Blessing. Sometimes it is necessary to search for the Guru though more than one lifetime. But knock and the door will open. Seek and you will eventually find. For as Rumi observed: "What you are seeking is seeking you."

Along the way, you might not find the Guru in a lifetime, but you can find Teachers along the way who can help you at every step. In the early years, the Guru might be found in your parents, or other family member, then through childhood, often through an inspirational teacher or mentor during the formal education years.

Think for a moment who has had the most inspirational, lasting positive impacts on you over the course of your lifetime up the present. That person or those persons are one form of your Guru.

THE RISKS AND PITFALLS IN THE SEARCH FOR FINDING THE GURU

There are many fakes, frauds, pretenders, and a surfeit of charismatic self-deluded cult leaders. It is at least a 100,000:1 ratio. That does not mean that sincere and genuine teachers cannot help you along on your journey to the Truth, but only that you must never place your full trust or faith in them.

How do you find the Guru? Do you look for long hair and beard, flowing orange, or white robes, an air of 'holiness' and 'wisdom'? Do you look for their ability to perform seemingly supernatural feats such as telepathy, healing or other 'powers?'

Do you find them where many throng to gather and pay their homage? Can you find them through internet searches or on television, radio or media?

Can you find them hidden in your own country or even your own backyard, or do you have to travel far overseas, far afield, and climb high mountains to seek them out in caves?

There are all too many numerous examples where charismatic, narcissistic and seemingly 'powerful' personalities have formed cults and followings around them, purporting to be this, that or the other. Some are outright frauds exploiting the vulnerable, and others are somewhat sincere but self-deluded false prophets.

Entire sub-religions have been founded and perpetuated by frauds purporting to be prophets. And there are always hordes of the gullible, awaiting to be hoodwinked and

'harvested.'

The simple reason is that human beings are ever so suggestible and so willing to be led by some 'higher authority.' History demonstrates conclusively that human beings are so easily hypnotized, deluded, and drawn to submit to 'strong men" who are authoritarian leaders both in the political and religious spheres.

"They shall be known by their Works, and not by their Words."

The Biblical wisdom of Gospel Matthew 7:15-20 is every bit as true in the present as it was in the ancient past. In every generation there have always been ravenous wolves outwardly pretending to be gentle sheep, and always gathering flocks of followers.

Most definitely you can know the one purporting to guide or lead others toward the light and out of the cave of the darkness of human ignorance by what they do and show and practice, and not by all they say. Otherwise it remains a matter of blind leading blind. The other old saying: "In the land of the blind, the one-eyed man is king," equally contains an element of truth to it.

Cult leaders strive to make their followers dependent and weak and unable to think for themselves. Cult leaders want their followers to adore them and even worship them, and to loyally defend them, regardless of what they have done. Cult leaders typically want their followers to isolate themselves from their families, their friends and from the outside, ordinary world.

Genuine Teachers are the opposite of all of that. Those who have undergone transformation have usually worked toward the singular goal of serving God for many more than one lifetime. They truly are selfless, and have the best interests and wellbeing and spiritual development of their pupils at heart as they are guided inwardly from far higher guidance.

Such exceedingly rare beings are living in ordinary life and operating in and on the Earth, and still dwell within planetary bodies, but they are not of this world. They have undergone transformation and the ego and identity they once were has died. They have literally been born again.

They have been called the Adepts, Saints, Prophets, Perfected Masters and known by many names and forms or many over times and through generations. They few have always been present when the Spirit of Guidance comes through them.

For purposes here, for the 21st Century, they might be referred to as *Resonance Beings.* That is, these wonderful rare benefactors of humanity have a raised vibrational emanation reaching the frequencies of the Divine.

Resonance Beings are exceedingly rare and not easy to find nor to understand for those not yet ascended. They may seem to think in very unusual ways and act in mysterious ways. Resonance Beings disdain material things and remain non-attached to everything. Resonance Beings eschew publicity and avoid the limelight. They may have a significant following in many countries as did Master Aivanov, or they teach only to small groups of devoted pupils and disciples.

If you are fortunate enough to find a Resonance Being who will accept you as a pupil you were meant to do so. Your luck and your providence is far beyond that of any 'lottery' winner.

The rare genuine authentic will practice and live full sincere humility. They pretend nothing. They often speak little. They say what them mean and mean what they say. They often have the most wonderful wry sense of humour and cause everyone around to laugh at the absurdities of life.

The authentic rare Resonate Being radiates Love. Radiates Love for all without distinction or comparison.

They may berate the ego of the pupil at times and give them a good 'growling,' they will always expose and challenge the fixed attitudes of the pupil, they may appear at times detached and distant, at other times warm and compassionate. They may appear sometimes as wise and old, and at other times seem and appear spontaneous as a newborn baby.

TEACHERS WHO CAN POTENTIALLY HELP YOU ALONG BUT HAVE NOT YET THEMSELVES ASCENDED

A fully realized and wise Resonance Man, a Human Number 5 once made the sage recommendation, "You can learn from the ducks." (AD 1981 Quest I).

What this points to is the fact that in the course of life, if you are constantly open to learning, everything, every person, every experience, every event, and every moment can be your teacher. As you develop discernment, you will be able to see and understand things in very different ways than you did in the past. This is an indication that the *Spirit of Guidance*, or the *Voice That Constantly Comes From Within* is connecting with you and working within and through you.

With such a positive and open attitude, it is fully true that the so-called lower animals such as the ducks, or the geese, or the fauna and flora can be our great teachers. And this reflects the wisdom of Hazrat Inayat Khan that the only book is the Book of Nature.

You can most definitely learn from books. Books and reading can give you a roadmap, help you understand your present location and global position, and inspire you. You can use the books as a form of teacher up to a certain point, but you must avoid becoming a 'book yogi.' It is the effort and the practice that counts and is vital on the path of spiritual development and voluntary evolution.

WHEN A BRIDGE IS NOT YET A BRIDGE

The profound truth of the quote from Sufi Master Irina Tweedie that the bridge can carry no one while it is being built, refers to the Teacher as well as the pupil. The bridge can help the pupil cross over to the Divine, but not until it is built.

This opens the lens on a further category of guru, who is the unrealized, uncompleted spiritual teacher. The imperfect master. This form of teacher might potentially be helpful to you on your journey, but caveat emptor as they are a bridge under construction.

This form of teacher can have genuine knowledge and possibly mostly pure motive and good intent, and even some unusual gifts and capabilities, but they still have feet of clay and are not perfected nor yet balanced.

To give a few short specific examples of teachers who came from India to the western countries in the late 20th Century and attracted large numbers of followers. This objective assessment is not intended to offend as some of these leaders did, without doubt, inspire and provide help to followers along their journey. But they also fell short of the mark.

Muktananda was born in 1908 near Mangalore to a wealthy family and named Krishna Rai by his family. At the age of 15 he first came into the presence of **Bhagawan Nityananda**, who was no doubt a pure, genuine and advanced *Resonate Being*, possibly a Human 5. In his early years Krishna Rai was initiated in the Saraswati line of ascetics and underwent training as a Hindu sannyasin. But by his own account his journey began in 1947 when he again met Nityananda to receive the darshan of the Master and to undergo the shaktipat initiation. *Shaktipat* is the direct spiritual energy transferred from an Avadhuta to a pupil which has the effect to open up the chakras and ascend up the spine. Shaktipat is very real and experiential witnesses have reported sensations like electricity or fire travelling up the spine, leading to a sense of ecstasy and bliss. From that point of initiation, he lived and meditated in an ascetic lifestyle and received the sublime name of Muktananda, or the Liberated. It was after this period when in 1956 Muktananda was given responsibility of leader for an ashram at Ganeshpuri. His fame and reputation spread.

From 1971 he began a series of world tours, where he demonstrated his method of direct transfer of Shaktipat through touching attendees with his fingers or through the tip of a peacock feather. For many it was a powerful personal experience. He then established his own line of teaching which he called Siddha and a foundation to spread and operate it. He arrived in North America at a time when generations were thirsty for knowledge, open to Eastern mysticism, and during the Human Potential movement. He and his core group of followers rapidly established Siddha canters across the United States. Wealth and fame came soon and in vast material abundance. When crowds witnessed Muktananda step from a black limousine to a waiting private jet, it was evident that the diminutive, orange-robed Indian was an American-style "success." Muktananda attracted a growing following including rock stars, political figures and even a former astronaut.

But Muktananda had a hidden side, a dark side, and a secret life. Investigative journalist William Rodarmor was justly credited with interviewing many former followers with direct experience at the time to reveal all of that. Muktananda preached chastity and *Bramacharya* practice but was, at the same time, sexually exploiting young women, including it was alleged, underage girls in his orbit. The testimony of victims and witnesses was conclusive, although it was denied by officials of the Siddha organization for years.

Muktananda died in 1982 at the age of 74. He apparently never responded to the allegations, nor did he own responsibility, express regret or attempt to make any repair for the suffering he caused his victims in the betrayal of trust.

So what is the legacy of such a man? On one side of the ledger, Muktananda helped introduce many seekers to Hindu wisdom and to the practice of meditation. On the other side of the ledger, he was unbalanced, and deeply flawed himself and hypocritically failed to practice the lofty ideals he preached to others. Muktananda soared high, but came crashing down because of his failure to purify his motives. Muktananda violated the trust of his pupils and followers, he let down his own genuine Guru Nityananda, but most of all, he let himself down and failed his higher self. In other words, he went against his Conscience.

In India, a number of Nityandanda's pupils strongly disputed Muktananda's claim that the Guru had passed the Siddha leadership on to him when on his deathbed, but that fact only came to light some years after. And by that time, Muktananda's fame and fortune was on the rise.

Years later after his death, a number of his followers still considered Muktananda a great master, and others are grateful for something he gave them on their own path, although they never considered him their guru. Almost all agree that Muktananda was a man of unusual power. The point of difference is what he did with that power and how he used it.

Yogi Bhajan was another guru who came from the Punjab of Pakistan and India to the western world in the late 20th Century and attracted substantial numbers of followers in Europe and North America. Yogi Bhajan, born Harbhajan Singh, brought the Sikh faith teachings of Guru Nanak which had been inspired and influenced by none other than the great Kabir. It was never clear exactly who was the actual Guru of Yogi Bhajan.

Yogi Bhajan brought the tradition of Kundalini Yoga, and fashioned it in his own way to give out to his western followers. Kundalini Yoga is reputed to be the most powerful form and potentially risky unless the practitioner is guided closely by a master. In Kundalini Yoga certain kriyas, postures and disciplines are given out with the 'breath of fire' exercise that causes the *kundali*, the spiritual energy force curled up like a serpent in the lower chakras at the base of spine to rise rapidly. It is very powerful, but also potentially dangerous, as the force of kundalini, when rising rapidly can lead toward enlightenment, but if unguided and untrained can also easily slam back down into the lower base chakras. Such an effect can be disastrous, as it can easily have the effect of ramping the material sex drive of the adherent to lead them to negative sex, and behaviors that will stop the person dead in their tracks toward spiritual development.

Yogi Bhajan brought his "Happy, Healthy, Holy" foundation knowledge and practices to many people in the western world and introduced them to the objective teachings of the Sikh Faith and the wisdom of Guru Nanak.

He used his yoga methods to rehabilitate drug addicts and his followers carried out good community works and charitable help in areas where his followers resided. Many of his followers reported how his teaching and the yoga practice had helped them improve and transform their lives.

Yogi Bhajan died at the age of 75 in the year 2004 in the State of New Mexico in the United States. In 2019 his former secretary Pamela Saharah Dyson published a book which reported the detail of what she and other women had experienced and witnessed around sexual exploitation and relationships with Harbhajan Singh. The Foundation which Yogi Bhajan founded, then bravely, wisely and prudently had an independent inquiry carried out to get to the truth. That investigation objectively came to the conclusion that, more likely than not, the allegations that Harbhajan Singh had sexually exploited some of his female followers with allegations of possibly raping three of them were true. It was also found that the claims by his followers that he remained celibate were completely false.

So here is another example of a guru who did some good and also did very wrongful things as well. Another unfinished bridge that helped some along the way, but left others damaged.

WHEN A BRIDGE IS ANYTHING BUT A BRIDGE - ONLY A CHASM

Then there was the extremely controversial Chandra Mohand Jain who called himself **Rajneesh**, and who subsequently became "Osho." Rajneesh was cynically referred to as "the honest guru" because he made no pretence of his purity or his honesty. He openly encouraged unrestrained free sex to his followers, which attracted many to him, and he enjoyed making displays of his vast accumulated obscene wealth. At one stage his followers tried to carry out a mass food poisoning against a local community his cult was in dispute with. Rajneesh was not even a partially completed bridge but rather an example of a negative cult leader, and a menace demeaning the name guru. In such cases, it is far better to be without any external guru at all than to follow or be connected to anything such as that.

Remember: What is good is what wakes you up, what is bad is what puts you farther asleep and unconscious (AD). There are numerous other examples of leaders in every faith and religion, and hypocrites in every institution who pretend to be one thing, and, in reality are something completely different. Although imperfect, some can help you along, and a few can harm you. Never give your full faith or trust to anyone or anything until you have objectively and thoroughly put it through yourself and assessed the evidence of their authenticity and **purity of motive.**

SEX ENERGY AS THE FUEL FOR SPIRITUAL DEVELOPMENT

The real, the genuine is difficult to find, but it nevertheless exists and is like rarest treasure.

Sex energy is a refined force which is produced in overabundance as it the drive of biological reproduction. It's important not to confuse the sex act with sex energy which is what the material-minded are apt (aped?) to do.

The basic drives of the human animal material body are for **oxygen from air, thirst for water, hunger for food, and the instinctive drive to reproduce.**

Sex energy is essential and necessary for biological creatures such as mammals to reproduce. Nature installed the sex energy drive program to provide for reproduction and survival of the species.

Apart from the instinctive drives for air, water and food, it is supremely powerful.

But following the natural laws, the sex energy is also a double-edged blade.

Sex energy can be likened to rocket fuel which crudely but effectively boosts satellites to escape velocity beyond the gravity of the Earth.

Rocket fuel is equally a volatile and potentially extremely dangerous chemical mix, but it can also power human bodies to visit other celestial bodies such as the Moon or Planets.

In the future, anti-gravitational technologies may deliver a different energy and means to provide the lift for space-going three-dimensional vehicles, but crude, volatile rocket fuel was what humans started out with. The same principle applies to Kundalini energy.

The **Sushumna** in the ordinary person is closed in lower root chakra of the **Muladhara** around the base of the spine. Once Yoga practice, devotional discipline or spiritual practice begins and is in process, the Sushumna starts to open as the lotus pedal.

Vivekananda reveals that the power of Kundali can be roused through love and devotion to God, through the mercy of perfected Sages or Resonance Beings, or through the analytic will of Jnana Yoga. The arising of the Kundali is fuelled by fine sex energy and, when channelled through purity, will lead to attainment of Divine Realization.

Sex energy is the rocket fuel propellant that can cause your rise or fall, depending entirely upon how awake you are and how you choose to use it. Tantric Yoga is known as the most powerful, direct and rapid path to enlightenment, but it can only be properly and safely applied by a conscious living master who can guide and help the pupil along every step, and only when the pupil who is prepared and ready to receive the teaching.

DANGERS OF ENTRAPMENT IN NEGATIVE SEX

Negative sex is, of course, one of the 12 chief features and a proportion of the population will have that particular feature or be prone to it at any one time. Lust is closely linked and more negative dense still. Again, the only positive of the 12 chief features is Love and that is also the rarest.

Strangely enough, an abundance of fine sex energy can be a decided advantage in realizing spiritual attainment, if it is properly controlled and channelled. For example, people that attain in ordinary achievements in life such as athletics or accumulating large wealth will usually have a high level of sex energy. They are choosing to use that sex energy to get wealth and/or power for themselves. Typically they may have alternating chief features of Greed, Sex and Power. You could accurately say they are 'driven.'

People without high levels of sex energy may have chief features of Dependence, of Laziness or Ineffectualness. It may be more of a challenge for them to find the energy to work on themselves spiritually. They will need to overcome and change those chief features to further their progression.

The landscape is littered by innumerable examples of those destroyed by negative sex. The 'celibate' Roman Catholic priest paedophile arrested after a lifetime of abusing innocent children and destroying lives. The throngs of people who become the slaves of addiction to pornography from the flood of internet images selling attachment to desire and flesh. It all only promotes pandering to the Law of 7 and to the tyranny of the prison of the biological body. The disgraced Christian Televangelist caught out in various sex scandals and shown to be an abject hypocrite. Every religion and institution harbors them, yet such people purport to be 'gurus' in their own ways.

The outer forms of the Christian Church infected many generations with their indoctrination of suppression of sex. Their objectively nonsensical falsity of "original sin" led to their portrayal of human biology, reproduction and sex as 'dirty' and 'sinful.'

It was the simple paradox of human psychology for people to inevitable **become most attracted to that which is "forbidden fruit."**

The Christian dogmas and negative indoctrination around sex directly led to untold damage to entire generations and contributed to the perversions the pious clerics so vehemently railed against.

It is equally true that the people who are spiritually dead, one half of the population, can objectively do anything they like and have any number of sex partners and indulge and wallow in their various sensual pleasures in whatever forms to their content. This is the last stop on their journey and there it ends, so they can enjoy whatever they choose.

But for the other half of the population, those with a Magnetic Centre or a spiritual seed or higher, such indulgences will only put them further to sleep and damage their possibility of fulfilling their high purpose and their potential.

"The Seventh Vase Will Never Be Filled." (AD - NEGATIVE ATTITUDES 1986)

Here is a very powerful truth given out in the wisdom of a Human Number 5, an evolved rare Resonance Being. No matter how much sex you have, how many sex partners you have it with, how much or how many material possessions you gather, no matter how much 'success' you have, it will never be nearly enough to fulfil your desires.

You may fill to the brim the first, the second, the third, the fourth, the fifth and the sixth vases with all your desires. **But you will never, ever be able to fill the 7th Vase.** *Your desires will keep coming and you will always remain a slave to them. A slave to the tyranny of the body and stuck in the recurrent Law of 7.*

This is the essence of the nature of suffering. It is the attachment to desires. Only the salvation of non-attachment to desire will lead to the cessation of all the suffering.

Negative sex is a powerful attractant and has been the ruin of many. It was attachment and obsession with sex that led to the failure of the Jinn, the prior Experiment of Consciousness on the Earth. It is a powerful obstacle for human primates as well but the greater risk for this particular species is far more from aggression, anger and violence caused by fear, selfishness and greed.

But for those who can master and channel the fine sex energy, it is pure rocket fuel to lift them into the Divine Cosmos and through all the barriers to Voluntary Evolution.

BRAHMACHARYA

Vivekananda linked morality with control of the mind, seeing truth, purity and unselfishness as traits which strengthened it. He advised his pupils to be holy, unselfish and to have *shraddhā* (faith).

Vivekananda also supported *Brahmacharya,* believing it the source of his physical and mental stamina and his presence. No doubt it most definitely was.

Brahmacharya is most certainly a discipline that can contribute to more rapid spiritual development and self-perfection but it is not easy to practice properly. True Brahmacharya is not just being celibate, but totally and completely avoiding all thoughts of not just lust or sex, but any and all impure thoughts such as anger or vengeance, or any of the many other negativities.

Brahmacharya is initially like walking on a tightrope but can lead to rapid development when practiced sincerely, genuinely and properly. This can be true even for short periods of time over

But, on the other side of the same coin, mere suppression of the instinctive sex drive can have detrimental and quite negative effects. It is only for monks or adepts or those under the guidance of a genuine Guru during the reproductive years of young adulthood. If Brahmacharya is to be practiced at all it must be done fully and properly or not at all.

THE BALANCED PATH OF THE HOUSEHOLDER

It is better for most young adults to take a balanced and very practical approach and to marry or have a life partner and live an ordinary life as a **Householder**. Working on self to become a good husband or wife and a good parent is every bit as potentially productive in gaining balance and spiritual development as living isolated in a monastery or a cave.

Through the life of the Householder, ordinary sex will be enjoyed as a part of the expression of a pairing marriage of Love. At the same time, in a loving home children can be brought up in a balanced way with emphasis on their own spiritual development. Holding the aim to be a good householder will most certainly force you to directly confront your selfishness and all the other negativities.

In latter stages of life, the practice of Brahmacharya or the path of the Sannyasin may open up, once the householder stage has been completed.

THE INNER GURU

That Teacher within is the *Ultimate and One Guru*. The Teacher Within is none other than The **Conscience** (The Active Force of the Sun) and your Guide to the Conscience within. The Conscience gives you the possibility to raise up from the animal to become a **Knowing Part of God**.

The **Conscience**, on the highest level of vibration in the **Solar System**, is so inconceivably great and powerful that an intermediary is required between it and a puny human being, and that is your **Guide to the Conscience**. All the same, the Conscience is God and the miraculous fact is that every human being alive has the Conscience within. Raising the Conscience is raising "Atlantis."

The Teacher within **is your own Higher Self.**

If you can tap into your subconscious mind, if you can learn to make contact and ask questions of the Guide to your Conscience, you have tapped into Being at a vastly higher vibrational frequency. If you can reach the level to learn communication with the Holy Mother the Earth, you have at your access, the key to what has been variously called the "Akashic Records," a very highest source of direct higher knowledge and objective reason.

Just to reconnect one further piece in the puzzle, the name for the **Star Antares**, the seat of **Holy Ahura Mazda at the centre of the Galaxy** was long believed to have derived from the Greek observation of comparing the Star to the planet Mars, both of red hue. Thus, Antares, was believed to have been called the 'rival' of Mars as a reference for physical identification in the celestial sky.

However, the far older Sanskrit conception of "Conscience" is Antaratma-mati अन्तरात्मा-मति.The compound is of two elements: **Antara** which means Inner and Atma which refers to the soul or self. Therefore, the **Antaratma** points to the inner **Self of the Innermost Essence**. **Mati** points toward something like the 'higher mind.' It points to something far beyond the realm of thinking, understanding or intellect.

The **Antaratma-Mati** points to the meaning of **Conscience as the Inner Force**, the spiritual organ or capacity within Self that guides Objective Ethics, the internal guidance system distinguishing what is objectively right from wrong, balanced from unbalanced, positive polarity or negative polarity.

What this confirms is that there is existing a ground of **Objective Ethics**, and that higher morality is never cast into a void of chaotic relativity of subjective values as modern human dogma presupposes. That ground of Objective Guidance is none other than the **Active Force of the Sun – The Conscience.** Going with the flow of that natural internal guidance system is what leads to life and consciousness, and going against it is what leads to unconsciousness and death.

ONLY DEATH OF THE EGO CLEARS THE WAY FOR THE REAL TO EMERGE FROM THE UNREAL

Of Mr Gurdjieff's many pupils, it was musician Thomas De Hartman who had the Chief Feature of Love (AD 1981). De Hartman **collaborated** closely with Gurdjieff to compose the ancient **Objective Music** which is so exceptionally compelling and unique. Gurdjieff remembered by heart the ancient chords from his own exposure in an esoteric school in Central Asia and worked with De Hartman to put them to piano. The unusual devotional music from ancient sources produces unusual vibrational effects on its listeners.

Thomas DeHartman and his wife Olga had been long term senior pupils, travelled extensively together through thick and thin, and loved Mr Gurdjieff as their Guru. They knew from direct experience he was an extraordinary man but also they understood well his weaknesses, his faults and his limitations at that point in his own development.

As a person reaches what can be called 'critical mass' in their transformation, they may begin to display certain qualities and 'powers' which may well seem to be 'supernatural' and very unusual. If they identify with those powers or misuse them, then their progress will abruptly halt at that point. In order to develop further, they must constantly purify themselves through devotion to God and through humility.

Their internal struggle between 'good' and 'evil' between positive and negative polarities reaches critical point. At this stage, they Adept will receive the calling from within that the time is ripe to destroy the ego. Destruction of the ego is a tremendous thing. It is a very real death before dying of the body.

The ego may be destroyed systematically and gradually through constant practice of Mantra as Swami Ramdas and Mother Krishnabai did, or through more rapid and extreme means, such as severe fasting, or other austerities and processes.

When Mr Gurdjieff had reached the stage of his own development of unbalanced Human Number 4, he was still incomplete, an unfinished bridge. He may possibly have lost contact because of war and turbulence of the times with his own Guru somewhere in Central Asia. He was very powerful, but also not yet balanced or completed in his transformation.

When Gurdjieff made an inappropriate gesture toward Olga, the DeHartman's took it as a message that they were meant to leave the Fourth Way school that they had been part of in France and continue their spiritual journey on their own. The DeHartmans left the Prieure and travelled overseas, influencing artists and architects and continuing to practice the teachings that Gurdjieff had given them.

It took enormous suffering and tragedy in his own life for Mr Gurdjieff to destroy his ego, but, **to the benefit of all humanity**, that is what he eventually did. His transformation was then complete. It is also possible that his 'disappearance' for a period in the years around WWII was because he had needed to return for direct contact with his own Guru.

When a Human Number 4 reaches a certain point in development, they require the direct physical contact with a Human Number 5 for knowledge and direct transfer of *Baraka* for the guidance to allow their further stage of transformation. They are told from within what they must do. This is clearly explained in a source in the references at the end of this book.

THE PROBLEM OF SUCCESSION

When a genuine Resonance Being dies, an enormous vibrational gap is left on Earth.

The evolved Resonant Being may have died from natural physical causes of the body, or may have gone into Samadhi without seed. Entering the Eternal Bliss of the Silence, entering the Samadhi without seed, the Adept will not return. If they enter, however, the Samadhi with seed, their work is unfinished and they will return to life in their planetary body.

The problems around succession of a living Saint or Resonance Being has long been a perplexing challenge for the pupils and followers. **The most important thing to always remember that is that it is never the Teacher who is important but the Teaching** (AD Probings 1979).

At the same time, the death of the Guru leaves a gap in many profound ways. Some Gurus have had the benefit of pupils who were able to rapidly progress to transformation in their lifetimes and they could confer responsibilities of succession to them.

Others do not appoint or anoint or even identify successors, for various objective reasons, not the least of which no pupil as yet reached the stage of development rendering them fit for succession.

When Gurdjieff died in Paris in 1949, he left an extraordinary legacy of Teaching but had designated no successor. Various members of his inner circle of senior longstanding pupils took up the mantle on their own accord to varying degrees of success. The problem was that not a single one of them had destroyed their ego nor attained balance. There was an underlying arrogance that developed in the way the teaching was passed on, the missing vital ingredient was Love (AD). The understanding and accurate transmission of the mission of Gurdjieff was left to someone born later and who had never physically met him.

The claim that each of them made, directly or implied, was that their direct contact and relationship with the Master qualified them to transmit his teachings. To a certain extent there is an element of truth in such a claim, and some of them certainly did help with the accurate and vital transmission of Gurdjieff's teachings. The farther away in time and distance from a living master, the greater the chances that there will inaccuracy, changes, embellishments or distortions of the Teaching. These may be not intentional at all, but simply the effects of the rust that never sleeps – the Law of 7.

Like every Master, Gurdjieff was able to help his pupils, those existing at the time, and future pupils yet unborn, from far beyond the grave.

The wise and loving Master Guru provides a conscious succession plan for his pupils that allows for the **Group itself to become the Teacher** following the death of his planetary body and transcendence.

As already made reference, great Christian Saints such as St Gregory, St Dominic, St Francis and others carried out exceptional work, but the problems emerged when succession failed as power-possessed beings vied for control and established institutions within orders and built organizations. Human nature is what it is and there is no point in denying it as petty jealousies, rivalries, cavilling and power struggles can afflict spiritual aspirants as easily as ordinary people.

The Guru directly helps the pupils and extends all that benefit much farther afield through books, and through subsequent generations who are inspired by the Teaching.

If you are exceptionally fortunate enough to come into the sphere of a rare, genuine Resonance Being as your Teacher, you are truly blessed by Grace. Do not use worldly criteria to try to understand or explain the Teacher. Have no preconceived notions. Outwardly, at first glance, the Resonance Being looks very ordinary and not much different from yourself. How much you will know the Teacher will depend upon your own vibrational state and level of evolutionary development. When you are able to formulate questions about transformative methods or of deep inquiry into your inner nature, the Teacher will respond to your unique circumstances and needs effectively. In order to receive you must ask.

Serve the Teacher selflessly. The Teacher is a manifestation of the divine energy and part of your own aspiring higher being. One of the best ways you can serve the Teacher is to accept the help and guidance given to sincerely and tirelessly work on yourself. Most advanced Pupils know how the presence alone of the Teacher is helping them every moment, calming the mind. Give to the Teacher homage, respect, gratitude. Love and Respect are the twin most high vibrational virtues necessary. Love without Respect may impede your own spiritual evolution. Respect without Love may prevent you from becoming close enough to the Teacher to receive the Darshan or the Light of Wisdom for the transubstantiation of your own being.

The Sufi Masters such as Hazrat Inayat Khan are continuing to inspire and guide initiates today and in each generation through their ageless wisdom.

Yet, every one of the Resonate Beings that help along humanity always guide us to seek and contact the inner Guru, the ultimate source of all knowledge and wisdom.

CHAPTER 28

Preparing for Death - Crossing Over the Transition Horizon

"All that lives is spirit, and all that dies is matter."

HAZRAT INAYAT KHAN

PREPARATION FOR DEATH
IS THE PURPOSE OF A LIFETIME

The course of any lifetime in a human primate body is for the purpose of dying. Everyone is either dying to live or living to die. How you live will determine how you die, and how you die will determine how you live.

Cut a small branch from a living tree and fashion a walking stick. Life and Death are simply opposite ends of the same stick. When one end of the branch was part of the tree, it was still living, once it is cut and dried, it is what can be described as dead, but it has two ends, and one end was once attached to the living tree.

You may observe that there are several kinds of people in their thinking and beliefs about the inevitable reality of death.

The Hyclics, or the Living Dead, which compose approximately half the population of human beings, believe that after death there is nothing. For the Hyclic, their belief is that death of the body is the end of everything. The body dies, decays and that's the end of it. Their philosophy is to enjoy as much as possible while the body is alive, as there are no consequences for what they do or what they don't do.

The second group is composed of people who would prefer to avoid thinking about death because of fear. That is, they believe there is something possible after death of the body but are uncertain and fearful about it. Fear of death is caused entirely by ignorance. Fear itself is one of the Chief Features and extremely common. Fear and Faith are incompatible. Fear is caused by lack of Faith. Faith or Conviction eliminates fear.

The third group is so attached, diverted, obsessed and engrossed in sense gratifications, they cannot bear to think about death. The death of a loved one or close friend may temporarily give them cause for pause, but generally, they want to put death out of their mind and pursue the many pleasures and diversions in various forms.

Death, just as Life, is omnipresent and all-pervading. Death means change.

Everything that is material and of matter withers away and dies.

Change is inevitable just as Death is inevitable. The human body changes constantly, originating as a zygote, then manifesting as a foetus, then an infant, then a child, then as an adolescent, then as an adult, then as senescence in old age. The planetary body is made up of impermanent material elements, but the Voyager is eternal.

The dense material world runs under the control of Time, or what Gurdjieff referred to as "The Merciless Heropass" or what the

Hindus refer to as Kāla. This is the cause of the deterioration of all that is material. *The Bhagavad Gita*, says that just as a person puts on new clothing, the Voyager (the Magnetic Centre or Soul) transmigrates to new material bodies, giving up the old and useless ones.

Mr Gurdjieff observed at the end of *All and Everything*, that perhaps the one best chance humankind has is for each person to realize, whenever looking at another person, that each had to die. The consciousness of mortality of the body is the great leveler, and can lead to awakening. Everything and everyone has to die. Equally, it is true that everyone has to live.

Stars and planets and galaxies have a nearly incomprehensibly far longer lifespan than a single human being, or even the entire species. But at the end of their allotment of time, even stars will exhaust their supply of fuel and are subject to decay and death. The observations of the birth and death of stars and the stages they can go through are among objectively the greatest things that human beings have been able to witness and grasp some meaning of.

Where there is an experiment of consciousness in a three-brained lifeform such as human beings, there is a reasonably long but distinctly limited time for that experiment to play out and fulfil its purpose or to fail and deteriorate. The Holy Father the Sun and the Holy Mother the Earth are objective in their celestial dance of love and will continue to give birth to vehicles of consciousness until the objective is attained for as long as they are capable. At the end of that cosmic life cycle, the Sun will expand to a red giant and subsume the inner planets and the Solar System will undergo transformation.

It is not all the play of Nature? Is it not the Lila of God?

"Death comes as a Lover. My breath Thou giveth and taketh away."

WHAT IS THE NATURE OF DEATH?

Celebrate Death as You Celebrate Birth as You Celebrate Life

Death is vibration just as life is. All is vibration. Always remember this one Truth. **All is vibration**. One level of vibration pours out and puts into motion rotation and circulation. It is the rotation of the planets and the circulation of the blood which gives rise to one level of vibration. The cause as well as the effect of all that exists is vibration.

What is called "life" and "death" can be recognized as a form of existence within certain degrees of vibrations. In ordinary language, when someone says, "this flower has died," what is dead is a change if vibrations. The leaf that has been removed from the tree and dried out is not the same as the freshly picked green one. The leaf no longer has the vibration that you might describe as "living?" It is called a 'dead' leaf. But, all the same, it hasn't lost its vibrations entirely. If the leaf was entirely dead, then herbal mixtures derived from it would have no effect as a form of medicine, would it? So some form of different vibrational quality remains for a period of time.

And so it is with the dead body of an animal or a man. We may say that life has gone out of it, but it is only the life which we recognize as life that has gone out of it, for we recognize as life only a certain pitch of vibration; anything beyond it or below it we do not recognize as living. Yet it has not died in the sense it is still vibrating. It is still going on, for nothing can exist and not vibrate, and nothing can vibrate and not be living in the real sense of the word.

It is only natural and fully understandable that human beings grieve at the death of family and loved ones. For they are grieving for the living being in the form that they knew them for so many years and in the way they experienced them. It is certainly true enough that the person who has died will never physically come back in the same body or exactly the same outer coating or form as they were in that particular lifetime. But the unique vibrational qualities, the real essence of who they were can go on. That real vibrational energy being is none other than the Traveler of the Voyage.

When we begin to see life from a closer-to-real point of view it will appear that birth and death are only our conceptions of life, that there is no such thing as death and that **all is living**. It only changes from one form to the other, subject to the law of vibrations. The difference in the vibrations of dead and living bodies is a difference of their frequency, intensity and resonance; it is a difference of rhythm.

It is also reality that the different stages of life such as infancy, childhood, youth, and old age and the different tendencies arising naturally out of them, are all phenomenon of vibration. Strength and weakness, the tendencies to action and repose, all come from the different speed of the vibrations. H. I. Khan observed it is no exaggeration to say that hidden behind every illness are wrong vibrations which are its cause. Vibrations are the cause and they are also the effect.

Nothing stays the same in the dense world of matter. And to hold onto any make-believe notion that it doesn't only causes suffering of the mind through a refusal to accept that everything about life is impermanent. No instruments have yet to be conceived or assembled to allow the most subtle measurements of vibration. That means what is moving beyond this dense present level we do not recognize as vibration.

But as there is no other word this 'vibration' and it's presently the only one we can use for it; for it is the same life force which sets everything in motion on the physical plane, and this continues on all other planes of existence, setting them all in motion. It also explains to us that it is vibration, a certain degree of vibration, which brings to the Earth the things of the inner world, the world that is perceived though not seen; and a change of vibrations takes away the things that are seen into the unseen world.

You might say that there is no movement in a dead body, that there is no heat in it, but do people not use fish and flesh of slaughtered animals as food? If these did not possess any life what nutrition or benefit would there be from consuming and digesting their flesh? If they were really dead, if all the properties which is called life was entirely gone from them, they would do harm instead of good, as is the case when they rot or further decompose? Yet this also shows that though we call them dead there is some life left in them, and that this change is only a question of degree in the vibrations.

When a fruit has decayed, when a flower has faded, there has been a change of vibrations. It is wonderful to watch a flower when it is still a bud and to see how it grows every day, how it vibrates differently every moment of the day until it comes to such a culmination that it begins to radiate, reflecting the Sun.

Apart from its colour and form we can see something living in the flower, something sparkling. It can best be seen when the flower is still on the plant. And then, when it has reached its culmination, it begins gradually to fade, and that again is according to the law of vibrations. Yet even when its petals have dropped there is still a form of life left, for even in the dry leaves of the rose there is a fragrance, and from the dried rose leaves an effective medicine can be made.

There is great difference between the eating of fresh vegetables and of preserved vegetables, a difference of vibrations. The former are nearer to our life, and the latter which have gone further from our life have less influence on us. And so it is with everything. When we begin to see life from this point of view it will appear that birth and death are only our conceptions of life, that there is no such thing as death and that **all is living**. It only changes from one form to the other, subject to the law of vibrations. The difference in the vibrations of dead and living bodies is a difference of their speed; it is a difference of rhythm.

THE EXTRAORDINARY GIFTS OF THE TIBETANS

All of humanity is deeply indebted to the Tibetan Adepts for the extraordinary contributions that have been made to the progress and consciousness of the species.

The Tibetans developed the highest form of technological advances that have ever been achieved in the course of history of humanity possibly since the ancient Sumerians. No, the Tibetan thinkers, Lamas, researchers and scribes didn't send human planetary bodies to the Moon, didn't split the atom or develop hydrogen bombs, didn't harness electricity or invent telephones, computers, televisions, or toasters, didn't find out about DNA, or decode the human genome, or explore the physical surface of the Earth, or the oceans, nor categorize and analyze plant and animal life, or send probes to planets of the Solar System.

What the Tibetan people achieved was farther advanced and much more objectively important than any of that. The Tibetans were the pioneers in the exploration of Inner Space and of Consciousness.

Only one of the reasons for their remarkable development and exceptional insights and contributions was physical isolation afforded through their habitat home in the Himalayas. The Tibetan people had long been adept and attuned to spiritual practices and were deeply connected to the Mother Earth and her wisdom even long before the arrival of Buddhism

When the Buddhist Teaching of Compassion eventually reached Tibet in what is believed to be around the 7th Century CE, during the reign of King Songten Gampo, the ignition point was reached.

Over time, Buddhism flourished in the fertile ground of Tibet. Buddhist teachings blended with indigenous beliefs to form a unique hybrid of belief, practice and research that became as distinct and powerful form of the faith.

Jetsun Milarepa was a Living Master Resonance Being who was a legendary yogi, poet and teacher who lived in Tibet circa 1052 to 1135 CE. Milarepa is a very great Tibetan figure so revered as a living example of the transformational power fulfilling human poten-tial. Milarepa lived a worldly life full of tragedy, suffering and strife until his meeting with Tibetan Buddhist Master **Marpa Lotsawa.** As a pupil of Marpa, Milarapa engaged in rigorous practices including asceticism, conscious suffering and labors, forms of advanced Yoga and meditation. It was Milarepa who demonstrated the potential of a human to transform from the animal through to complete libera-tion in a single lifetime.

THE BARDO AND THE BARDO THODOL

The 1927 publication of the translated **Tibetan Book of the Dead**, or the **Bardo Thodol** which had been the lifework of anthropologist W.Y. Evans-Wentz was a pivotal, landmark event for introducing the advanced Tibetan knowledge and practices to the wider consciousness of humanity.

The Tibetans have a saying: "In life you make the mind. But in death the mind makes you."

The term Bardo refers to the **intermediate state between death and rebirth**, for lack of a remotely adequate linguistic description, this 'placeless place' might be referred to as multi, micro and macro-dimensional, beyond matter, or the 'Interdimensions.' After death and final separation from the body, the vibrational core, the essence of the person being passes through transitional chambers or zones of the Bardo. Each Bardo can be understood as providing a vital opportunity for spiritual liberation.

The three major phases of the passage:

1. **The Chikai Bardo – Moment of Death**: Bardo begins at the point of terminus at the moment of death and through the transition entry point where the consciousness fully separates from the body. This is the launch window opening.

   Some symptoms of the first stage: **Earth** melting into molten metal elements such as lead, mercury or liquid iron; **Water** and ice coldness, freezing; Water element evaporating into **Fire** element, hot, intense, still, unbreathable atmosphere; Fire into **Air**: intense sensations

on the edge of explosion, dispersal of self; **Air into Clear
Light**- Aloneness, purest Peace, beyond space or time, sense
of deep ironic knowing, profound wisdom, full recognition
of remembrance.

2. **The Chonyid Bardo of Luminosity**: the second
passage in the sequence wherein is the confrontation
with the **Clear Light of Highest Luminosity**.
Luminous and visionary experiences. The crucial
opportunity for recognition and remembrance.
The unfolding formlessness of the Endlessness, the
moment of encounter with the pure reality and the
opportunity for merger and absorption.

3. **The Sidpa Bardo of Rebirth**: The third reconciling
phase of the passage at the point where the individual
being-consciousness prepares for rebirth in a new
form. Drawn down to the planetary material realm of
the Earth again and seeking, irresistibly, magnetically
attracted toward another rebirth in a new womb.

During the first phase (these words "first" and "phase" are indicative only and cannot come close to describing the indescribable, but provide a kind of practical roadmap for the Traveler).

The sacred text of the **Bardo Thodol** provides for 49 Days of the Reincarnation process through a series of "chambers" and phases. It is essential to grasp the reality that "Time" as it is conceived, experienced or imagined in the material world does not exist. Whether the time for reincarnation is 49 days or each 'day' equaling 10 years for a total of 490 Earth years is irrelevant and meaningless in the Interdimensions of the Bardo.

TERMINAL MIDWIFERY

Anyone who has volunteered or worked professionally in a hospice or similar setting providing care for the terminally ill and dying will have remarkable experiences and many observations to share. For many hospice workers there is the common observation that each and **every death is unique**, just as **every single birth is unique**.

Some will exit peacefully and quietly, some will exit in unbearable pain and suffering, some will exit quickly and some will exit very slowly. Some will die young, some will die old. Some will welcome and embrace Death and some will resist and fight furiously against the 'dying of the light.' Some will go out surrounded by family and friends, some will go out all alone. Some will go out fulfilled by their lifetime, and others will go out with regrets, resentments and dissatisfaction. Some will go out content, some will go out angry, some will go out grieving, some will go out fearful, some will go out fearlessly. All will go as they go, just as in birth all will arrive as they arrive.

Is it unique, it is singular, it is deeply, profoundly personal. It is the Lila of God and the unfolding story of us all.

To create the best possible environment for the dying person is to help them prepare for the transition into death and across the Bardo.

Because each death is unique it certainly isn't always possible to prepare immediately prior. An airplane crash, a road accident, dying in an earthquake, or by cyclone or natural disaster, dying by violence at the hands of another person through war or crime, dying in despair or dying doing what is their passion, dying for love, dying without love, dying by sudden accident, dying by drowning, dying in fire or flood, dying in every way, shape and form. This is the Law of Accident pre-empting the Law of Fate.

Each of us is given so many allotted breaths in a lifetime (AD). When the last breath has been breathed within us, then that is our Fate. Each breath inhaling is a little life, each breath exhaling is a little death in itself. Learn to savour each breath given and be breathed with profound gratitude.

Each and every birth and each and every death is singularly unique. For those whose death comes suddenly and unexpectedly or through violent circumstances it is shocking. But the process of the transmigration through the Bardo remains the same and constant. It will require a period to recover and regather consciousness and to realize the reality that death has come and life, as it was known, is over.

The main purpose for the Tibetan Book of the Dead and similar sacred texts is to help the liberation of beings.

The Tibetans developed what could be described as 'Terminal Midwifery' to help the dying person prepare and negotiate the way through the Bardo. The Bardo Practitioner connects with the dying person, creates the right atmosphere and setting, and reads verbatim from the text to help the Traveler realize what is happening and how to respond at each point along the way.

The time to prepare for death is within the course of a lifetime and best not to be left until the last moment when you are in the queue for the 'departure lounge.'

Volunteers and workers in hospices often observe how very unwell, severely suffering and dying patients will seemingly mount a powerful rally of lucidity and clarity right before the death of the body. This is nature naturally taking her course and an act of Grace.

SOME OF THE SIGNS THAT TRANSITION IS IMMINENT – THE THRESHOLD OF TRANSITION

1. Loss of control of muscles, face, bladder, sphincter
2. Sounds such as rolling thunder, high frequencies, buzzing, whistling, rumbling
3. Visions, hallucinations or blindness
4. Chain-stroke breathing (Cheyne-Stokes breathing), struggling with each breath
5. Intense sensations of cold, teeth chattering, uncontrollable shivering
6. Agitation, anxiety, irritability, restlessness
7. Deep lethargic calm, sudden inexplicable absence of previous pain
8. Deep peacefulness, calm, at rest

During such crucial times in the prelude to death, you can witness and observe the ego melting away. The Traveler is emerging. The person is no longer concerned about trivial things such as toileting or appearances. The person is often, for the first time perhaps, open to the reading of sacred texts such as the Bible, the Quran, or the Bhagavad Gita or the Bardo Thodol. There is a different air or atmosphere around the dying person and some subtle, perceptible time and space distortions in the house or place where the dying may also be occurring. It is the process of the *Sacred Rascooarno*.

The Tibetans pioneered terminal midwifery and modern esoteric Teachers such as E.J. Gold had adapted it for practical application.

Terminal midwifery is sacred and valuable, but the time to prepare for death is during the course of a lifetime prior to entering the launch zone into the Bardo. That is the purpose of self-work and raising the vibrational resonance.

WHAT HAPPENS TO DIFFERENT PEOPLE AT DIFFERENT POINTS AFTER DEATH OF THE BODY?

The Hyclic

For approximately 50% of the population, death actually is terminal and so it's fairly straightforward and simple enough. For the Hyclic or Living Dead who have no spiritual magnetic centre, death of the body is actually the final end, just as they believe. Their last life was their last go round. Rest in Peace.

For the Hyclic, upon the death of the body, it is fade-to-black and into oblivion.

There is a 'shadow body' made up of the three canters and residual components of personhood that can persist in ethereal form up to maximum 21 years post death trapped in attachment to the Earth. These departed entities are the 'Hungry Ghosts' referred to in the Bardo Thodol and other scriptures. The 'Hungry Ghosts' will frequently hang around places and things that attracted them in life such as bars or nightclubs where alcohol or other drugs are served, homes, workplaces or familiar surroundings. They are 'hungry' because they crave rebirth into a body to continue to fulfill their sense desires. They can see and experience food and drink with unbearable thirst and hunger yet cannot partake of it. Some sensitive people and so-called 'psychics' can perceive them or try to communicate with them, but this would only worsen their suffering.

Once the maximum period of around 21 years is passed, the components that comprised them will be recycled into a kind of 'galactic compost heap', nothing is ever wasted. But their chance at individual identity and accension is over as they are a failed individual experiment of consciousness.

Those With the Magnetic Centre or Even the Soul

The other 50% with the seed of the Magnetic Centre or even a Soul will be drawn back into the Bardo and transmigrate again through their own personal journey. Even an unbalanced Human Number 4 will have to reincarnate again, (AD Quest 1, 1982) unless they are granted Grace or can gather themselves in the Encounter with the Clear Light. This will occur within 7 days of the death of the physical material body.

Presence of Mind? Presence of Consciousness.

After death of the body, the mind and spirit separate, at whatever level of development, as all choice is lost and gone, as the inner being is irresistibly drawn to the vibration it has made, what it resonates with, on the level and nature of that frequency. There are Karmic energies and a range of other forces acting in this process as described in detail in Yoga and related disciplines. The overall principle is how the force of vibration is operating like a magnet.

After the death of the body in the material realm, what is done is done, and there are vibrational, subtle gravitational, and resonance attractants that take over and the will or faculty that was once the mind no longer holds any influence or force, as the time of choice is concluded for that lifetime.

This is where the exercises, rituals and practices of meditation, focused concentration, sensing and attention learned and done over a lifetime come into play and reveal their benefits and value.

Presence of mind and spirit are critical through each 'step' of the course through the Bardo.

It is first necessary to know that your body has died and that you are now separated forever from it and have entered the Bardo. Leave it all behind and let go. You are now the Traveler. The Traveler has at last reemerged.

It is vital and critical to know and constantly remember that, in the Bardo, you are already dead and cannot die any more than you have already died.

No need to fear death at all or anything that you perceive or experience because you can't be any more dead than you already are.

The Dream Time

Many so-called "primitive" cultures of native peoples, or rather more accurately, those still more closely directly connected with the Holy Mother The Earth speak about their origins in the 'Dream Time.'

This is objective knowledge and truth as everyone and everything has their origins in the non-material spiritual world of the "Dream Time."

You enter the Dream world during your sleep cycle every night or when you are in the deepest sleep cycle of REM and Theta. One of the reasons you feel so refreshed in the morning from a sound night's sleep is because, for a brief period, your spiritual part is drawn back to the planet you are in harmonic resonance with (AD Quest 1, 1982). The farther away from the Holy Father the Sun, the denser the vibration, the closer to the Sun the finer the vibration.

This will be a fantastic and incredible notion for the materialists who could not conceive of such instantaneous travel or survival in the harsh three-dimensional conditions of another planet.

It was natural for our ancient ancestors to observe members of their clan or tribe who had died and to grieve and to wonder. To them it seemed like the person had fallen asleep and could not awake again. At first, they buried them in the trees to keep the wild animals from the body, and later learned to put the corpses into the ground or burn them.

To a significant extent, dreaming is a facsimile of the experience of the Bardo, although those who have experienced Near Death Experience NDE, have often reported that the "dream" seems far more real than anything in the material world.

After death and in the Bardo, it is vital to know you are in the Bardo as you know and have awareness that you are in a dream in ordinary sleep. Whatever unfolds in the Bardo is the unwinding of your own consciousness. If you are able to realize this and make a separation from it and recognize it for what it is, you can achieve stability.

If you are unprepared and are identified and swept away by it, it can seem overwhelming as well as strange beyond conception and wondrous.

Lucid Dreaming

Only one way, not necessarily at all the best way, of preparing for the Bardo is to learn the art of lucid dreaming. The main thrust is in the awareness that you are dreaming, and that you know it is only a dream. The next stage is to gain the ability to direct the dream without awakening from the sleep state. There is some reluctance to give out this practice as people often had a tendency to make a deva of it, and focus too intensely trying to achieve some 'goal.' You may ask for dream if you need to confirm the truth of something or to receive guidance from your Guide or from your Subconscious mind.

WHAT 'OCCURS' IN THE BARDO DOES NOT ALWAYS STAY IN THE BARDO

There are 7 veils between this life in the material world and the entrance to the gates of the Bardo. Some people have experienced **Near Death Experience** and returned to the body. There is a growing body of research around this phenomenon and canters studying it such as at the University of Virginia in the United States. The stories of the people who have experienced the NDE are remarkable, and although different and unique, they have some common themes.

Some of the themes are the sense of entering a dark tunnel and travelling through to intensely bright luminous light. Other experiences reported by those who have clinically died and returned are coming out of their bodies and hovering overhead watching ambulance staff or medical teams trying to revive them. Other experiences reported are of meeting deceased loved ones and family members or of amazing journeys accompanied by some figure seeming to be a guide.

These are very helpful testimonies and can be inspiring for those who are skeptical of anything beyond the material body, but it is unlikely that the NDE Traveler has penetrated any farther than the first veil, or they would not return. One particularly compelling story was shared by Neurosurgeon Dr Eben Alexander who was trained and steeped in the scientific method and was able to assess and review his NDE experience of being in a long-term coma and very close to death over a considerable period of time. Dr Alexander came to the informed conclusion that existence beyond death was very much real, a view that was reportedly a 180 degree opposite turn from his views prior to the NDE.

At the same time, there are further credible testimonies of people, particularly children who are able to recall something, sometimes some details of a prior life, some fact which can be confirmed. This is very rare but much more common to observe in some children who have not yet developed the false identity of the ego. The search for the successor of the Dalai Lama, for example, through reincarnation in a child has been well known and documented and is now in the Common Consciousness.

THE REALITY AND THE EXPERIENCE OF THE BARDO

Without going too deeply into the distracting fine details, the most vitally important thing to remember when entering the Bardo is that you are in it but not of it and what you are experiencing is the

unwinding of your own consciousness. It is real reality and reality more real than real, but will also be somewhat like watching a holographic film of your life before you.

Think again of **energy, vibration, frequency** and **resonance**.

Think of a rubber ball dropped from the 100th story of a tall skyscraper on to the pavement below.

At the first bounce the energy and momentum and force is at its maximum. At the first bounce the ball will rebound higher than at any point afterward.

With each bounce the ball will bounce lower and lower following the natural law of gravity in the material world.

Encounter With the Clear Light

The greatest opportunity of any existence is the encounter with the **Clear Light of Objective Reality** at the transition point after death. This is where you meet God. The **Clear Light** is indescribable, inconceivable, it is the **Atman**.

If you have prepared and through Grace you may be able to stabilize within the Presence of the Divine Clear Light and become or rather know you are One with it and be totally absorbed and merged into the **Clear Light of Objective Reality**. This is the acme, the essence of everything that can be experienced by any being, human or otherwise.

On the second bounce, you will still have the chance to know and merge with the Clear Light. With each successive bounce, the momentum is diminishing and you are being drawn deeper through the Bardo in the chambers leading toward rebirth in another body.

For the advanced Buddhist, for the advanced Hindu, for those who have worked in some way on some form of self-perfection, you will try to go out at the moment of death through the top of the head saying the sacred **OM** in your heart and in all of your being or for a Muslim reciting the sacred **La il la ha, il ha La Hu** (there is none save Allah) or The Christian mantra: **Lord Have Mercy**. The adept tries, through whatever struggle or difficulty to be sitting up and go out through the fissure on the top of the cranium known as the Brãhmarandhra. This is above the physical cerebrum in the uppermost area of the Lotus Blossom that is soft tissue located on the crown of the head when the infant enters this world. The ideal is not always possible or practicable, and in many cases the spiritual consciousness will exit from the 9 apertures of heart, solar plexus, the mouth, the nose, the ears, or any other escape exits down below the navel through to the 'lower orifices,' to put it delicately. This is a specific reason that the Hindus and Buddhists traditionally tie the legs of the corpse together, to prevent the exiting spiritual part from attempting to return, as well as other, practical considerations.

The **Clear Light** in Gnostic cosmology is the **Pleroma** which points to the precious, highest plane of divine resonance of fullness, eternal, timeless, infinite, endless perfection. The **Pleroma** is the ultimate ground and source of all and everything experienced in the encounter with the **Clear Light** through the **Matrix of Space**.

In stark contrast is the dense material world of matter which is marked by the pairs of opposites, ignorance, suffering and separation from the Divine.

THE DEATH CHAMBER AT THE POINT OF TRANSITION AND THE FUNERAL

Once again, the room, the atmosphere and the environment of the place where the deathing is occurring can be very helpful and conducive to the peaceful transition of the dying. Soft music, incense, candles, family close by and witnessing but not becoming overly emotional or loud are but some few examples. Prayers and readings from sacred texts as the departure window opens will assist.

You will notice how family and friends crying and grieving or celebrating the life of the deceased will stop once the coffin has been lowered into the grave or when the fire is ignited in the cremation pyre. For both the grieving and the deceased this is the moment when everyone recognizes "the game is over." There is an immediate change in the atmosphere, and in the personal interactions. Pray for the beloved, wish them well eternally and let them go, send them on their continuing journey of sacred adventure. Go and live your own life and give them your respect and your love. Hold on to the memories but never, ever call them back in any way.

One of the worst things that medical science has done in recent generations is to try to keep people artificially alive beyond the time they have would, by Fate, have died. There is now a growing and increasing awareness in the Common Consciousness to avoid this abhorrent practice. Trying to hold someone who is dying tied to the material world through artificial life support beyond a certain point is cruelty.

WHAT ARE SOME OF THE EXPERIENCES AND "WHERE" DO PEOPLE GO?

"All the gods, all the heavens, all the hells, are within you,"

JOSEPH CAMPBELL

Following the Encounter with the **Clear Light**, the Traveler will move through the phases of the Bardo in the encounters with the Peaceful and subsequently the Wrathful Deities.

In the earliest phases, the devout Christian will see and experience Jesus and the Heavenly Host as they had visualized it all. Radiant angels play divine music upon their golden harps, above the clouds, all are singing praises of the Lord. They will experience precisely what they expect to experience, as this is their heaven and reward.

The same will follow exactly for the devout Muslim who will also experience precisely as they expect, such as the glories of the higher Heavens or seeing the Holy Prophet, or marvelling in the most magnificent gardens where pour fountains of kousar, the divine, intoxicating wine. Attendants such as houris and malayaks with radiant faces will serve them. Every person entering djennat, the heaven, will become young.

The devout Hindu may experience the presence of Krishna, of Shiva, or Ram or any manifestation of God in accordance with expectations.

All encompassing and glorious, indescribably powerful experiences of pure joy. At first. Some will experience and talk with long departed dear family members or friends or teachers. Some may experience the presence of their Guru.

It will continue and it will go on for a phase. Yet with each bounce of the ball, the energy force is gradually decreasing and the buoyancy lessening as the phenomena of the Bardo come into play.

The effect of spiritual gravity on the bouncing ball inevitably results in descending into the lower chambers of the Bardo unless Liberation is attained through recognition- absorption in the **Clear Light** initial stages. Attention and focus is essential. The **Clear Light** is not above, below, behind, in front, or around you. You are not a human primate and never were. You are the **Clear Light**. You are One. For the Traveler recognizing and knowing the **Clear Light**, Liberation is instantaneous.

This is your true, one home. You cannot be born, you cannot die, you cannot exist or change. All is Vibration. When know you are the Clear Light, you become One with the Clear Light. After your very long journey, you return. Welcome home.

DESCENDING ON THROUGH LOWER CHAMBERS OF THE BARDO TOWARD REBIRTH, THE PEACEFUL AND THE WRATHFUL DEITIES

There are helpful Guides explaining the details of the voyage into the lower chambers of the Bardo for those prepared to seek them out. But knowing any of that is not anything nearly as important as being prepared for death itself. The transition into the real world of the Bardo is only very much going home, but it may be equally shocking and overwhelming for the unprepared to be wrenched from a physical body and discover your true nature stripped bare.

This why it is so vital during life to reach the point of knowing you are NOT your body.

In the journey through the Bardo, the Traveler is faced with ongoing challenges and uncertainties. Each phase is a test. Knowing and constantly remembering that is all a dream, only **a projection of your own unwinding consciousness** will allow the Traveler to maintain composure and balance. Whatever you experience may be shocking, but it is all coming from yourself.

As the Conscience unwinds, the Traveler may experience the Corridor of Judgement, particularly if that was part of their conditioning or religion. For most travellers this is revealed almost as a holographic, and wholly objective film-like replay of their whole life in many details. So many NDE witnesses have reported "My whole life flashed before me." It is totally objective and it is devoid of judgement in the sense that one is praised for the good deeds or condemned for the bad. It is purely objective and it is exactly what it is as it unfolds.

The crucible of a lifetime in a human primate body dwelling on the Earth is a tough assignment.

At the beginning of the assignment you had to come back to learn some things and to repair some things. How well you learned those things and whatever else you have yet to learn will be revealed before you.

There is an accounting of sorts, yet Karma, however certainly real, yet is purely vibrational.

Everything is recorded in your Conscience, every little detail. A divinely ingenious, infallible, miraculous natural system.

In the Peaceful Deities stage you may witness and experience visions of gods and angels, deities of every spectrum that emerge from your own consciousness.

Few know that the Christian Biblical Book of Revelation was less about the "End Times" of the whole of humanity which theologians have analyzed in detail, but far more derived from the much earlier Egyptian Book of the Dead about the 'end times' journey through the Bardo of the individual soul.

Then following phases in the spiralling descent through the lower chambers of the Bardo come the encounters with the Wrathful Deities. The Wrathful Deities are the negative mirror images of the Peaceful Deities. In this phase you may witness and experience visions of demons, ugliness and horrors. It is for a purpose.

THE RAYS OF PURIFICATION AND THE PITFALLS OF THE SEDUCTIVE ILLUSORY LIGHTS OF ATTRACTION WHEN WANDERING IN THE LOWER SIX DIMENSIONS

The brilliant white radiation bathes you to dissolve the vibrations of violence, anger and hatred. It is like acid, it is intense. Remain in it and persist, refuse to be drawn in by the soft, seductive, smoky light coming from the portal to the hell dimension. Refuse to be drawn to the seeming 'haven' of the dense grey smoke of the hell dimension where a sentence in suffering awaits. The Ray is very harsh. Bathe in it in willing acceptance and surrender to have the primate habits of anger, hate and violence dissolved and washed away. Rejoice in it.

The brilliant intense yellow radiation is savage in different ways. It is cleansing and dissolving the vestiges of pride, vanity and false ego. Bathe in it and persist. At the same time, the soft blue light portal opens to the human dimension of the material world. Resist the impulse to flee the cleansing yellow radiation to escape down into rebirth in the lower human world. This portal is tempting to those who were 'big people' back in material primate life.

The full exposure to the dazzling red light is the purifying radiation to dissolve the habits of attachment and possessiveness. At the same time, the portal will open with the soft yellow light of the insatiable hungry ghosts. Avoid the temptation to seek refuge in the soft yellow light portal. Overcome your aversion and bathe willingly and fully in the red radiation purifying your being of attachments and possessiveness and greed.

The emergence comes of the brilliant, dazzling clear green light of radiation emanating from the Heart of Wisdom of the Guide of the Air element of the Labyrinth. It is also intense and very difficult to bear, but persist as it purges your being of jealousy, envy and ignorance. Opening as a portal of seeming haven from the ray of radiation is the soft red light flowing from the Purgatory dimension. Avoid repulsion and disgust. Quell the impulse to run, or to seek refuge there. Bathe in the dazzling green radiation with gratitude and persist.

In the realm of the Wrathful Deities, ugly, slime-drenched bloodthirsty gruesome monsters are there to devour the unwary Traveler in every shape and unimaginable horror manifestation. In the hell-worlds and in purgatory, every torture and suffering conceivable and beyond is on tap and available for necessary cleansing and purification purposes. For those requiring a thorough scrubbing, you came to the right dimensions. The good news is that what they probably told you in Sunday school that it's for keeps and for eternity was all bogus. **Even this shall pass away**.

As you travel downward through the latter chambers of the Bardo, increasingly you will be attracted to rebirth in another human womb. Shocking ambushes of sights, sounds and visions may well be expected to attempt to trick you into rebirth. As only one of innumerable examples, you might find yourself chased by a vicious pack of wild animals with fierce fangs and glowing red eyes. If you run to hide from them, you will have been easily tricked into entering the seeming safety of a cave which is actually a random womb of rebirth.

Yet, if you continue to realize and know you are already dead and in the Bardo you will simply remain where you are and stay calm and detached. The vicious pack of terrifying beasts will circle you and go quiet and leave you alone. You can then go on through the Bardo to more consciously choose the higher birth of a womb that will give you what you need to progress in your next life, if it is back into the material world you must come. It is a far better rebirth to come back consciously rather than be thrown into the world.

In this lower phase of the Bardo you are asking to be born again. As you are drawn farther down the Bardo and toward the point of no return before rebirth, you will witness lovemaking couples projected in beams of pale blue light visions before you. Or possibly you will even be attracted to that scientific test tube containing the ovum and the sperm of your parents if your re-entry is through artificial means?

You are asking to be born to parents, to a family, into a culture that is best for your personal development. You are being drawn by your vibration. If you choose rashly and unwisely from some negative vibration such as fear, you could, for example, risk being born into the smoke-filled grey world of the brutes. There are indeed certainly hell-worlds on the Earth as well as in the Bardo, so choose wisely and carefully if you are going to be drawn back into this world in yet another lifetime on the Planet of Choice to start all over again.

THE ORGAN AND FACULTY OF KUNDABUFFER

From his training and deep knowledge from within esoteric schools, Mr Gurdjieff transmitted the concept of the faculty of **deep forgetting** which he called the organ Kundabuffer. This faculty was installed by higher beings as a kind of simulation program in humans early on in their evolution as a vehicle of consciousness. The reason for the faculty of deep forgetting is to compassionately shield the Traveler from the suffering of holding the experiences of prior lives and through the journey of the Bardo.

It is practical: the overwhelming majority of human beings have enough on their plate of contending with the present lifetime on the Earth without the burden of memories of past lives. A being progressing in life on the spiritual work journey will come to a point where they are prompted from within that something about past lives is to be known. For the majority, it's an unnecessary distraction from the main course of contending with the here and now of the present lifetime. The other compassionate reason for the deep forgetting faculty is to erase the traumas of the journey through the Bardo which would be unnecessary and painful. The deep, everlasting familiarity with the Bardo will be remembered when the time comes.

There may be fragments or remnants of very distant dreamlike memories in some individuals. For example, people who are attracted to horror movies or scary novels with dark, sinister themes will have some vague sketchy shadow memories of the journey through the Lower Six Realms and encounters with the Wrathful Deities, purgatory or hell dimensions.

It is not punishment. It is pure compassion. It is purification of Karma and negative vibrations accumulated over lifetimes. *If you can bear it with gratitude you will be liberated.*

REMEMBER ALWAYS: What seems to be happening to you during the journey through the labyrinth in any form must not be resisted. Never try to flee in fear nor never, ever try to fight or display aggression in any way. You can't die any more than you already have. You can, however, experience exquisite pain and suffering, but not if you continually know it is only the **projections coming from yourself**. It is you and nothing more or less. The animal survival instinct is powerful, but let go of it and leave it because there is nothing left to survive. You are already as dead as you can ever be.

Resisting the purifying radiations will result in spontaneous rebirth or descent into the lower dimensions. Focus your attention on the **Beloved**. Say the name of the **Beloved** and ask for succor. At nearly any stage, you can still attain liberation through Consciousness or you can stabilize in the chambers of the Bardo and attain a higher rebirth if you are compelled to return to the Earth.

WHATEVER IS SO IS ALSO SO HUM

The powerful ancient mantra **Om So Hum** is a very valuable tool in this life, and particularly so when constantly remembered in traversing the Bardo. It is a combination of three sacred vibrations: **Om** and **So** and **Hum** which are of the breath, and of the Prana. **Om So Hum** is the awareness of one's true nature.

As with any mantra, it may be repeated continuously through the chanting of the voice vibrations or inwardly silently in the heart. When practiced properly, the mantra helps quieten the chatter of the mind, cultivate conscious awareness and connect with the universal.

So Hum may be translated literally as "I am That." It also means "I am that I am."

It is a powerful reminder that **ALL is God**. In this life the thief that steals from you is God, your worst enemy is God, all that you love and all that you despise is God. Everything beautiful and wonderous is God. Everything ghastly and repugnant is God.

Within the Labyrinth of the Bardo, remembrance and repetition of the **Om So Hum** carries you through the strange radiations, through the shocking ambush of sound, sensations and visions. Through the Peaceful and the Wrathful Deities. Through the Purgatory and Hell World dimensions. Whatever you perceive, whatever you see, whatever you witness: **"I AM THAT."** The visions are coming from you and you are the visions.

Through holding the Mantra in your heart and through constant remembrance you will, through Grace, transcend immersion in the Labyrinth and rise above it by the epiphany of being one with it. Nothing can ever harm you again.

This might provide you with some hint, some clue, some spark of an idea that the practices of self-work and meditation just might be a worthwhile while still alive in a breathed human primate body dwelling on the Earth?

THE VITAL IMPORTANCE OF PREPARATION OF LIFETIME IS ABOUT VIBRATION AND RESONANCE

Always remember: Nothing "happens" in the Bardo. Nothing has ever "happened" and Nothing ever will "happen."

Such notions are remnants of the human primate conditioning.

The whole purpose of a lifetime of work-on-self, through purifications, through devotion, through service to others, through meditation, through prayer, through self-improvements of every sort is about vibration, only vibration. **It is all about raising the vibration.** You have the possibility, **the choice**, of doing this only while still alive in the dense material world on the **Planet of Choice, the Earth**.

Just as attitude determines altitude in material life, in the Bardo, vibration determines escape velocity, either rising and ascension or succumbing to gravity of the dense material realm, thus remaining trapped in the cycle of death and rebirth.

In order to fully appreciate, contemplate and benefit from any of this, you must first have the **Seed of the Need**.

HAZRAT INAYAT KHAN IN THE GAYAN, VADAN, NIRTAN:

Death, what are you
I am the shadow of life
Death, of what are you born
I am born of ignorance
Death, where is your abode?
My abode is in the mind of illusion.
Death, do you ever die?
Yes, when pierced by the Seers glance.

Death, whom do you draw near to you?
I draw closer who is attracted to me
Death, whom do you love?
I love the one who longs for me
Death, whom do you attend?
I readily attend those who call on me
Death, whom do you frighten?
I frighten the one who is not familiar with me
Death, whom do you caress?
The one who lies trustfully in my arms
Death, with whom are you severe?
I am severe with the one who does not readily respond to my call
Death, whom do you serve?
I serve the godly, and when they return home
I carry their baggage

CHAPTER 29

The Need And The Acceptance

"The fluteplayer puts breath into a flute,
and who makes the music?
Not the flute. The Fluteplayer!"

— RUMI

And who gives breath to the flute player? What was your purpose for coming into this material density? Was it for the purpose of accumulating material wealth, fame or power? Was it for the purpose of outstanding achievements in sport or physical games of competition? Was it for creating great works of art or music? Was it for the purpose of having a career or parenting or family or descendants? Was it for the purpose of pursuing ever more sense pleasure experiences? Was it for the purpose of learning, exploring and travel? Was it for the purpose of doing 'good works,' of helping your fellow human beings who are suffering in this life? Was it for the purpose of advancing scientific research or medical knowledge? All of those things you may be called to do along the way, but they are secondary diversions and none of those were ever nor will ever be your primary purpose. **This offer will be repeated ... but not indefinitely.**

If anyone proposes to teach anything at all about how to increase the power, variety and range of bodily sense-enjoyments and fleeting pleasures there are multitudes always thirsty, hungry and ever eager for it.

How to accumulate wealth, how to gain power and influence, how to make the body more healthy, how to cause the body to live longer and become more 'attractive.' How to invent or use the latest technology, how to build things, how to grow things, how to manipulate things, how to do 'self-improvement.' How to 'get ahead.' How to cook tasty foods and become a 'celebrity chef.' How to acquire or enjoy the latest lust objects or to follow the latest fads and trends, or about how to attract the most 'followers.'

At the same moment, if anyone proposes to share knowledge and experience of the supreme goal, one finds few prepared to listen. Only a proportion have the need to seek knowledge of the higher, fewer have the energy or patience to engage in practice to reach for the higher, and fewer still have the inner drive, the patience, the strength and persistence to progress toward attaining it.

There are two polarities driving the course of the story of humanity and they magnetically attract and lead in very different directions to separate **possibilities.**

THE MATERIALIST POLARITY

The materialist polarity is the dense vibrational frequency of the material world. The material dimension of the body and the five portals of the senses. The world of dense matter, the world of animal existence. The biological, the physical, the economic, the political, the commercial, the spatial three-dimensional, all of what is taken to be the so-called 'real.' In this realm, matter is all that well...matters.

In the polarity of the dense material, the drive is to make life ever more comfortable for the animal primate body and to seek the 'utopian' goal of finding ways to make it survive longer. The tendency is to pander to the root of evil which is the worship of the Profit Motive. The world spends trillions in currency on 'defence' in weapons of mass destruction whilst billions are left homeless, hungry and suffering. The tendency is for most human beings to bury the awareness of the stark reality of being in prison, and to lapse farther into sleep and into the delusional realm of Maya. It has always been practical truth that in order to escape from prison it is first essential to know you are in a prison.

In the Anthropocene Age of the dense realm of the materialists, it is fully acceptable, indeed expected, to exploit the Earth, to destroy her habitats, to upset the balance of Nature, to mine and pillage, to pump up oil and dig up fossil fuels, to set fires and carry out logging and clearing that destroys ancient forests. To domesticate, farm and slaughter animals. To drive into extinction without a care innumerable animal and plant species sharing the Earth. To pollute. To spew carbon, smoke, chemicals into the air and water. To overpopulate and drain and excavate and ruin, to despoil every habitat. Why? Because their external "Sky God" dwelling up in 'heaven' told them the Earth was for exploitation and nothing but a rock made for them to dwell on so as to freely use and abuse.

THE SPIRITUAL POLARITY

The spiritual polarity also has a substantial magnetic pull of vibrational frequency but is more subtle and passive to the Material. Passivity certainly never means 'weak.' There is more strength in passivity than can be conceived. The spiritual polarity is the First Force, positive and the Material is actually the second negative, denying force. This is the reversed opposite of what most assume. What is still missing is the third, neutralizing, balancing force. This is the conception of the Holy Ghost.

The spiritual polarity upholds the ancient Truth that everything in the material world is constantly changing, finite and very temporary. The spiritual polarity holds the Truth that dense material world is a manifestation of God descending into the solidified lower realms. The first polarity holds the Truth that all is God and the purpose of a life is the potential given to return to God in a knowing, conscious way.

The spiritual polarity Truth is that human primates have an important enough role in the Solar System as the current Experiment of Consciousness but are absolutely not the 'Centre of the Universe' that they long assumed themselves to be. The next stage of the Copernican Revolution is just ripening for opening.

The Spiritual Polarity holds the Truth that the Holy Mother the Earth is a highly conscious being that co-created humankind with the Holy Father the Sun, and indeed all the Stars and Planets are highly evolved conscious three-brained beings. Humans were, in reality after all, actually created in the image of God.

Wouldn't it follow that the human species must radically change all attitudes and begin to learn to revere the Holy Mother the Earth and cooperate and consciously work with Her under Her guidance?

This will predictably be the most difficult-to-swallow Truth for the materialists who have long assumed that the Earth is 'nothing-but', an insentient globe of rock, water, minerals and magma, a dead clump of materials, a planet which just happened by happenstance and sheer luck to be the venue where life formed.

They ever predictably will call heresy and scoff and deride and belittle the very notion.

But how could such a controversial idea of the Earth as a holy, conscious, living being be proved or disproved?

Time will tell. Those who know **vibration, frequency and resonance know**. And those Rare Resonance Beings who know, know, but for the time being, remain unknown.

THE COMMON CONSCIOUSNESS

It would seem undeniable that throughout most of modern human history the Materialist Polarity is decisively dominating and winning out most of the time. That is true enough on one level, but there is a subtle change gradually gathering force as more humans from different cultures, philosophies, faiths and perspectives have begun to interact and share knowledge and experiences.

There is gradually emerging what could be called the Common Consciousness of like-minded people around the world of the 21st Century. These are people who come most diverse genetic, geographic, linguistic, educational, cultural, scientific, and spiritual backgrounds and faiths. They typically bring open minds, and are not satisfied to accept the orthodox, conventional explanations and long-held fixed assumptions of how the world they live in operates.

Through the 21st Century, at a time when there are critical convergences of crises facing humankind, there is an openness to new ideas, novel and different ways of thinking, of cooperating, of collaborating. There are potentially previously unknown perspectives emerging to help understand and grapple with how problems are formed and resolved (without the creating further new problems).

Never before in recorded human history have there been greater dangers and opportunities, and never before has there been such interactive collaboration, cooperation and transformational potential. The problems will not be solved by the next generation of technology, nor by the old mindsets that created the problems. The solution is not found in "changing the world" just as it never has been.

The only solutions will only come from transformation of the Self. Whenever an individual begins to make spiritual progress, the vibration changes within and around them. This affects others and there is a snowball effect. If only approximately 144,000 human beings awakened and attained consciousness, Rare Resonance, the life on Earth would change in astonishing ways for the better. The Resonance Beings would transform human vibration upon the sacred Earth. As inner life changes, outer life follows.

INNER VERSUS OUTER TRANSFORMATIVE DEVELOPMENT

That does not necessarily at all mean that the advance of human knowledge, science and technology is wrong or not of potential substantial benefit. The risks arise when the technology advances much faster than the consciousness of the species which invents and builds it. The same principle has been the 'Great Filter' tipping point for prior species and earlier civilizations as the Law of 7 predicts how the cycle repeats.

The developing maturity of the species which is the Experiment of Consciousness will determine its survival and its ascendence. Rising away from and above the dense vibration of animal-primate aggression, away from the penchant for reciprocal destruction (war), and from the negative vibrational effects of Selfishness, Fear and Greed is required for collective species evolution.

With half of the population coming back in as the Hyclic or spiritually dead, there is a lot of dense negative vibration dragging the chain. The crime, the violence, the war machine, the greed machine, and most of the causes of the way the world is can be largely attributed to the pernicious influences of the proportion of the populace among the living dead. It is rather unlikely, that a beneficent extraterrestrial higher species is going to intervene to remove the Hyclic from the Earth to another planet for rehabilitation and enlightenment. It can only from within themselves to reignite the spiritual flame, and miraculously in some rare instances, by Grace, it does happen.

THE WISDOM: THE STRUGGLE BETWEEN THE OUTER AND INNER DEVELOPMENT INTERSECTS AND CONVERGES AT ONE POINT IN THE QUEST TO MASTER NATURE

The external world is but a gross form of the internal, the subtle. The finer is always the cause, the grosser the effect. Allow this truth to absorb by putting it through yourself.

The external, material world of the body and senses is the grosser, dense form of the spiritual. In the same way, the external forces are simply grosser, dense manifestations of the fine, subtle, spiritual inner forces. We must use the word 'spiritual' because we lack adequate language to come close to the mark of explaining the vibrational quality of the subtle inner force. Wherever you are, the Force is with you.

The Human Number 5 Resonance Being Vivekananda presaged all of this in the 19th Century. Vivekananda observed that the human being who has discovered and learnt how to apply the Internal Spiritual Forces will bring forth the whole of Nature under mastery. So the Yogi proposes no less a task than transcending the ordinary laws of Nature to the point where the laws of the Universe will have no influence. This is the actual nature of the "Supernatural." Through realizing the Atman, the Allah, the Supreme Source and attuning the vibrational resonance with the highest realm, the Adept gains the mastery of the whole of Nature, internal and external.

The progress and civilization of the human primate species can be understood as the drive to "control" Nature. From the discovery of how to make fire, through learning how to make tools from chiselled stone, the arising of agriculture, to the invention of the wheel, to the invention of the sail, through to the invention of the steam engine, through to the first aircraft, through to harnessing electricity through to achieving nuclear fission and onward.

But the unbalanced intense focus on externally controlling nature risks the ignorance morphing into arrogance. Playing God is the game of an abject fool, and this is precisely where humanity is potentially heading with access to genetic manipulation, cloning, and artificial intelligence. Pride and arrogance always goeth before a fall. A technologically advanced ape is still just a clever ape.

Vivekananda went on in his exposition of Raja Yoga to observe different branches or spheres of humanity have taken different approaches and processes to mastering nature. This is essentially describing the axis of polarity between "East" and "West."

Just as in some societies, individuals want to control the external manifestations of Nature, other societies seek to master the inner manifestation of Nature. Some contend that by controlling Internal Nature, everything may be controlled. Others contend that by control of the External Nature, all Nature will be controlled.

Vivekananda aptly observed that, carried to the extreme, **both are right**. This is because in Nature there is no such division as Internal or External. The division is only fictitious and attempting to place limitations and boundaries where none ever existed.

The Internalists and the Externalists are destined to meet at some point, when both reach the extremes of their knowledge. Just as when the Physicist pushes knowledge to its limits, it starts to melt away into the realm of Metaphysics. So it is that when the Metaphysicist tries to find the boundary between mind and matter, there is only reality along a spectrum, beginning and ending in the reality being of **One**.

Here is Truth. The end and aim of all science is to reach the Unity. The balance. The **One** out of which the manifest is being manufactured, the **One** existing as many.

Even a limited knowledge of all this can only lead to profound humility. Nature can only be mastered through Nature, and through inner voluntary evolution and transformation through Grace.

The human body is a masterful work of Nature and each human being potentially a great being. In one sense humankind, as a Vehicle of Consciousness, is higher than all the other animals. In another sense, higher than even the Angels, or the Devas (Lesser forms of Gods). Even the Devas will have to come down again to Earth in order to attain salvation through imprisonment in a human body and to traverse the course of a lifetime. It's a tough assignment, no doubt about it. Yes, it's puzzling and baffling, but there are clues and signs along the way and guides to help you through the Labyrinth.

And there is the **Grace of the One Supreme Source** if we will open ourselves and attune our vibration to it. For Grace to descend, we must consciously open ourselves to it.

THE SEED OF THE NEED

"If you are on the right path, you will find that invisible hands are helping".
JOSEPH CAMPBELL

Where do you find the need to progress along the spiritual self-development path to reach your potential? Every single living human being has the Conscience within. The Seed of God is in every living human being.

If the need is not there, nothing external will force it upon you. If you have even the tiniest fragment of need to know and confirm that there is something more, something beyond yourself, that your life has intrinsic meaning and purpose, then doors will open for you.

It cannot be forced. It can only be cultivated from within yourself. The Conscience, your Guide to the Conscience and your inner Subconscious mind are all there awaiting with the seed but only you can bring the need.

Only when you have a burning aspiration for God can your mind stay fixed on God.

We come as we are. We can only start from where we are. We may start from the motive of any of the 11 primary negativities but our motives will be purified as we persist in the journey. It is not necessary to find any new religion. You can go deeper into the same religion you were born into, only to understand it from a different light. You can develop your own personal faith.

It will help if you are open to seeing the underlying same Truth at the core of all other faiths and not only the one you were born into or brought into.

The practice of faith in the future will not take place principally in churches, temples, mosques, synagogues or venues, although those structures will still have their place and purposes.

The practice of Faith in the coming future will principally be in homes by study, worship and practice of small groups of like-minded people. In the 21st Century, the practice of traditional spiritual faiths has increasingly fallen away as too many young people are left devoid of any anchor, or any internal guidance system, attracted by materialism, cynicism and nihilism, and falling into despair.

Young people look at the conditions of the world around them and see so much that seems out of control and going in the wrong direction, from climate change and pollution, to war machines, to the obscenely unequal distribution of wealth, to the profit motive.

This self-work of conscious evolution is not for everyone, it requires belief and sustained effort and consistency. Or put differently, it is for everyone, but not everyone is open and yet ready to make the commitment to undertake it. But by applying some of the principles, practices and methods such as meditation, prayer, fasting, the aim of selfless service, you will absolutely and most definitely raise your vibration and begin to resonate with higher frequencies. You will certainly go out far better than you came in. Each and every lifetime is a precious golden opportunity.

If you want knowledge, you have to actively seek it out. It's unlikely if you didn't want it or or weren't ready or it if have continued reading up to this point.

Some references and resources and contacts will be provided in the conclusion and acknowledgements.

There are and will be turbulent times ahead navigating through the 21st Century with the convergence of human-made climate change and atmospheric heating resulting in droughts, floods, and the increase in natural disasters. There will be the ongoing spectre of the age-old madness of reciprocal destruction and war, as well as periods of potential economic collapse ahead. It will get worse before it gets better. Nothing has really changed since the 20th Century except more of the same and just more advanced technology. The proportion of the population of the Hyclic, the living dead, is not going to decrease but they will have access to levers and to power and to technologies to make living for ordinary people potentially more difficult than ever before. Drug-fuelled 'zombies' and extremist zealots will bring mayhem and violence as they always have, but during desperate times, that will magnify.

As a practical advice for young people raising families, the "back-to-the-land" movements of the 20th Century were most definitely on the right track. Living away from dense urban areas in small communities of like-minded people as self-sufficient as possible, "off the grid" and with their own source of high-quality water, alternative power such as solar, wind and hydrogen, and capacity for food production will be the best way for raising a family. With coming failures of multiple systems, living in and around large cities is going to be difficult, problematic and filled with risks.

The back-to-the-land movement was small but significant and founded on principles of simple, sustainable living in harmony with our Holy Mother the Earth. It is interesting that in the 21st Century some of the young people of formerly 'developing' countries such as India and China are making a conscious decision to move back to simple farming and life on the land after the prior generations had deserted in rural communities for the jobs, excitement and opportunity of massing into the cities.

The concept of living in communes was somewhat impractical in the long term and problematic in the 20th Century but some of the experiments found a degree of success. J.G. Bennett, a prominent pupil of Mr Gurdjieff, was a proponent of the establishment of 4th Way communities in which organic farming and self-sufficiency was established with facilities for training, education and spiritual work practices. Mr Bennett was a visionary who was ahead of his time, and the principles he espoused for self-sufficient communities are more relevant than ever.

The idea of small landholding of self-sufficient like-minded householder families in cooperatives as part of a small collective community is likely to be the most practicable. There must be a constitution for the cooperative and a democratic structure to make decisions to contain and circumvent the inevitable human ego tendencies toward bickering and power struggling.

But you can carry out self-work in whatever environment you are in, urban or rural, and regardless of what is going on around you, peaceful serenity or chaos and mayhem, the only thing important is what is going on inside. Just like the Saint asked about the imminent end of the world, always just keep sweeping the floor and carrying out your self-work and improvement and you will transcend in the end.

THE REALITY OF THE SITUATION CAN SOMETIMES SEEM DAUNTING AND CRUSHING

The vast majority of people will avoid by every means at every turn the opportunity to awaken out of deep slumber and realize the reality of their predicament and true mechanistic state. At some point in time nearly every individual will come to glimpse the fact that ordinary "life" is shot through with nothingness, futility and absurdity, as they find themselves staggering from one attachment to desire on to the next negative vibrational state, and on to the next. It is as in the Myth of Sisyphus.

Many inevitably turn to various pastimes, diversions, and myriad 'entertainments.'

A proportion turn to alcohol and other drugs to deaden the involuntary suffering of the pain factory, some turn to the outer forms of religion, increasingly a substantial proportion turn to consumerism, obsession with sex, technology and the religion of materialism. Some of the most unfortunate are sadly crushed by the tides of life and, in desperation, tragically self-destruct or 'suicide' their biological bodies with the aim of escape. They don't know or care that self-annihilation offers no enduring escape at all, but will only result in a far worse state, and far more dense vibration.

Yet, God is forever merciful and compassionate, and Hope springs eternal. The very best that can be done is to live a lifetime in a way to open yourself to Grace. To raise your vibration and resonate with the higher frequencies to escape the density of the lower. Everyone will make mistakes along the way, and everyone will have regrets for the choices made on the path through a lifetime. But the Eternal Source is ever merciful and correcting. With sincerity and persistent effort, you are on the path to self-improvement and higher vibrational resonance. You have the possibility to attain liberation.

ACCEPTANCE LEADS TO LOVE

The Dharma teaches unconditional Acceptance as the key to everything. The problem is not what happens to us, but our lack of acceptance of what is. Swami Ramdas lived this principle and demonstrated it in everyday of his life and teaching. Read through the life story of Ramdas for inspiration of how every setback, every defeat, every pain he experienced he always saw as the Will of God. Other Saints of other Faiths attained rare resonance by precisely the same practice. Ramdas expressed it so clearly and eloquently for the modern aspirant.

His secret was to apply Acceptance to the extreme, attuning and totally submitting his will to the Will of God. His book, *God Experience* (1963 Anand Press) is the essence of a map for how complete acceptance leads to the direct experience of the Divine. It is in the Socratic form of questions from his pupils and answers from the Master.

The practice of Acceptance leads to the higher state of vibrational attuning. Every situation presented daily offers the opportunity of practice. The practice of Acceptance leads to beholding God everywhere in everything. Ramdas testifies there is nothing but God and only God and experiencing it is Purest Love.

The **primary stage of Love** is that in which the lover entirely surrenders unto God, the Beloved. This is Acceptance.

The **middle stage of Love** is that in which God's presence is felt everywhere.

The **final stage of Love** is that in which the Lover and the Beloved become as one, and beyond that a state where is left no sense of Love, Lover or Beloved.

All the love songs, the poetry, the music, the lyrics of love speak of love for a woman or a man. But in deep reality, they are only subconsciously pointing toward the only love which is the love of the Beloved One Source.

When we are in love we can see no faults in the Beloved. This is the secret of Acceptance if only we can remember it.

The Seven Aspects of Acceptance

1. **Understanding** Awareness, balance objectivity. Knowing that you are not the body and are beyond the body
2. **Trust and Faith** Trust in something higher than ourselves. God as you conceive God. Full and total trust.
3. **Humility** Meekness, order, simplicity, awe, serve others
4. **Tolerance** Never judging others, external considering, openness to differences, realizing everyone is part of God; suffering 'fools' gladly
5. **Sincerity** Honesty, being true to yourself, purify motives, staying real, pursue Truth
6. **Gratitude** Receiving and giving; grateful for all that happens, both 'good' and 'bad.' Take it as it comes and be grateful
7. **Non-attachment** Letting go, surrender, freedom, liberation

THE DIVINE MOTHER'S LOVE

This journey through life is all about learning and a series of constant tests. Everyday is Judgement Day. We are beset with desires and negativities along every step every day.

And so we stumble and fall, and get up and get lost and later found throughout the course of one lifetime of learning until the day when we draw our final breath and die.

Throughout all of the many trials and tribulations on the path of learning, the Holy Mother selflessly gives constant, unconditional Love. As a Mother does, she picks up her infant who has strayed and fallen in the dirt, or wandered into danger. She washes us, clothes and embraces us. She watches over us with sweetest unconditional love.

Even many animals will sacrifice their own lives for their offspring.

The Holy Mother is the highest ideal. Her profound power is in her Passivity. She may manifest as Gaia, as Lakshmi, as Kali, as Mother Mary, and in so many other names and forms known and unknown to the world.

For a human being who experiences the joys and pain of Motherhood in a lifetime, often the love and attachment for her children is extremely strong. It can be one of the final barriers to detachment along the spiritual path. This is the test is loving with detachment.

From the internal knowledge coming through the writer, there is the deepest subtle connection between Child and Mother throughout life. There are three stages of the Umbilical Cord which have come through.

1. **The first stage at birth when the physical umbilical cord between Child and Mother is cut.**
2. **The second stage at age 7 years when the etheric umbilical cord severs.**
3. **The third stage upon the death of the Mother (or of the child) is the final cutting of the cord.**

This same principle is relevant to the growth of a single individual and to the progress of humanity as a vehicle of consciousness.

While most of us no longer believe that human beings are the centre of the Universe, or that people are living on a flat plate around which the Sun revolves, we continue to be subject to other, even more profound illusions about ourselves.

Why persist in the illusion that we are awake, conscious and free, able to do what we want, able to make and carry out decisions, that we are a single, permanent person whom we refer to as "I" and have a positive will?

So as long as we are bound up in this myth, this matrix, this delusion, and fail to see the prison bars, we cannot become free, for why work to achieve capabilities that we already imagine we have? When we start to wake up, we can see our mechanical selves as we are like Pam in the classic limerick below, and make every effort to bring about an awakening.

> *"An earnest young seeker named Pam*
> *Said, "I think I've found out just what I am.*
> *I'm a creature that moves*
> *In predestine grooves.*
> *I'm not even a bus; I'm a tram."*

Pam no longer holds illusions about herself. Her situation is far less desolate and hopeless than she first thinks. Not everything is predetermined, and certainly not for those who are prepared to work on improving, purifying and perfecting themselves, of raising their vibration. She has realized she is in prison, which is to first step to finding the keys to escape from it.

All the characteristics we ascribe to ourselves and take for granted are our inherent birthright; they were created when homo sapiens was designed, but they are not yet all fulfilled or operational. Only we ourselves can activate this potential by making continuous personal efforts in the right way through the process of self-perfection.

Until we learn to start to practice this we cannot really do new things. Until we have started the transition, time will always go around in a circle, and everything will merely be a repetition of old situations, thoughts, problems and feelings we have already experienced. We will always "fall for" the same types of people and always find ourselves in the same difficulties.

The launch gates have opened, and each one of us must now find the way to make the present lifetime in the **ever-present-here-and-the-eternal** now count for something. It is Kipling's *filling the unforgiving minute with 60 seconds worth of distance run.* It is illusion to imagine we can spare ourselves the effort by paying membership fees in a religion or buying indulgences. No god, no holy man or woman, no guru, no -ism, no book, no mantra and no journey to holy places can help us attain more consciousness, higher vibration, and personal responsibility while we still take our old ego everywhere with us.

Death to the ego! Liberation from attachment to desires!

Like the other animals that have evolved of the Earth we humans still have our feet still planted on the ground, but our consciousness is stretched out to the Cosmos, for we are, to some extent, self-aware and imbued with the third brain of the intellect, and the seed of the spiritual. We are created "in the image of God", and we carry this potential for voluntary evolution ingrained in ourselves.

Yet it's not principally a collective evolution as in the case of the other animals. The individual can achieve completion and transcendence, independently of whether the whole of humanity will become better or worse. At the same time, by undertaking conscious evolution, by raising vibration and resonance to enlightenment, the individual can help guide others to raise themselves.

In this process the experiment of consciousness that is humankind has the possibility of fulfilling its purpose and its reason for being, that of ascension.

Acknowledgements

The singular acknowledgement is to Pir O Murshid **Shaikh Abdullah Isa Dougan** whose extraordinary original ideas, revelations and teachings form the core foundations of the book and to whom everything is attributed. The first meeting with Abdullah in the early 1980's changed the course of thinking, understanding and life for the writer. Any expression of gratitude falls short of the mark for conveying profound thanks for all that has been taught and given by Abdullah, whose perfect work is the Source of everything imperfectly contained herein.

40 Days – An Account of a Discipline (Gnostic Press 1979) is the best introductory story of Abdullah's striving from the unconscious to the conscious, his pathway through Gurdjieff's teachings and eventual initiation as a Naqshbandi Sufi. In order to destroy the ego, in 1974 Abdullah undertook a 40-day fast on water alone while travelling through India, Afghanistan and thus culminating in the Hajj in Mecca. The unfolding of the transformational discipline is seen through the eyes of Abdullah as well as two witnesses, both pupils, an emotional man Number 2, and an intellectual man Number 3 travelling with him.

Disclaimer: the writer makes no representation whatsoever of representing the Gnostic Press or the Gnostic Society or any official body. All the concepts, ideas and truths delivered in the book are conveyed as accurately and faithfully as possible and are the responsibility of the writer. At the same time, they are only an introduction and nothing can come close to serving as any facsimile or substitute for the direct teachings contained within the books and stored as direct audio recordings from Mr Dougan's meetings with pupils over the course of years.

Abdullah taught through the Socratic method of questions from pupils to the Teacher which requires critical thinking on the part of the questioner. The quality of the question is determined by the level of knowledge, understanding and the vibration of the pupil asking the question. The meetings were subsequently edited into a series of books which can be studied and applied.

Abdullah also created Objective Art through a series of paintings and prints to illustrate some of the ideas coming through to him, and as a means of conveying concepts that words could not express. He also composed music in the form of the Solar Suite.

The writer wishes to acknowledge and thank my life love Pratima Devi Prasad for support provided during the undertaking of writing the present work.

References

Abdullah Dougan, **The Quest: Part 1: Ideas**, Gnostic Press, 1981

Abdullah Dougan, **Probings**; Gnostic Press, 1979

Abdullah Dougan, **40 Days – An Account of a Discipline**, Gnostic Press, 1978

David Bohm, **Wholeness and the Implicate Order**, Routledge 1983

Hazrat Inayat Khan, **The Unity of Religious Ideals**, Motilal Banarsidas Pub, 1990

Steven Strogatz, Sync: **The Emerging Science of Spontaneous Order**, Theia, 2003

Steven Strogatz, **Infinite Powers: How Calculus Reveals the Secrets of the Universe**, Houghton Mifflin, 2003

I.A. Ezekiel, **Kabir the Great Mystic**, Radha Soami Satsang Beas, India 1966

Omraam Mikhael Aivanhov, **The Mysteries of Yesod**, Prosveta Publishers, 1988

Mother Krishnabai, **Guru's Grace**, Anandasharam, 1964

Swami Ramdas, **God Experience**, Anandasharam, 1963

Tibetan Book of the Dead, Translated by W.Y. Evans-Wentz, Oxford University Press 1960

Vivikananda, **Raja Yoga**, Advaita Ashram, 1896

About the Author

G. E. Poole is a nothing and a nobody. Outwardly leading an ordinary life as a householder, from an early age he was drawn to physics, logic, science, philosophy and the quest for consciousness. At age 22 he entered The Work through the J. G. Bennett line of transmission through Sherborne House and the Claymont Society. In 1982 he migrated from Hawaii to New Zealand to become a pupil of Sufi Shaikh Abdullah Isa Dougan.

Subsequent to the passing of Abdullah in 1987, he continued to study and practice his teachings for over 30 years. In 1990, he met Sufi Master Irina Tweedy in London, and in 1992 had substantial direct close ongoing personal contact with Taoist Master Hua Ching Ni. He presently resides in Australia.